MEASURED SPIRIT

MEASURED SPIRIT

How Sam Allardyce Made Bolton Wanderers a Top-Flight Force

Sam Bradley-Green

pitch

First published by Pitch Publishing, 2025
1

Pitch Publishing
9 Donnington Park,
85 Birdham Road,
Chichester, West Sussex,
PO20 7AJ

www.pitchpublishing.co.uk
info@pitchpublishing.co.uk

A CIP catalogue record is available for this book from the British Library.

ISBN 978 1 83680 144 3

Typesetting and origination by Pitch Publishing

MIX
Paper | Supporting responsible forestry
FSC® C010615

Printed and bound on FSC® certified paper in line with our continuing commitment to ethical business practices, sustainability and the environment.

Printed and bound in India by Thomson Press

Contents

To 'Big' Sam Allardyce for the amazing memories, and to all who follow the Wanderers.

Foreword by Stelios Giannakopoulos

MY YEARS with Bolton Wanderers have been some of the most memorable of my life. I feel for ever connected with the town and the team.

But from a football perspective, those years were something extremely special under the inspirational and masterful leadership of Sam Allardyce.

In my humble opinion, success came through the ingenious management of all factors of team management, from the player selections and transfers to the tactical formations and the players' dietary needs.

This was not an easy achievement for Big Sam, bringing together so much talent from so many different nations, perspectives and ages.

But success could not have come without the great support from the team's corporate management that backed Big Sam and also created a great environment for the team to flourish.

I will never forget the team's special welcome when I returned from the Euro 2004, where, as part of the Greek national team, I reached the pinnacle of my career, winning the European Championship. The welcome was simply amazing! I felt that the whole team honoured me in a way

I never expected. It made me feel I wanted to achieve every goal with Bolton as well.

I believe that Sam Bradley-Green's book has managed to capture all those little details that allow this achievement of the great Bolton team to be appreciated even more.

Having lived the experience, reading these pages took me back in time, filling me with the emotions that drove me and my team-mates to success.

Thank you Sam Bradley-Green for bringing all this back to life with this wonderful book.

Every true Bolton fan will appreciate it. Those who lived it will remember and the newer generations can learn and feel proud to be Wanderers fans.

Stelios Giannakopoulos
Bolton Wanderers 2003-2008
(177 Apps & 28 Goals)
Euro 2004 Winner

Preface
Living the dream

THIS BOOK has been written from the heart to the heart. It is a trip down an incredibly happy memory lane for Bolton Wanderers supporters who remember a distinct period of time at the Reebok Stadium. The era under Sam Allardyce is without a doubt the club's most successful since the 1950s and put not only Bolton Wanderers, but also the town, on the map.

Sam built a team to be feared by many in the English game and also on the European stage with his team's symbiotic relationship of heart and flair. This mixture can be known as 'measured spirit': the ability to use statistical, analytical, and quantitative means while also using heart, spirit and fight to achieve their goal. Bolton would use this to conquer many mountains and go from the bottom half of the First Division to the top six of the Premier League within Sam's eight-year spell at the club. The names of Okocha, Djorkaeff, N'Gotty, Stelios, Hierro, Davies, Nolan, Anelka, Diouf, Guðjohnsen, Jääskeläinen, etc., would grace the pitch at the Reebok and bring some of the most amazing memories that the supporters of one of the oldest clubs in the world had ever seen. In a town with such proximity to Old Trafford, Anfield, the Etihad and

Goodison Park, it is clear to see that it is sometimes hard to support Bolton Wanderers, especially in more recent times. However, Sam and his backroom team, adding with the support of Phil Gartside and Eddie Davies, gave the town a club to be proud of and gave the supporters their own fair share of bragging rights over their local and national elite clubs.

I have been a season ticket holder at the Reebok Stadium for 23 years and my first experience of football was with Sam Allardyce, I didn't know any different at Bolton and thought and hoped the good times would never end. I remember my grandfather, before his passing, speaking about the passing ability and greatness of Fernando Hierro and him helping Bolton get into the UEFA Cup, saying to me, 'Make the most of this, it won't last.' I did not understand at the time and felt this was the norm. Now, in 2025, and with hindsight, it really was the top of the hill and I understand his words, as instead of yearly trips to Old Trafford and Stamford Bridge (which I took for granted) it is Barnsley, Burton and Cambridge.

This book highlights Bolton's journey to the Premier League and beyond under the leadership and guidance of Sam Allardyce. The transition from perennial strugglers to a force capable of competing with the best was nothing short of spectacular as Sam used a combined relationship of English grit, continental flair, and analytical approaches. This book is for the believers, the dreamers and for those who were there and saw the most successful period in Bolton Wanderers' contemporary history. In reflecting on this golden era, one cannot help but marvel at the journey of the club. It was a period where passion, perseverance, and pride converged to create something truly special at the Reebok Stadium. The legacy of this time lives on for all who don the famous white shirt and acts as a dream that one day, the club will return to the promised land and start the next phase of their Premier League legacy.

As the next phase of Bolton's story unfolds into the 2020s and beyond, the period in the early to mid-2000s will for ever remain a cornerstone of the club's famous history and a period that could only be described as 'measured spirit'.

'The most important thing for me is the opportunity that you have. I think I maximised my opportunity at Bolton, changing the mindset of the people from when I arrived till the time I left. So, when I look back at what I achieved at Bolton, it makes me very happy.'

Jay-Jay Okocha, November 2017

1
Todd-al change

'COME ON Bolton! Come on Bolton!'

Stamford Bridge was awash with fans in white and blue but both sets of supporters were singing loudly and encouragingly from the bottom of their hearts for the men in white. Sunday, 10 May 1998 may have been approaching the dawn of the new millennium but for many Bolton fans, it was the dawn of a potential Armageddon.

As news came through of Coventry's equaliser at Everton in the 89th minute thanks to a goal from Dion Dublin, Bolton fans gained hope that the impossible could be possible. Wanderers needed only to match Everton's result to stay in the Premier League for the first time in their history. After 1997's amazing First Division title-winning campaign, manager Colin Todd's team were trying to look at the influences of the great nights at Burnden Park under his former boss, Bruce Rioch. Bolton had made a much better go of their top-flight season compared to their last efforts in 1995/96 and had taken this chance of Premier League stability down to the last day. With this, they had the chance to stay up but also to relegate the 'grand old team' of Everton.

Everton v Coventry stood at 1-1 in the 89th minute at Goodison Park as Bolton were trailing 1-0 at Chelsea thanks to a 73rd-minute strike from player-manager Gianluca Vialli. The Bolton fans knew that just one goal would save them and ensure another go at the Premier League at the Reebok Stadium, less than 12 months after its opening. Bolton had struggled to turn the Reebok into a fortress a la Burnden Park but certainly had regained form and had also bought wisely with a mixture of experience and quality. As the away section of Stamford Bridge started to put their ear to their wireless radios and start to hear about Dublin's equaliser in Merseyside, the news spread throughout not only the away end, but all four stands of Stamford Bridge.

The 34,845 attendees felt that history could be made. Chelsea fans caught themselves joining in with Bolton chants, and at one point, the home supporters were starting to boo their own players for tackling Bolton players. The confusion among the 22 on the pitch was a unique sight as Chelsea had consolidated fourth place three weeks earlier with a home victory against Liverpool, and were effectively playing for nothing. Yet, with that in mind, they still fielded a strong line-up and many of the players who had helped Chelsea win the League Cup in March and would start the Cup Winners' Cup Final three days later, such as Frank Leboeuf, Mark Hughes, Roberto Di Matteo, Gustavo Poyet, Vialli himself and top goalscorer Tore André Flo, all played against Bolton on that summer's day in west London. Three days away from Chelsea's major European showpiece, it could be argued that this fixture was in fact Bolton's cup final.

Bolton had started with a 3-5-2 formation with a defensive unit of Guðni Bergsson, Mark Fish and Gerry Taggart then a midfield of Neil Cox, Per Frandsen, John Sheridan, Alan Thompson, and hometown hero Jimmy

Phillips. Phillips, more comfortable as a defender, had filled in and showed his Bolton spirit and stated he would play anywhere to help his hometown club. Up front was the partnership of Bob Taylor and the previous season's First Division hero, Nathan Blake. Taylor had proved to be a fine acquisition as the record signing Dean Holdsworth was yet to start firing for the Whites as Bolton looked to replace the iconic John McGinlay who had departed for Bradford City earlier in the season.

'Sad but true, Bolton have looked a bit short when it mattered the most,' stated the commentary team as Bolton started to build up a move to try and bring the scores level. John Salako, wearing McGinlay's former number ten shirt, began to show glimpses of the player who had earned international recognition with five England caps in 1991. The Nigeria-born midfielder had arrived on a loan from Coventry City but had not really pulled up any trees during his time at the Reebok Stadium. However, he began to shimmy and shake with the ball down the left-hand side, took on three Chelsea defenders and found himself with the ball at the edge of the box. His cross was then deflected into the path of club icon Alan Thompson. The ball fell on to the Geordie's unfavoured right foot in the D; he then chipped it into the six-yard box. There stood the unmarked Swiss striker on loan from Nantes, Gaetano Giallanza, another Hail Mary attempt from Todd in March to try and replace the goals lost by the sale of McGinlay. However, the ball moved towards him in only his third appearance for Bolton. Could he be a hero for the Lancashire side? The stadium held its breath, and the ball came drifting towards him. With one flick of his head, he was due to be a hero, keep Bolton in the Premier League and have his name etched in the history books of one of the founding members of the Football League. Alas, the ball sailed past him and out for a goal kick. It needed the slightest nod, the smallest touch and he would be for ever remembered by the Bolton faithful.

The camera would pan to Colin Todd, whose expression said more than the expletives of the away end could. It was over, that was the big chance, surely. Then in the next move, substitute Gus Poyet, never one to shy from the dramatic, started to drive forward with the ball in midfield. At this moment, the Chelsea fans began to boo Poyet; they wanted Bolton to stay up.

Poyet threaded a lovely ball with his right foot through the visiting defence to youngster Jody Morris. Morris was expected to be a future England hero but never reached the heights of his childhood friend and academy scholar John Terry; he is, however, still fondly remembered by Chelsea fans. The 19-year-old took the ball forward and hit a low strike across Keith Branagan and into the bottom-left corner to get his first league goal. With 90 minutes on the clock, the score was now 2-0. The crowd knew it, the players knew it and Todd knew it. Bolton's time in the sun, in the greatest league of all, was over. Back to the First Division they went. Coventry's equaliser was irrelevant, Bolton could not do their bit. Chants were replaced by tears: the hopes of the faithful, travelling fans turned to sorrow as the players bowed their heads. Some knew it would be their last appearance in a Bolton shirt, some had no idea what was to come. Just a year later, there was more heartbreak in the capital for Todd and his white army.

After that relegation in 1997/98, a run of positive results at the back end of the 1998/99 First Division season had seen Bolton manage to book a play-off position with some difficulty. A high-end play-off place or the potential of an automatic promotion looked very much on in late February. However, a stuttering end to the season saw Bolton lose four of their last ten games as they slumped to sixth in the table, secured with a final-day victory over Portsmouth at Fratton Park.

Bolton, very much the outsiders for that final promotion spot back to the Premier League, would face Ipswich Town who finished third under George Burley and were disappointed not to make the top two after ending up just one point behind Bradford. Ipswich held a greater goal difference than Bradford as well so could see themselves unlucky not to be a Premier League club. This would be some fight on Todd's hands: not only to get to Wembley but also, if the worst happened, to keep hold of his best players. Sharks had been circling around the talents of Claus Jensen, Per Frandsen, Mark Fish and up-and-coming youngster Eiður Guðjohnsen. If Bolton could not secure Premier League football for these international players, then they would run the risk of another club prising them away from the Reebok.

However, Bolton managed to get through the play-off semi-final by the skin of their teeth. An 84th-minute strike from one of the Scandinavian Whites, Michael Johansen, earned a 1-0 win at the Reebok and something to take on the long journey three days later to Portman Road. Ipswich were furious as they felt they should have been awarded a penalty prior to Johansen's volley as Fish tripped David Johnson in the box during the first half.

However, if the first leg was a damp 1-0 affair, the second leg was anything but. On 14 minutes, Ipswich's Irish-by-proxy midfielder, Matt Holland, evened the aggregate with a lovely finish, before Bob Taylor equalised in the second half from close range after some great work from

Jamaican teenager Ricardo Gardner who laid the ball off to Guðjohnsen whose shot was saved before it was smashed in by Taylor; 1-1 on the night, 2-1 Bolton on aggregate. However, the basketball-esque match continued to rage on and just one minute later, future England international Kieron Dyer put Ipswich ahead as the Portman Road crowd could smell blood; 2-2 on aggregate. The madness continued and Bolton had a corner in the 84th minute. Johansen floated the ball in; it evaded many a head but eventually fell to his Danish compatriot Frandsen who struck it in a way that would make many a Viking proud. He slammed his shot past the keeper to make the game 2-2 on the night, 3-2 Bolton with six minutes left to play.

Many in the crowd and at home thought the drama was done. How wrong they were, and Ipswich still felt they could add another twist in the evening. Fabian Wilnis, a signing that January for Ipswich from Dutch side De Graafschap, had the ball on the right. The Dutchman, who had cost Ipswich £200,000, almost paid that back in one moment. His pass found the run of the pacy teenager Dyer who once again broke Bolton hearts. The floated ball came in and Dyer got the deftest of nudges on it with his head just inside the box; the attempt had enough pace to loop in the air. The back spin caused the ball to dip at a speed which caught Bolton goalkeeper Steve Banks off guard, landing behind him and into the net; 3-2 Ipswich on the night, 3-3 on aggregate. Extra time was looming.

Six minutes into extra time, the crucial goal of the game was scored. Taylor hit a ball from Guðjohnsen into the back of the net; 3-3 on the night, 4-3 Bolton on aggregate. Bolton fans looked relieved, the plans for Wembley were on, many already thinking of excuses to tell the other halves. Still, Ipswich had other ideas and Holland scored his second, but though it gave Ipswich a richly deserved victory on the night, it was not enough; 4-4 on aggregate but due to the now cancelled away goals rule, Bolton progressed. Skin of their teeth does not even cover it. It was the third consecutive year that Ipswich's hopes of reaching the Premier League had been dashed at the play-off stage but never so cruelly. Throughout the evening, the side who had occupied that second automatic promotion position for much of the season were within reach of a place in that Wembley final on 31 May 1999. Ipswich would have their day in glory a year later by beating Barnsley 4-2 at Wembley to reach the Premier League. Yet, it was Bolton who would be marching up Wembley Way and reaching those two towers to face Watford in 1999.

A crowd of 70,343 fans attended Wembley for the final. Watford had beaten Birmingham City via a penalty shoot-out after a two-legged 1-1 aggregate score. Watford won 7-6 from the spot at St Andrew's to book their place in the final. They were managed by a man who was no stranger to Wembley, former England boss Graham Taylor. Taylor, who was a victim of cruel media taunting during his time in the big job, had started to rebuild his career and had worked hard to build a strong Watford team who had caused some teams problems and had surprised many in the First Division.

The media projected that the winner of this tie would take in around £10m in TV rights and sponsorships and both the bookies and pundits predicted a comfortable Bolton victory. However, Watford had done the double over Bolton that season with a 2-1 win at the Reebok in October and a 2-0 success at Vicarage Road in April, a result that would very much still be in the minds of both sets of players in the build-up to the final.

The match kicked off at 3pm with South African defender Mark Fish captaining Bolton. Colin Todd and Graham Taylor would lead their sides out at Wembley in front of a cascade of fireworks and expectation. The game began with Bolton dominating early on. Chances from Taylor and Guðjohnsen scared the Watford faithful but there was nothing to show for both efforts. Then, in the 37th minute, a corner from Watford left-back Peter Kennedy was whipped in but cleared by Neil Cox and Colin's son, Andy Todd. Yet a moment of sheer brilliance by Nick Wright silenced the Bolton faithful into silence. Wright performed an acrobatic overhead kick which the youngsters of 1999 would refer to as a bicycle kick, from inside the box, slamming the ball past Steve Banks and into the far corner of the net before being mauled by his Watford team-mates and stunning everyone in a white shirt. The sea of fans in yellow were elated and the rocket man, Elton John, celebrated in his own way: a glass of bubbly from his private live stream in Seattle. It was not even half-time yet, Elton!

By the second half, the game dragged on with no real events in the game. Todd brought off Cox and Johansen and brought on young Dane Bo Hansen, and the ever-reliable Scott Sellars. Bolton were pushing and pushing for an equaliser: it felt all too similar to that final-day game at Stamford Bridge a year earlier. With Wanderers stretched and out of position, Watford took their chance. In the 89th minute, Sellars lost the ball in the middle of the park to Kennedy who passed it to substitute Allan Smart. Smart, upset not to be starting after eight goals that season, took the ball in his stride and calmly placed it past Banks to confirm Watford's place in the Premier League for the first time to the elation of Taylor and the supporters in the stands. Once again, in London, Bolton hearts were broken on the last day with a 2-0 defeat.

Todd looked defeated, by the result as well as the job. Had he taken this team as far as he could? From his humble start as Bruce Rioch's number two in 1992 to this Wembley defeat, Todd's association with the club had had its fair share of ups and downs but 31 May 1999 was Watford's day and once again, not Bolton Wanderers'.

But from the demise, a phoenix would rise. It is always darkest before the dawn they say: this epitomises Bolton Wanderers perfectly.

That summer brought an air of change and a sudden dose of reality to Todd and his squad before the 1999/2000 season. For many of the international superstars at the Reebok, it was either goodbye or soon to be goodbye. Chairman Gordon Hargreaves stated in the summer, 'This club is still geared financially for Premiership football, and we have to address that situation and bring it into line with Division One status before we can mount a renewed challenge.' In short, Hargreaves was saying that Bolton had a Premier League squad with a First Division budget and wage structure. Something had to give: there needed to be a recoup of some money after the failure to return to the Premier League.

Todd had been a figure of stability and reliability since his move to Bolton in 1992 to act as assistant to Bruce Rioch. He had followed Rioch before and after their stint together at Middlesbrough, so it was a natural next step after a short-term spell as first-team manager on Teesside. After Rioch left for an ill-fated tenure at Arsenal following the play-off final win in 1995, Todd originally took up the role of joint manager with his former Derby team-mate Roy McFarland. However, after McFarland was dismissed in early 1996, Todd was officially given the role of first-team manager of Bolton Wanderers. Both of Todd's attempts with Bolton in the Premier League ended in relegation but his title-winning team of 1996/97 went on to be one of the supporters' favourite eras and gave Burnden Park the most perfect send-off as Bolton made the move to the Reebok Stadium.

However, after relegation in 1998 and play-off final defeat in 1999, the cracks were beginning to show and maybe it was time for all parties to start a fresh adventure. Todd knew that in order to reach previous heights again, he would need further backing in the transfer market, something Hargreaves and the board were not too keen on after substantial financial outlays in the mid-to-late 90s had already been put in place, namely a brand-new, state-of-the-art stadium in Horwich.

During the summer, the rumours surrounding Danish anchor Per Frandsen were all over the local press, namely in East Lancashire as Blackburn Rovers seemed to take a serious interest in taking the midfielder to Ewood Park. Frandsen had become a cult hero at Bolton with his performances at Burnden Park to help secure the First Division title and his reliability in tough times. Frandsen had also been part of the Danish squad which competed at the 1998 World Cup so was very much a jewel in the crown for Todd and Bolton. He was seen as one of the best players outside of the Premier League by the summer of 1999. Although the financial writing was on the wall for Todd's non-existent transfer kitty, he was assured that Frandsen would not be sold.

However, Todd was deflated at the free transfer of Scott Sellars to Huddersfield Town: this one stung Todd as he felt Sellars was vital to Bolton's push back to the top flight. Sellars had arrived in Bolton during the 1995/96 season for a fee of £750,000 from Newcastle United and had gained great stock with the supporters and his manager due to his leadership qualities, great ability and superb attitude. Fifteen goals in 111 appearances displayed those attributes and many in BL6, including Todd himself, were disappointed to see him cross the Pennines to Huddersfield. Yet, if Todd was given the choice of losing Frandsen or Sellars then he was surely happy with the conclusion of his summer outgoings.

The season started and Bolton had spent a grand total of £0.00 on transfers in the summer; the future looked bleak for a team fighting to win the title. Three defeats in six kicked things off as they struggled to find form. Bolton still had a great plethora of quality, but a lack of fresh blood was always going to hurt especially with a Wembley hangover. After a 2-2 draw away at Barnsley on 18 September 1999, Todd was brought into Hargreaves' office to discuss something serious. A bid had come in for Per Frandsen from Blackburn. An already depleted squad would not only struggle without the Dane but would flounder and Todd made it noticeably clear if this bid was accepted and went through then he would have to leave the club as his position would become untenable. The board did not take Todd's remarks seriously as they knew of his family ties to the town, with a home in the brand-new Turton Heights estate in Bromley Cross as well as his son, Andy, being a member of the first-team squad. Todd was in fact informed that before any new signings could appear at the Reebok Stadium, he must first sell off any valuable assets. Again, he made his position clear.

At 50, Todd felt he had no reason to be playing games and waited for the decision from the board regarding

Frandsen's future. On 22 September 1999, after seven years at the club, Todd resigned. Bolton had accepted an eventual £2.25m offer from neighbours Blackburn and Frandsen had made his way through Darwen over to Ewood to sign the papers; just like that, Bolton had lost arguably their best player and their manager in the space of a day.

Todd stated, 'My position had become untenable after the club accepted an offer from Blackburn for Per last Thursday. I wanted to wait until that transfer was complete and now, it is, I have resigned.' Todd's anguish was obvious and how torn he was about this decision. 'I felt the club could have gone further without the financial constraints that have held back my personal ambitions,' he added.

Todd also revealed that he'd had some free transfers and loans rejected by the board in the summer after assurances that high-profile players would not leave. He seemed resentful since the club had recently sold the land at Burnden Park to a supermarket developer two years after their departure and recouped £6.7m for this. This would, at first, become a 'Big W' – a form of Woolworths where in its present-day iteration it is a large ASDA superstore. However, it must be remembered that they were only two years down the line from purchasing the Reebok Stadium for the sum of £35m, a move which would go on to cost the club over £100m.

Todd had left and the last remnants of that iconic Bruce Rioch side that swept through the lower leagues and killed many a giant was gone. It was time for a fresh change and a new era to begin. Roy Evans, formerly of Liverpool, was heavily rumoured to be taking over but it never materialised. In October, Bolton's board chose Phil Gartside of Leigh to replace Gordon Hargreaves as chairman and on 19 October 1999, a decision that would change the club for ever was made. On his 45th birthday, Bolton Wanderers announced their new manager: welcome, Sam Allardyce.

The legacy began.

2

He's one of our own (ish)

SAMUEL ALLARDYCE was born on 19th October 1954 in the Midlands market town of Dudley. Although he would later be classed as a Boltonion and would make the north-west town his home, the young Allardyce was a proud West Midlander and followed his beloved Wolverhampton Wanderers when he was not playing for either his school or Dudley Town. But it was a different Wanderers where he would cement his legacy, first as a player but more recently and more famously as manager.

Born from two Scottish parents, Robert and Mary, Sam didn't excel in education due to undiagnosed dyslexia but would go on to be one of the most successful names in the academic and statistical side of the modern football game.

'Big Sam', as he would be affectionately known, signed an apprenticeship with Bolton Wanderers just before leaving school at 15 and, to supplement this, he worked in a factory producing record decks. During this time, the Bolton first-team manager was the great – and soon to be Sir – Nat Lofthouse. Upon signing for the club, Allardyce and his father met Lofthouse at Burnden Park. Little did the universe know that the names of Lofthouse and Allardyce would become arguably the two most famous names associated with Bolton Wanderers' history. If Lofthouse was the King of Burnden, then Allardyce would surely be able to take that crown in the club's modern ground for his contribution at the Reebok Stadium a mere 30 years later.

Inspired by fellow Dudley-born legend Duncan Edwards, who would unfortunately die in the infamous Munich air disaster of 1958, the same year Lofthouse lifted the FA Cup for Bolton, Allardyce wanted to make his time in Lancashire successful but also saw an opportunity to make his mark and put down some roots in the town. After an early feeling of homesickness, Allardyce became right at home after meeting his future wife and rock, Lynne. They both still live in Bolton to this day in the village of Bromley Cross.

Upon reaching the first-team, Sam would go on to make a combined 294 appearances and score 26 goals over two separate stints at the club, playing in the top three tiers of the Football League for the Trotters over the 1970s and 80s. Before, between and after, Allardyce had stints for Sunderland, Millwall, Tampa Bay Rowdies, Coventry City, Huddersfield, Preston North End, Irish side Limerick and his boyhood rivals West Bromwich Albion, a team he would go on to manage in 2020. The burly central defender recorded 578 appearances and 42 goals over a 21-year playing career and, although he never gained the recognition in the English game – he and others felt he deserved it – it was in the manager's seat where he would gain his global fame.

Allardyce's first foray into management was during his time in Ireland as player-manager of Limerick after originally being a player-coach during his time at West Brom. At Limerick, he would guide the team to promotion into the League of Ireland Premier Division after winning the First Division in 1992 all while still being a playing member of the first-team squad as well. Sam returned to the north-west of England and took over the role of caretaker manager at Preston North End. His time at Deepdale was promising but not enough to guarantee the job on a permanent basis and he would then move to Preston's great rivals Blackpool for his first full-time managerial role in England. From 1994 to 1996, Allardyce made his home in Blackpool as he was appointed as the Tangerines' manager. A change he made at Bloomfield Road was one that would help create a great friendship for years to come when he promoted former Bolton captain Phil Brown from player to coach. Blackpool finished 12th after losing steam at the end of the season despite putting on a healthy promotion push for most of the campaign. The following year, Blackpool lost in the Second Division play-off semi-finals to Bradford City and Allardyce was dismissed from his role by chairman Owen Oyston who sacked him by a phone call made from inside a prison cell. Some informed Sam that he dodged a bullet on the seaside.

By 1997, Sam was back in management and took over the reins at Notts County in the Second Division. He arrived just too late to save them; they were relegated to the Third Division and he found it hard to get some of the older players to respond to his newer methods as the team went 18 games without a win. However, in the 1997/98 season, Allardyce led Notts County to the Third Division title by a massive 19 points and then helped the club survive relegation the season after. However, by October 1999, he was on his way back to Bolton, this time as manager.

Big Sam's move from Meadow Lane to the Reebok Stadium was not a clean break and there was some doubt on its legality at certain points. New chairman Phil Gartside had made it very clear from the start that Allardyce was his man, and the hiring of a new manager was made all the more complicated coming in the middle of the investment from Eddie Davies and the transitioning from previous owners to new ones. Brett Warburton, of the Bolton-based bread baker, was a close friend of Sam's from his early days at the club and had invited the potential new manager to his house to meet the incoming board and the incoming investor, Eddie Davies. Davies had made his fortune from thermostats on electric kettles and was happy to be a silent investor of his hometown club. Educated in Farnworth and brought up in Little Lever, Davies was keen to give something back to his community in the form of helping bring back the glory years to Bolton Wanderers.

The deal was nearly confirmed. However, Sam was still technically the manager of Notts County. After a player dinner, Sam tactically decided to sneak off early and arrive at Meadow Lane early the next morning where he knew no one would be due to nursing heavy heads. Allardyce put his resignation letter on the desk of chief executive Geoff Davies and headed off to the Reebok. Magpies chairman Derek Pavis had initially rejected the resignation but eventually it was cleared, and Sam was back home in Bolton. However, one small hill to climb first involved his old mate Phil Brown.

Brown had been Colin Todd's number two after leaving Allardyce at Blackpool and had been given the role of caretaker manager after Todd's departure, making it clear he wanted the job on a permanent basis. His record of three wins in four games had also raised some eyebrows in Bolton and had made Brown feel he had a shot. The north-east native was also a cult hero in Bolton like Allardyce due to his career in the late 1980s and early 90s and felt disheartened at not getting the role. Allardyce and Brown were good friends, but this threatened to jeopardise that. Allardyce met with Brown and made it clear that if he wasn't happy then he could leave, but more than anything, he wanted Brown to be his assistant. Sam and Phil came to an agreement and an iconic duo was firmly in place – they would create history at the Reebok Stadium.

Allardyce's first duty was a gesture of goodwill as he allowed Brown to take control of the first-team one last time, when Bolton faced Crewe Alexandra at the Reebok Stadium in front of 12,676. A tough 2-2 draw ensued in which Bolton looked poor, and without the goals from Eiður Guðjohnsen and Dean Holdsworth, it would have ended up in defeat in BL6. However, Allardyce admitted that, despite the result and performance, there was a team with great potential and clear quality. Future club legends Jussi Jääskeläinen and Ricardo Gardner were there and embarked on a career in English football that would eventually etch them in Premier League folklore alongside the experience and reliability of Guðni Bergsson, Mike Whitlow, Holdsworth and hometown hero Jimmy Phillips. However, it was Phillips himself who would inform Allardyce of his first big issues as manager of Bolton Wanderers.

On 6 November, Bolton recorded an impressive victory over Crystal Palace at the Reebok Stadium thanks to goals from the Scandinavian duo Guðjohnsen and Claus Jensen. Allardyce had started brilliantly as he had lost only one of his first four games as manager of his beloved Wanderers. In spite of this, he didn't really know his players and the winds of change at the club at both boardroom and changing room level meant that Sam needed to create an air of calm and togetherness among the squad. With this in mind, four days later, Allardyce took his squad and backroom staff on a team-bonding session at the Mottram Hall golf resort in Cheshire. It had been made clear to Sam that unless there was a return to the Premier League and fast, then he would not be able to add to his squad substantially, so he was aware that the players he had needed to become a team.

The plans were for some golf, a few quiet drinks, a meal and togetherness. Sam went to bed early on Thursday night while he let the players have some fun. However, during the night, a thumping pound at Allardyce's door startled him. As he opened it, Phillips, Mr Bolton, was at the door. Phillips, one of the elder statesmen of the dressing room, was someone Sam felt he could trust. Phillips informed Sam that he needed to come downstairs to the main hotel toilets. Upon approach, Allardyce saw Phil Brown's face covered in blood, a crowd of players and staff surrounding him and there stood Andy Todd showing no emotion. Phillips had informed Allardyce on the way down that Andy had attacked Brown. Phillips even remarked he might have killed him. As Allardyce approached the centre-back, Todd informed Sam that Brown 'deserved it'. Apparently, during his time as caretaker manager, Brown had made some insensitive comments about Andy's father Colin and his tactical approach; Andy had bided his time and waited for the moment to get his revenge. Brown was taken to hospital to have his jaw wired and Todd was placed on suspension by the club.

Todd showed a lack of remorse for his actions and continued to state that Brown deserved the attack. Allardyce decided Todd's contract should be terminated and he should lose his job, but this posed a sticky situation. Todd was an up-and-coming quality player in a team that couldn't afford to replace him. As if by luck and fate, before Todd was sacked, Sam received a call from Charlton Athletic boss Alan Curbishley, who was inquiring about none other than Andy Todd. Bolton agreed to sell Todd to Charlton for £1.5m and a potentially catastrophic situation was made a little less dramatic. However, Sam had lost a player and his assistant manager for a considerable amount of time. Todd's career would continue to be marred with issues and he was later sold to Blackburn amid a violent event with Charlton goalkeeper Dean Kiely, and had also previously been fighting on the Reebok Stadium pitch with Stan Collymore a year previous during a Premier League clash against Aston Villa.

As the season moved closer to the millennium, Bolton were starting to progress up the table and by the end of November they had gone seven games without a loss including four victories on the bounce against Swindon, Crystal Palace, Sheffield United and Grimsby. The Swindon result was particularly pleasing with two goals in the last three minutes from Bob Taylor and Bo Hansen giving the Trotters a 2-0 win in front of 12,486 at the Reebok Stadium. With only one defeat in his first ten games, the crowd had really started to get behind Sam and the team and although the crowds were not flocking back, the positivity around the club and the town started to return. However, a trio of losses against local and old rivals Tranmere, Blackburn and Stockport brought the elation crashing down to earth as Sam started to think about the thinning of his squad and the chance of losing his star player, Eiður Guðjohnsen, to the Premier League sharks in the new year.

Guðjohnsen was grabbing the headlines and was classed by many, including Allardyce, as the best player outside of the Premier League. The Icelandic striker had come to Bolton in 1998 under Colin Todd to rebuild his career after finding himself at Dutch giants PSV Eindhoven in 1995 at the age of

17 with the small task of competing for a place up front with the Brazilian Ronaldo. *O Fenômeno* is today classed as one of the best strikers of all time and at that time was using PSV as a stepping stone to heighten his career, which of course he did. Guðjohnsen struggled in the Netherlands and after a return to Iceland with KR of Reykjavík, he found himself in BL6 ready to go again with another chance in high-level football outside of Scandinavia. In 1999, Guðjohnsen was still only 22 and was becoming a hot commodity in English football. Before the end of the year, Chelsea and Derby County had made enquiries about his availability, but Allardyce did all he could to persuade the board to hold off until the end of the season. If Bolton did not reach the Premier League, then he would allow Eiður to be sold.

Guðjohnsen was enjoying his time in Bolton and the goals were flowing; between 1998 and 2000 he had scored 18 league goals for the club, impressive considering he didn't cement his place in the first-team until March of 1999. His league goals were impressive and kept Bolton ticking in the table, but it was his goals in cup competitions that season that attracted the eyes of many. With seven goals in 13 cup appearances, Guðjohnsen was on fire and in the lead-up to the League Cup quarter-final against Wimbledon in December, many were hoping that Guðjohnsen could be the man to help Bolton progress to the semi-finals.

Bolton had already defeated two Premier League sides on their way to the quarter-finals, beating Derby County 2-1 away and Sheffield Wednesday at the Reebok Stadium thanks to a 53rd-minute strike from Robbie Elliott. Cup games and triumphs were a key part of the success brought to Burnden Park under Bruce Rioch in the early to mid-90s so there was an air of expectancy as Bolton faced Wimbledon at the Reebok.

Wimbledon themselves, no stranger to cup drama and giant-killing, were fielding a strong team in a hope to gain some glory from that season as they would eventually face relegation after 14 successive seasons in the English top flight. However, the attacking line of John Hartson and Jason Euell were hoping to book a place in the semi-finals of the League Cup.

Wimbledon started the stronger of the two under the lights on 14 December 1999 and deservedly took the lead in the 17th minute. Welsh man-mountain Hartson had picked up the ball and played a lovely through pass to young striker Carl Cort who effortlessly drilled it past Jääskeläinen. Wimbledon continued to control the game and had other chances to double their advantage. Manager Egil Olsen demanded that his side continue to turn the screw and try to put the game out of Bolton's reach early. Against the run of play, the 'Iceman' Guðjohnsen picked up the ball and zigged and zagged past four Wimbledon defenders before smashing his shot past Scotland goalkeeper Neil Sullivan to tie the game at 1-1 in the 33rd minute. Game on. Bolton could see the nervousness begin to impact the Wimbledon players. This was Eiður' s tenth goal of the season and he wanted more. Eleven minutes later he was with the ball and met with an open net. However, he was unable to control it and Sullivan was able to recover.

The pressure from Bolton continued and many in the ground felt that Wanderers should have been awarded a penalty after Gayle pulled back Bob Taylor in the box. So did the referee; penalty. Many expected Guðjohnsen to take it but it was the Dane Michael Johansen who stepped up. The number seven, one of the few remaining members of the First Division-winning team in 1997, started his run-up and made no mistake as he smashed the ball past

Sullivan to give Bolton a 2-1 lead just before half-time. In the second half, Olsen asked for more of his Wimbledon players and they looked much more creative and fluid in their movement and their 4-3-3 formation was stretching Bolton. Allardyce could see that Bolton needed to show fight and grit and despite the onslaught of Premier League quality, they weathered the storm and defended heroically. Bolton cleared a shot off the line in a six-yard box scramble just as the referee blew the full-time whistle.

The inspirational form and performance of the eye-grabbing Guðjohnsen had got Bolton into the semi-finals of the League Cup where it would be an all-First Division affair against Tranmere Rovers.

Guðjohnsen would leave Bolton in the summer of 2000 for £4.5m to Chelsea, where he would become a double Premier League champion and League Cup winner. He would then move to Barcelona where he would pick up a La Liga, Copa del Rey, Supercopa de España, UEFA Super Cup and win the Champions League in 2009. Not bad for a kid from the Reebok. He would also return to Bolton in 2013 as a free transfer under Neil Lennon after a plethora of European clubs. His short reunion with Bolton produced five goals and a memorable FA Cup penalty against Liverpool and, although it may not have been the same Guðjohnsen from that night against Wimbledon, he was still loved and always respected anytime he returned to the place that gave him his break in English football.

3

Sam's semi heartbreak

THE GIANT-KILLING victory over Wimbledon had been sandwiched within a run of poor form; Bolton had lost three out of their four league games in December 1999 and were looking to pick up form and use the result against the Dons to kick-start their season. Sam Allardyce, still only less than three months into the job by the turn of the millennium, saw 2000 as a fresh start for Bolton and an opportunity for he and Phil Brown to really put their stamp on the team, and what better opportunity than a chance at reaching Wembley?

The League Cup had been named many things due to various sponsorships, most famously the Coca-Cola Cup between 1992 and 1998 and latterly the League Cup between 2003 and 2012, and in modern-day terms the Carabao Cup. However, the brewery Worthington's would hold the naming rights between 1998 and 2003 and the cup was seen as an opportunity for less glamorous clubs to gain a day at Wembley as Bolton were more than aware thanks to their 1995 appearance against Liverpool. Wanderers and Tranmere were First Division sides and would jump at the chance of a cup final in their season as well as a potential place in European competition for the eventual winner.

Additionally, the chance of another Premier League meeting lay for the winner of the semi-final as the other tie was between Aston Villa and Leicester City.

On 12 January 2000, Bolton welcomed Tranmere to the Reebok Stadium for the first leg of the semi-final. There was an air of expectancy as almost an extra 4,000 Bolton fans attended the game compared to the quarter-final. There was also an added edge as a small rivalry had been brewing between Bolton and Tranmere due to the Merseyside club's defeat of Wanderers in the 1991 Third Division play-off final thanks to an extra-time strike by Bebington-born striker Chris Malkin. Additionally, when Bolton arrived at Prenton Park as First Division champions in 1997 and needing a win to reach the record-breaking 100 points and 100 goals to end their season, Tranmere equalised in the last minute to salvage a 2-2 draw. Fuel was added to the fire further by gestures to the visiting fans from striker John Aldridge, A man who would later go on to become the sole role of Tranmere managerr.

Yet, with all this bad blood in the air, there was a sense of expectancy that Bolton would reach the final after their more recent experiences in the big time of the Premier League compared to Tranmere's lack of top-flight history.

As the teams lined up, Bolton were to be without their defensive lynchpin, the South African Mark Fish. Fish, who had arrived from Lazio during the 1997/98 Premier League campaign, was an imperious defender and was certainly playing below his level in the First Division. Yet he was out of action for the semi-final first leg due to international duty with *Bafana Bafana*. A wealth of experience would plug this gap as Guðni Bergsson returned to the side and in front of him a midfield of Michael Johansen, Claus Jensen, Ricardo Gardner and former Marseille man Franck

Passi, with the hot-shot Eiður Guðjohnsen and Bo Hansen up front.

Although only 13,303 fans were in attendance at the Reebok Stadium, it felt as though there was double that. The place was a cauldron of noise, and the Trotters supporters were willing their team on to give them a day out in the capital. The game started as a feisty affair with rash tackles flying in from both sides and with some tame efforts early on the first real chance came to the home side as Guðjohnsen laid the ball across the edge of the box to Johansen who drove a fierce shot low across the goal which was palmed on to the left-hand post by Rovers keeper John Achterberg and cleared out.

The game was nicely poised early on, and Tranmere had received a throw-in far into the Bolton half. Future Stockport County manager Dave Challinor launched his famous long throw deep into the box as the Bolton defence stood ball-watching. The only player who was able to reach the ball was Tranmere's David Kelly who poked his head towards it and with Steve Banks stretching it sailed past him and clipped the left-hand side post and out for a goal kick. Both teams had hit the woodwork, and the game was in the balance early on. The dangerous throws of Challinor continued to be a problem for the home defence as Challinor's arms were almost as useful as a corner or free kick. It was obvious that the game plan was to take advantage and try to nick a goal to take back to Prenton Park in two weeks' time. Alan Mahon had tested Banks with a looping volley, but it was the most unlikely of sources that broke the deadlock. From the resulting corner, Bolton were yet again caught ball-watching as Gary Jones flicked on with his head across Banks and found defender Clint Hill waiting at the back post to finish into the empty net.

The number six had made it 1-0 to Tranmere on 23 minutes and had not only given his team the lead, but also a precious away goal.

Bolton pressed and pushed for an equaliser but were met with defiant defending from Challinor and Hill as well as superb goalkeeping from Achterberg. Bolton keeper Banks was not having his best game either as he received a yellow card for a very questionable challenge on Kelly. Banks, who was in for Jussi Jääskeläinen, was not doing himself any favours. Alas, despite great work from Gardner and substitute Dean Holdsworth, the game ended 1-0 to the visitors. A big job lay on their hands at Prenton Park in a fortnight's time. Tranmere manager Aldridge, in his usual 'classy' fashion, made the Bolton fans very aware of who had won on the night.

Sandwiched between the two semi-finals were two league games for Bolton. The first was their first win in eight, 1-0 away at QPR thanks to a 64th-minute strike from Claus Jensen, then a 1-1 draw at home to the previous season's rivals and promotion-chasing Ipswich Town at the Reebok.

The second leg at Prenton Park was do or die for Bolton who knew they had to overturn the first-leg result and try to get as many away goals as possible. However, they knew this could leave them open and another goal from Tranmere could kill the tie early. The stadium was full to capacity with 15,834 filling the stands. This was a big night for Tranmere. Usually in the shadow of trophy-hunting Liverpool and Everton, this was a chance for Merseyside's 'third club' to have their moment.

Within five minutes any hopes that Bolton had looked over. A scramble in the box created an opportunity for Nicky Henry who blasted a ball from 18 yards into the top corner, the strike sailing past the diving Steve Banks to make it 2-0 on aggregate. In the 20th minute, Mike Whitlow hauled down former Bolton striker Scott Taylor in the box and referee Graham Poll pointed to the spot; it seemed Bolton were only there to make up the numbers. Poll blew his whistle and Alan Mahon, the player who had tested Banks in the first leg, sent the keeper the wrong way and made it 3-0 on aggregate after 21 minutes. Game and tie over, it seemed.

Tranmere added a third in the 70th minute as Kelly made up for his miss in the first leg by sliding the ball past Banks after a quick free kick, and the Wirral club celebrated long into the night after a 4-0 aggregate win. Aldridge again celebrated this achievement to all four corners of the ground including once more, the Bolton supporters. He and Bolton would meet again the following season and let's just say that fortunes had changed for both clubs. Tranmere went on to play Leicester in the final and lost 2-1 in a spirited performance at Wembley that February. However, they had done the region of Merseyside and the First Division proud.

Alas, it was back to the drawing board for Big Sam and Phil Brown as they had a league campaign to contend with and also an unexpected second chance at cup glory in 2000. The season had seen an upsurge in form after the disappointment of the Tranmere semi-final and the Wanderers were slowly heading towards the top six of the First Division. The players and Sam felt that they owed the fans one and what better way than a 3-1 derby win over Blackburn Rovers at the Reebok Stadium in February in their first league game since the defeat on Merseyside. It was a Scandinavian slammer that day as Iceland's Guðni Bergsson, Great Dane Michael Johansen and of course a goal from Eiður Guðjohnsen sealed the points in front of a bumper 17,687 crowd in Horwich. In fact, Bolton would only go on to lose three more league games in 19 before the regular season came to a close. Prior to this, however, Bolton had also won 3-1 at Cambridge United in the fifth round of the FA Cup to progress to the quarter-final after previously defeating Cardiff City 1-0 and Grimsby Town 2-0 in the winter months.

For many First Division clubs, the FA Cup was an opportunity to get a giant in an early round, maybe some exposure on TV and potentially for some players to put themselves in the shop window. Allardyce had no dreams or visions of going far again in another competition after his already stretched squad had gone so far in the League Cup. The league was the priority and with the run Wanderers were starting, the chance of promotion back to the Premier League was very realistic.

Yet Bolton had somehow reached yet another quarter-final and on 19 February 2000 they faced Charlton Athletic at the Reebok Stadium in the FA Cup. Yet again the Trotters were one win away from Wembley. This had an even bigger incentive for Bolton as the next year, the grand old stadium, which had seen the 1966 World Cup Final, Live Aid in 1985 and of course, Sir Nat Lofthouse lift the 1958 FA Cup for Bolton, was due to be demolished and in its place a state-of-the-art facility which in reality wouldn't be ready to host a game until 2007.

Charlton arrived at the Reebok on the back of some good form and like Bolton, a First Division club who felt they belonged in the Premier League. Alan Curbishley was considered a great up-and-coming manager in the English game and had begun to create a legacy at Charlton. It was in fact Curbishley who would be one of the men Sam would be competing against during his unsuccessful England interview in 2006. They were as determined as Bolton and had the returning Andy Todd in their line-up with eager eyes on he and Brown before and after the game.

Bolton's biggest crowd of the season piled into the Reebok Stadium as 20,131 fans came to hopefully, this time, see their side make it to Wembley. This was their biggest non-Premier League attendance at the Reebok Stadium and the atmosphere was bouncing. Unlike in the semi-finals against Tranmere, Allardyce was able to call upon Mark Fish and Jussi Jääskeläinen, but an unpopular choice was Ricardo Gardner being named among the substitutes and an unlikely start for academy youngster Dean Holden. Holden, who would actually eventually become Charlton manager, had started to bring himself into the Bolton first-team. The number 41 was a life-long Manchester United fan and had turned down trials at Old Trafford to join the Wanderers in a more realistic opportunity of first-team football. He would go on to make 13 league appearances for Bolton before an horrific series of injuries would ruin his career. Holden would go on to tell the *Bolton News* in 2016 that he felt his injury issues at the Reebok cost him four to five years of his career. However, he went on to forge a solid vocation around the Football League as well as a good progression to management.

The Reebok pitch was not at its best as the game kicked off, and resembled Blackpool beach more than a football stadium as sand would begin to get stuck in players' boots. However, the tie started at a breakneck speed and early on Guðjohnsen saw a strike flick off the bar. The crowd was lively and very much 'up for the cup'. At the other end, Jääskeläinen was forced into a close-range save from Swedish striker Martin Pringle in what was proving to be a good old-fashioned end-to-end cup tie. Due to the condition of the pitch, both teams felt they needed to play the ball in the air more than the ground which meant both sets of defenders needed to be alert and ready to head their way out of trouble.

Club president and FA Cup hero Nat Lofthouse was in the crowd, hoping that his beloved Bolton Wanderers could have one last stab at the cup before Wembley was to be demolished. With every tackle, pass and throw-in the fans, Lofthouse included, were cheering as if it was a goal and Guðjohnsen was leading that pack with exciting play and demanding the ball at every opportunity. The game reached fever pitch when on-loan midfielder Allan Johnston whipped the ball into the box to meet Robbie Elliott whose shot was blocked in the six-yard box by Todd, with Elliott's resulting strike firing against the post. It was coming and it was all Bolton as half-time approached. Strikes from Johnston, Johansen and even defender Mike Whitlow came in as the home side took advantage of the pitch and launched many a cross into the Charlton box.

Mark Fish marauded forward and played the ball over to Johansen who laid it to Guðjohnsen, who took his moment – and drove a shot into the top of the South Stand much to the joy of the away fans. Bolton were fired up and the team and Allardyce, for that fact, were refusing to let another chance at Wembley slip through their fingers. Yet Charlton were no pushovers and had come to Bolton on the back of 11 straight wins and would eventually win the First Division that year after the disappointment of relegation the season prior.

The second half started and again Bolton were in charge. Claus Jensen won possession in midfield and the ball found its way to Whitlow who played it towards

Guðjohnsen with his back to goal. Guðjohnsen looked up and played a quick one-two with Michael Johansen then found himself inside the box with the ball at his feet but at a tight angle. That didn't stop the Icelandic striker who swung his right foot and smashed the ball past Dean Kiely to put Bolton 1-0 up. The stadium erupted and Guðjohnsen ran over to Jensen for a celebratory hug. Bolton had their goal as the ball flew in off the post as Guðjohnsen had now scored in every single round of the FA Cup. However, the game was not over, and Charlton were not going to take this lying down. As they got into the game further, despair for Bolton approached: surprise addition Dean Holden was sent off due to an off-the-ball incident with winger John Robinson. Holden admitted his stupidity in the moment as there had been some bad blood between the two due to a collision in the first half. Both players squared up to each other in the second half after some vicious words from Robinson, Holden was seen to potentially head-butt the Charlton winger. Holden would go on to serve a four-game ban and, of course, receive an almighty rollocking from Allardyce. Unfortunately for Holden, upon his return to the first-team he would break his leg against Sheffield United and would never feature for Bolton again.

The second half progressed as Charlton started to feel their way into it after Holden's dismissal and they started to make the advantage count as Allardyce brought striker Bob Taylor off for defender Paul Ritchie. Countless charges on the Bolton goal ensued as Pringle forced a clearance from Whitlow and then Robinson, the pantomime villain of the day, fired over the bar from the resulting corner. Pringle then laid the ball off to Robinson again and this time his strike was firing towards the corner of the net, but Jääskeläinen was able to get a hand to it and turn it away.

Allardyce brought on Ricardo Gardner for some pace and energy to try and weather the storm as Mark Kinsella's shot whistled past the post. Other than a header over the bar from Carl Tiler, which was met like a goal by the Bolton fans, Charlton hadn't done enough and as Graham Poll blew the whistle, the stadium reached pandemonium levels. They had done it, and they were off to Wembley in the FA Cup semi-final. What an achievement. Only six months earlier Allardyce had been at Notts County, he was going to be leading his team out in their second semi-final in the space of two months, and this time he would be doing it at Wembley. Lofthouse looked on in the directors' seats swollen with pride and anticipation of what this next chapter could bring.

Many of the Bolton setup, including Allardyce, were strangers to Wembley but of course, the club was not. Bolton had been the first-team to win the FA Cup there back in the infamous 'White Horse Final' of 1923 and many around the club were eager to create a romantic swansong at the soon-to-be demolished stadium and add the last Wembley winners in 2000 to the first Wembley winners of 1923. Near the top of the list of those trying to achieve this was striker Dean Holdsworth.

London-born Holdsworth had started his football career at Watford, a mere handful of train stops away from Wembley, and was keen for his return to the capital to be much more fruitful than the club's last appearance there the season prior, that 2-0 play-off final loss to Watford under Colin Todd. Holdsworth had floated throughout London clubs before making his way to the Reebok Stadium in the summer of 1997 as Bolton were looking to replace the goals of the ageing John McGinlay with an experienced Premier League striker to accompany Nathan Blake. Eventually

'Deano' would even take McGinlay's prized number ten shirt at the Wanderers.

His £3.5m transfer in 97 was a then club record signing and a weight of expectation was placed upon his shoulders, but unfortunately he only produced three goals for Bolton in that season as they faced relegation in 1998. However, it was in the First Division for Bolton where Holdsworth would start to replicate the form he had shown for Wimbledon in his Premier League days between 1992 and 1997, where he had amassed a total of 76 goals in 208 games for the Dons. In the First Division Holdsworth scored 42 goals over a three-season stretch at the Reebok to become a vital cog in the team under Todd and then Allardyce. It was under Sam that Holdsworth showed his best form in a Bolton shirt and was highly valued by Allardyce as he commented on his excellent moments and crucial goals in building up Bolton's history. It was, however, in the FA Cup semi-final of 2 April 200 where Holdsworth would go on to be most remembered by Bolton fans, not necessarily for the positive.

Ever since the semi-final place was confirmed, the town had been in a frenzy. This had the potential to be the final time a Bolton team would play at the original 'Empire Stadium' at Wembley and fans flocked to ensure they did not miss out. Postal, telephone and physical queues were formed at the Reebok Stadium ticket office as every man and his dog wanted to join in for what they hoped would be the first of three potential visits to the national stadium before it was knocked down. Some 25,000 Bolton fans packed out their end at Wembley and if it had been possible, there could easily have been another 10,000 marching up towards the famous twin towers as Bolton looked ahead for yet another giant-killing.

However, on the pitch the odds were against Bolton as Aston Villa were no Charlton and would not take their opportunity for an FA Cup Final appearance for granted either. The Midlands team hosted a variety of big names of European football and glittering international players. In goal stood David James, England goalkeeper and former winner of trophies at Liverpool. In front of him stood future, present and former England stars Gareth Barry, Gareth Southgate and Paul Merson, with others on the bench in Lee Hendrie and Dion Dublin. Mix this with the international flair of George Boateng and Benito Carbone, and it was clear Bolton had an uphill challenge on their hands. Wanderers felt they could combat these superstars with their own level of quality and measured spirit as Sam picked a team he felt were good enough to go toe-to-toe with John Gregory's titans. Jääskeläinen, Bergsson, Fish, Johansen, Jensen, Guðjohnsen and Holdsworth all stood on the Wembley pitch ready and raring for kick-off.

Allardyce looked back on the last six months of his career. Never did he expect that, after putting his letter of resignation on that desk in Nottingham, he would be leading his beloved Bolton Wanderers out at Wembley, potentially 90 minutes from an FA Cup Final. Yet, there he was.

The game was kicked off by Paul Merson who laid the ball back to midfield as the crowd cheered. Prior to the day there were rumours of discontent around Merson who was believed to have questioned Carbone's loyalty to the Villans due to his refusal to sign a new contract. However, both Merson and Villa stated that their full focus was on the semi-final at this time and would deal with contracts at the end of the season. Villa attempted to control early on, but Bolton fought to ensure this did not happen as Holdsworth had the first strike of the ball straight into the hands of

James from outside of the box. The forward was up for it. At every opportunity, Jensen and Johansen were trying to feed the ball to both Guðjohnsen and Holdsworth and it was Holdsworth once again who came close as his glancing header sailed just past the post and past the diving James.

Villa were rattled and couldn't get a hold of the game, just what Sam had planned on, as Ian Taylor went down early due to a heavy tackle from Allan Johnston and was replaced early on by yet another England international, Steve Stone, in the 14th minute. This break in play gave them a chance to reset and former Arsenal playmaker Merson started to dictate play and pull the strings in the free role. Yet Bolton tested the Villa defence again as Guðjohnsen spun past Southgate and the Iceman's shot was palmed away by David James. The game started to calm down as Bolton passed it across the backline which was being marshalled superbly by Mark Fish. Every time the South African touched the ball, over 25,000 Trotters fans could be heard screaming 'FIIIIIISH!'. Fish had been given the unenviable task of marking the pacy duo of Julian Joachim and Carbone but in all fairness they offered very little as Fish was at the top of his game and on the rare occasion either got through, Jääskeläinen was also on his game to deny them.

The game passed with very little action of note and in the 70th minute, John Gregory brought on former Manchester United striker Dion Dublin to support the attack, to replace Carbone. Carbone showed his disgust in this by kicking a bottle of water towards the Villa bench. The Italian star had been humbled by little old Bolton. Dublin had recently returned after a suspected broken neck in December and was keen to get his career back on track and create history for Villa. As the 90 minutes came to a close, both teams were locked into a midfield battle and the final whistle went at Wembley to set up extra time with the tie still poised at 0-0.

As the additional period started, both sets of players – and managers for that matter – seemed exhausted. The mental and physical toll of playing in such a high-pressure situation had got to the players and it seemed like one moment of brilliance or stupidity could change the fortunes for either club. In the second half of extra time, Aston Villa were privy to a moment of stupidity. Young defender Mark Delaney was bombing down the pitch trying to keep up with winger Allan Johnston. As Johnston pulled away from the right-back, the Irishman hacked at the legs of the Scot to which the referee David Elleray blew and booked Delaney for a vicious foul, joining Holdsworth and Ugo Ehiogu in the notebook. Moments later, Delaney's lack of experience showed as Johnston once again jinked and bombed past him so he performed an almost identical sliding hack on the winger and saw his second yellow card; and the resulting red meant Villa would go into the final ten minutes of extra time with only ten men. Could Bolton make it count?

From the resulting free kick both Guðjohnsen and Holdsworth looked over the ball as Villa's wall was being assembled. Everyone thought Guðjohnsen was surely going to take this but in a quick moment, Holdsworth hit a sweet right-footed shot that curled past the wall and bent around towards the goal. The ball seemed destined to hit the net before it cracked against James's post and out of play. Allardyce could be seen, glasses and moustache too, with his head in his hands as Jimmy Phillips behind him on the Wembley bench with his mouth agape could not believe the Trotters hadn't taken the lead at the death. How close do you need to go?! Even closer it seemed.

Minutes later, Holdsworth had the chance of the game, the season and potentially his career. The ball broke to Guðjohnsen who had slipped past the Aston Villa defence. Wildly, James came storming out of his box attempting to get the ball on the left-hand side but Guðjohnsen was able to take it past the diving keeper. With James out of his net, Guðjohnsen had two choices: smash the ball in from a tight angle like he did against Charlton or lay it off to another player. Up stepped Holdsworth. Guðjohnsen played a pass to Holdsworth who was unmarked on the penalty spot with a clear shot at the open goal. Two Villa defenders were on the line, but Holdsworth had all the time in the world to pick his spot and put his name next to icons such as Nat Lofthouse, Frank Worthington and John McGinlay by slotting the ball into the Wembley net. The ball came to Holdsworth at a slow speed and the number ten stepped forward and crashed it into the – oh, no.

Holdsworth had leant back and blazed the ball over the target, much to the amazement of everyone in the stadium and much to the joy of the travellers from Birmingham. Allardyce stated that if he was going to back anyone to score that, it would have been Holdsworth. The manager dropped to his knees screaming expletives. Minutes later the referee blew the final whistle and the tie went to penalties. Heartbreak for Holdsworth who had dominated the Villa defence all afternoon. He had his moment waiting for him, yet it was not to be. He would be remembered by Bolton fans for ever but not for the moment he wanted, for this moment indeed.

The shoot-out began with tension in the air as many in the Bolton end were still in disbelief at Holdsworth's miss. Villa stepped up first as Steve Stone scored his penalty in the bottom-left corner, and in a moment of bravery, up stepped Holdsworth to take Bolton's first kick. 'Deano' chants scrambled from the crowd as Holdsworth placed his penalty in the right-hand corner, sending James the wrong way. Fair play and some real guts needed there.

Hendrie scored for Villa as the score turned to 2-1 despite Jääskeläinen getting a touch. Next, up stepped Johnston. The man on loan from Sunderland looked as though he wanted the penalty over and done with, and his tame shot was saved by James. Nineteen-year-old Gareth Barry put his penalty away calmly as Villa rose to a 3-1 lead in the shoot-out. The future Villa captain would be called up to the England Euro 2000 squad that summer and go on to forge a successful career for himself. Next, up stepped Michael Johansen, the Dane originally signed in the double deal with Per Frandsen by Colin Todd. A hero due to his part in the farewell to Burnden season and a man who had helped get Bolton to both semi-finals. The winger stepped up and smashed his penalty straight at James as Bolton hearts began to drop and it seemed a miracle was needed to secure a return to Wembley. Dublin stepped up and had the chance to be a hero to so many. He sent Jääskeläinen the wrong way and put Villa into the FA Cup Final. More semi-final heartbreak for Sam and for Bolton.

As many Wanderers fans were making their way back home, Sam was holding court in the dressing room and made his pride clear to the players, 'Be proud of yourselves. Now let's get on with making the play-offs'.

Bolton couldn't afford the time to wallow, especially Holdsworth who had missed the chance to be a history-maker. Yet the Trotters needed to forget the heartbreak quickly if they were to have any chance of returning to Wembley in the play-offs. Allardyce and Phil Brown plotted out the remainder of the season and ended up winning five of their last six games, finishing with a 2-1 victory at home over Wolves – to end the West Midlands club's play-off dreams – and then a 1-0 victory over Norwich City at the Reebok thanks to a late goal from Holdsworth. Bolton had made the play-offs by sneaking into sixth place by two points over Sam's beloved Wolves and looked forward to facing an old foe over two legs, a team that had been plotting their revenge for 12 months. The semi-final would be a repeat of the season before as Bolton would face Ipswich Town.

4

Rise from the ashes of defeat

THERE WERE 12 points between Bolton and Ipswich in the 1999/2000 regular season, in the Tractor Boys' favour as well. Ipswich had progressed since losing to Bolton over two legs in 1999 and were ready to gain their revenge in a carbon copy of the tie from the previous season with the first leg being at the Reebok and the second being at Portman Road. The first leg created more drama in this most random of rivalries as Bolton sailed into a 2-0 lead within 30 minutes thanks to Dean Holdsworth and Eiður Guðjohnsen. They looked ready to ruin the script by dumping out the team that marginally missed out on automatic promotion for the fourth season running. However, Ipswich had strengthened and the lethal Marcus Stewart scored two goals to end the game in a 2-2 draw. On a scorching day in BL6, Ipswich had shown fight to bring the score even and Stewart's first goal was a particular highlight after firing a half-volley from all of 30 yards into the top corner past Jussi Jääskeläinen. Stewart had cost the Tractor Boys £2.5m only months earlier and was very much seen as a last-ditch attempt by Ipswich to guarantee promotion. His transfer from Huddersfield Town was a club record signing at the time. Stewart would prove to be a shrewd signing and would go on to score 19 goals the following season, this time in the Premier League.

That line will give you an insight to how the second leg went for Bolton as the two teams lined up at Portman Road on 17 May 2000.

This was the eighth time Bolton and Ipswich had faced each other in the space of less than 18 months and both teams were sick of the sight of each other. By the end of this game, Wanderers would be sick of the sight of one man in particular, referee Barry Knight. Knight, from Kent, was given the role of referee for the highly important second leg and would make the game very much the 'Barry Knight Show', much to the disappointment of Sam Allardyce et al. However, after this game, Knight would never referee Bolton again in his career.

Much like the second leg the year prior, the night started off at a wicked pace with Bolton lining up in their usual home strip but with the change of yellow socks due to Ipswich's white socks. It was being screened live by ITV Granada and the coverage was extended due to the events of the game. Both teams sprinted out of the tunnel to a fanfare of support from all four corners of the ground. There was a carnival atmosphere in East Anglia as the boys in blue were looking to right the wrongs of 1999.

In the build-up, Bolton were handed a killer blow as Guðjohnsen was ruled out with an injury that many in the away end felt was a potential precaution due to a rumoured move away. In reality, Guðjohnsen was actually injured, but he had unknowingly played his last game in a Bolton shirt anyway, moving to Chelsea for £4.5m in the ensuing summer.

This changed the shape for Bolton as Allardyce decided to trust Holdsworth on his own and move to a

4-5-1 formation with a midfield three of Paul Warhurst, Claus Jensen and Robbie Elliott supporting the wingers of Michael Johansen and Allan Johnston. This was also supplemented by unusual full-backs of Guðni Bergsson and Mike Whitlow who, by trade, were centre-backs. However, no motivation was needed as every player on the pitch knew what victory would bring: another day at Wembley and a chance to get back to the Premier League.

The match kicked off with blue balloons dotted around the pitch. However, it was Bolton who started the brightest with Johansen grazing the bar from 50 yards as he saw Richard Wright off his line to test the nerves of the Portman Road crowd. The midfield five were overpowering Ipswich and making their possession count as Johansen played a ball over to the wing towards Bergsson who played it back to him and the Dane launched a looping cross into the box. Elliott challenged keeper Wright who caught the ball then dropped it into the path of Holdsworth who nudged home to make it 1-0. Holdsworth peeled away with his hand cupped to his ear, probably waiting for the responses after his miss at Wembley earlier after getting some grief from the Ipswich fans. Bolton had gone 1-0 up after six minutes on the night and 3-2 on aggregate. Allardyce celebrated but was more than aware that the tie was nowhere near over.

The hosts replied on 18 minutes as Jim Magilton jinked past the Bolton defence and went down, rather dramatically after a tackle from Elliott in the box. Magilton stood up and sent Jääskeläinen the wrong way to equalise on the night; the Irish midfielder would prove to be a pest for the entire match, and not for the first time, causing a furious response from Mike Whitlow who accused Magilton of diving to gain the penalty.

Holdsworth then gave Bolton the lead once again with a sublime free kick in the 39th minute after Allan Johnston was fouled on the edge of the box. Once again, however, Ipswich had a penalty as Stewart went down in the box. On second look it was obvious that there was no foul and Bolton had been hard done by. Referee Knight was chased by Bergsson and Whitlow who were fuming with the decision. It also seemed that Magilton had swung at Warhurst in the melee. This was missed by Knight as Magilton put the ball down for Ipswich's second spot-kick of the half. Magilton stepped up and hit a sweet strike that was heading to the side of the net before Jääskeläinen got a strong hand to it and pushed it out for a corner to the elation of the away fans, Allardyce and the great Finnish keeper himself who celebrated by shaking his fist at the Ipswich supporters. Jääskeläinen would become a club legend at Bolton and although he would be more remembered for his exploits in the Premier League years, his exploits in the First Division were very much a stepping stone to get Bolton to the level above. When looking back on those iconic Premier League moments, it's hard to deny that if Jääskeläinen had not put the hard yards in in the lower divisions then he would not have been given the chance to show what he could do in the top tier.

Upon the ball going out for a corner, Whitlow and Warhurst returned to Magilton to show their joy at the save. Magilton was left with 'pie on his face'. Going into half-time, Bolton were on their way to Wembley, yet this was all soon to change. With the second leg still poised at 2-1 and the tie at 3-2, Ipswich started to pile on the pressure and five minutes into the second half Magilton created a piece of magic, picking the ball up in the box and jinking past two defenders to then drive the ball in the back of the net; 2-2. However, just a minute later, Bolton scored again through a half-volley from Allan Johnston. Not a marquee signing, Johnston had arrived as Allardyce's first transfer for Bolton on a short-term loan deal from Sunderland. His hard work, furious running and drive had been a great addition to the team and his 19 games for Bolton that season were enough to convince Glasgow Rangers to sign him in the summer of 2000. Johnston had made the match 3-2 and with 40 minutes remaining Bolton had a one-goal aggregate lead and were going to Wembley.

Wanderers almost made it 4-2 when Wright saved a close-range shot from Jensen but Allardyce and Phil Brown worried that there was still life in the match. Going into the 90th minute, the ball was launched into the box and with time almost up, Magilton completed his hat-trick and made himself an East Anglia legend by placing the ball into the bottom corner to take the match to extra time at 3-3 on the night and 4-4 on aggregate.

Just before Knight blew for full time, there was more drama. As Ipswich hunted for a last-minute winner, Stewart was seen to have been brought down by Whitlow on the edge of the Ipswich box. Stewart made the most of it and Knight awarded a free kick to Ipswich. Knight approached Whitlow and stated that he saw the hdefender bring down Stewart with a drag on the edge of the box. However, any neutral watching the game would be stunned with what would happen next: Knight showed Whitlow a straight red card. The referee would go on to say that Whitlow had denied Stewart a goalscoring opportunity, this despite around eight players being in front of the pair. Bolton had lost their captain on the night and Whitlow handed the armband to Bergsson as he walked off in disbelief, he and most of the stadium too. Luckily, Magilton's free kick flew over and Knight blew the whistle for full time.

Four minutes into extra time, Knight struck again and handed Ipswich a third penalty of the night. With the ball bouncing in the box, David Johnson attempted to head it into the Bolton net, but he was expertly shepherded by another Scot on loan, Paul Ritchie. The 25-year-old centre-back turned around ready to carry on with the game after Johnson had climbed all over him and fell over to see Knight once again point to the spot.

Jamie Clapham stepped up and slammed the ball into the net to make it 4-3 so Bolton started to push for a goal. They tried to get the ball to the other end but as Clapham played a pass down the line towards Martijn Reuser, Elliott slid in with frustration but got the ball perfectly as the Dutch midfielder made a meal of the challenge. Elliott, already on a booking, saw the writing on the wall as soon as he heard the whistle; his second yellow card was soon followed by a red and Bolton were down to nine men. They still pushed and pushed but as the numbers were in the home side's favour, Ipswich went on the break and Reuser slammed the ball past Jääskeläinen to make it 5-3 on the night and 6-4 on aggregate. The Portman Road faithful invaded the pitch and celebrated long into the night. Ipswich would later win on their day in Wembley and beat Barnsley 4-2 in the final to reach the Premier League.

However, a night that should have been remembered for two First Division titans going to battle would be remembered for a man who didn't kick a ball on the night, Barry Knight. By the end of extra time, Knight had sent off two Bolton players, awarded Ipswich three penalties and booked a total of eight Wanderers men with not one home star receiving as much as a yellow card. Allardyce fumed at this and, not in a spirit of being a bad loser but a feeling of injustice, went in on Knight after the game. The manager would later state that it was indescribable what he wanted to do to Knight and marched down to the ref's door screaming and shouting and demanding an explanation. However, the official refused to open the door. Allardyce would tell the media that night, 'Knight's performance was unacceptable, he lost control. That referee shouldn't be allowed to referee another game.' Allardyce was later charged by the FA for his comments as was Bergsson for his words on the same topic. Allardyce added fuel to the fire by informing journalists that he 'didn't give a shit' what the FA charged him with. After the dust had settled, it was still hard for Bolton fans to rewatch that match and Allardyce and his team enjoyed a drink the night after still fuming with injustice as they started to plan for the next season. Bolton had been beaten in three semi-finals in 1999/2000 and while they couldn't argue with the first two, the last one left a bitter taste of injustice.

The impact of missing out on promotion was already starting to show as Bolton sold Guðjohnsen to Chelsea then star midfielder Claus Jensen went to promoted Charlton Athletic for £4m. The fallout from failing to reach the Premier League was there for all to see.

Heartbroken from their semi-final defeats, Bolton went into the summer transfer period with realism abounding. The prospect of having to lose their cup heroes had become a distinct reality and with little money to replace them, the challenge of promotion would be even harder than the previous two seasons. However, Sam decided to invest off the field and thus, his legacy of being a frontrunner in sports science was starting to take shape.

Following Jensen and Guðjohnsen to the Premier League was Mark Fish who joined Jensen at Charlton for £1.5m. Adding to this, Paul Ritchie and youngster Hasney

Aljofree would leave to join teams in Scotland as well as club icon Michael Johansen returning to Denmark with Akademisk Boldklub. The team that had done so well during the season was starting to become decimated but Bolton had been able to recoup an impressive £9.5m and would end up only spending around £3.5m of that on transfers.

Sam knew he needed to buy wisely and though Danes Jensen and Johansen left, one familiar Danish face returned in Per Frandsen. Not even a year into his move across Lancashire to Blackburn Rovers, Frandsen had become unsettled and Allardyce stated he 'saved him' from Ewood Park. Bolton paid £2m to bring Frandsen back to the Reebok, a saving of £250,000 from the sale less than 12 months prior. Imagine the look on Colin Todd's face when he saw that deal pop up on Sky Sports.

Joining Frandsen would be experienced defender and former Scotland captain Colin Hendry. Hendry had won the Premier League with Blackburn in 1995 and was a vital part of the Scotland team who reached both Euro 96 and the World Cup in 1998 and would bring a wealth of experience and quality that had been lost from the defence due to the sale of Fish. The 35-year-old cost an estimated £250,000 from Coventry City after an initial loan deal. Allardyce brought in shrewd free transfers in full-backs Simon Charlton and Anthony Barness as well as powerful striker Michael Ricketts from Walsall for £400,000 to try to replace the goals left by Guðjohnsen's sale to Chelsea. Veteran striker Ian Marshall would join later in the summer as well.

Sam had made some impressive on-field signings but the real investment was behind the scenes. Bolton had purchased a brand-new training complex in Euxton, near

Preston, and the manager was keen to build a successful team both on and off the pitch and that needed to start by getting the fundamentals right firstly.

During Sam's time in Tampa as a player, he had seen first-hand the importance of a backroom staff in American sports, especially in the NFL. He would label this 'the team behind the team'. Even in the early 1980s the use of data and science was there to see Stateside and this is something Sam always thought about during his route to elite management in football.

Sam made it clear to the Bolton board that in his eyes, for the club to compete, they needed to gain a competitive edge where other teams hadn't: behind the scenes. He wanted sports scientists, focus on conditioning of players, nutritional experts, psychologists, higher quality scouts and the software Prozone to use for a clear analysis of his team's performance. Bolton needed to be cutting-edge to be able to compete with big money-spending teams and Sam was able to convince the board that in the long run it would make their own players better, last longer and be an incredible investment for the future. How right he was.

When Allardyce arrived the only computer in the club was in the secretary's office so he managed to get a deal for second-hand laptops for his new regime. The first off-field acquisition was Jack Chapman as chief scout from Blackburn Rovers. Chapman was 69 by the time he arrived at Bolton and Allardyce would later recall how Chapman would ensure that he would be 69 for the rest of his working life in order to avoid being phased out at 70. Chapman had worked with Sam at Blackpool previously and would later follow him to his future clubs until his passing at the age of 82. Chapman's influence would be huge on the future of Bolton Wanderers as he supported the club in the famous deals for Jay-Jay Okocha, Fernando Hierro, Youri Djorkaeff and Radhi Jaïdi in years to come due to his scouting network that covered the globe and left no stone unturned.

Joining Chapman would be a host of academics and scientists not normally seen in football. Mark Taylor joined as head of sports science and medicine, Faz Page was promoted from kitman to sports therapist before Sam arrived but was highly regarded by Allardyce, Dr Tim Weighman joined as the club's sports physician, Matt Hocking arrived as match analyst, Mark Howard arrived as strength and conditioning coach, and the jewel in the crown was Mike Forde. Forde joined as the club's sports psychologist, arriving from Lancashire County Cricket Club. His responsibilities would be looking into the motivation and barrier-breaking of the players' mindsets to ensure they could be effective on the pitch but also effective human beings. This approach was questioned, especially by Dean Holdsworth and Guðni Bergsson at first. Forde would go on to be made performance director at Bolton and would later become head of football operations at Chelsea before moving to New York, advising sports teams around the world.

Sam would also promote from within by moving coach Chris Sulley up to take over as academy director and appointing Geoff Davey as the head of youth recruitment while also creating a pathway for Jimmy Phillips to move into youth coaching upon retirement. Sam would also hire outside help from time to time, and support from external companies and the facilities from Liverpool John Moores University were used to help give Bolton the competitive edge. Bolton could not compete on the transfer fund with many other clubs but they could beat them behind the scenes. The initial sceptics in the first-team would eventually start to see the results of this in their own performances, no more than Bergsson who was able to extend his career by another three years thanks to the work on nutrition and happily gave up his cup of tea and a steak for energy drinks and vegetables.

Allardyce's men, however, had a torrid start to pre-season in 2000. During a tour to Denmark, Bolton lost 2-1 to Brøndby, 6-0 to Lyngby and 6-1 to Odense. Adding to that, Sam's team toured the USA and lost 1-0 to the country's under-23 team. Not great as many worried about the season to come, although one shining light was the emergence of youth talent Kevin Nolan.

Nolan was 16 when he first joined Bolton after being invited to a youth training session by a friend. He was handed a year-to-year contract after the training session and did enough to impress Chris Sulley who would then speak to Allardyce to help persuade Big Sam to offer Nolan a professional contract. The Scouser had been released from his boyhood club Liverpool prior to this; the Reds' loss was Bolton's gain. Nolan had played four games the season prior and by the end of 2000/01 would rack up an impressive 31 appearances by the age of 18. His combative style and never-say-die attitude impressed Allardyce who was happy to use Nolan in the position vacated by Claus Jensen. Nolan would go on to become a fans' favourite and would make 345 appearances for the club over a ten-year period, scoring 50 goals. During this time, Nolan would become captain, score on the continent and score goals in wins against Manchester United in back-to-back seasons. Although England recognition never came, Nolan was always classed by many in the game as being very unlucky never to play for the Three Lions. Nolan would leave the Trotters in 2009 to join Newcastle United before a move to

West Ham United in 2011, later embarking on his coaching career in 2015.

With the dismal pre-season behind them, Sam's team needed a fresh start. The boss needed to be able to justify the massive changes on and off the pitch to the board and a strong start was imperative. In the first nine games of the season, Bolton won seven of them including a slice of revenge with a win over Tranmere at Prenton Park.

However, the match, yet again, would be remembered for other reasons thanks to the ever-brewing rivalry between Allardyce and Tranmere's ever-so-modest manager, John Aldridge. Still feeling the sting eight months after that League Cup semi-final defeat, Bolton returned to the Wirral for the first time since that awful evening. Keen to make a point and get the points, upon inspection, Allardyce found the facilities provided to the visitors were not satisfactory. Given Bolton's investment in off-field ventures, Allardyce felt the facilities at Prenton Park were not worthy of his forward-thinking team so had his players get changed at the Reebok Stadium before travelling late to the match. Some would say mind games, Aldridge would take offence, but whatever happened, it worked and Bolton came off the pitch celebrating a 1-0 victory thanks to Mike Whitlow, who had lost the armband to Guðni Bergsson. After the game, Allardyce stated that his team 'didn't want to spend too long here' and that they 'went there with a job to do and did it'. Tranmere chairwoman Lorraine Rogers took deep offence to this and labelled Allardyce as 'peculiar' and stated her lack of understanding at his approach to football. Well, that peculiar approach would do Bolton OK as six years later while Wanderers prepared to face Marseille in the knockout stages of the UEFA Cup in 2006, Tranmere would finish 18th in England's third tier.

Bolton moved towards the back end of September unbeaten before they faced eventual champions Fulham. The west London club came to the Reebok and decimated Bolton with a comprehensive 2-0 victory in front of 19,924 supporters. Fulham would go on to win the title by amassing an amazing 101 points in May and with players such as future France international Louis Saha, future Champions League winner Steve Finnan as well as former Arsenal winger Luis Boa Morte, it was no surprise that Jean Tigana's men finished ten points ahead of second place.

It was clear from around October that it was highly likely that Fulham would be taking one of the automatic promotion places and the fight for second was majorly fought between Bolton and close neighbours Blackburn Rovers. The two famous Lancashire clubs were in a near dead heat most of the season and the fight for second was on. They shared a point each at Ewood Park in September thanks to a last-minute equaliser from Bo Hansen cancelling out James Thomas's opener after only 48 seconds. Blackburn were a strong outfit and only five years from their 1995 Premier League-winning glory. However, ups and downs at both playing and board level had brought the Rovers down to the First Division in a league with local rivals Burnley as well as Bolton. Iconic owner Jack Walker, the man who had brought the glory days to Ewood Park in the 1990s, had died shortly before the start of the season and manager Graeme Souness made it clear to his players that they were to fulfil the late wishes of Walker by getting Blackburn back to the Premier League as soon as possible and by 2001 if they could.

After a tricky start to the season which had seen Blackburn lose four games in five between September and October, they would go on to fight their way back towards the summit of the table by losing only one match between 18 October 2000 and 9 February 2001, then only one more defeat before the end of the season. A man who was proving to emulate the days of Alan Shearer at Ewood Park was striker Matt Jansen who would end the season with 23 league goals and would eventually earn an England squad call-up the year after. Adding to this was local lad David Dunn, Irish winger Damien Duff, former Burnden Park hero Jason McAteer and Bolton-born Gary Flitcroft. Factoring in the experience of American keeper Brad Friedel and Champions League winner Henning Berg, many argued that Blackburn already had a team and a manager ready for the Premier League after their dismal 11th-placed finish the previous season. Blackburn had seen Manchester City clinch promotion at their ground in 1999/2000 and were hungry for some of that glory.

By the time the two clubs met again in late February 2001, Bolton looked comfortable in second and were seven points ahead of their local rivals. Many believed that a win in this fixture would near enough cement an almost certain promotion for Bolton. As well as the league fixture, the clubs had also met in the fifth round of the FA Cup at Ewood Park, which once again ended in a 1-1 draw. The replay would be played after the league game, meaning they would play each other three times in the space of three weeks.

The league game at the Reebok on 23 February promised to be a tasty affair with two rivals fighting for the promotion chances. Blackburn arrived in their away kit of black and red stripes with a strong front line of Duff, Jansen and Marcus Bent. A crowd of 20,017 turned up and the game kicked off at a very tense pace; it wasn't until the stroke of half-time that the first goal was scored, and it was first blood to Rovers. A defensive mix-up between Bergsson and former Blackburn defender Colin Hendry meant the ball ended up at the feet of Bent on the edge of the box, where the striker took a touch and smashed the ball past Steve Banks, in for the injured Jääskeläinen. That was Bent's tenth goal of the season and the away end limbs were everywhere.

Blackburn went into the break with a lead so in response, Sam brought on striker Michael Ricketts for Bo Hansen on 60 minutes. Ricketts was on 16 league goals by February after his summer move from Walsall and was proving to be known as a supersub for Bolton and someone who could change games. However, on 74 minutes disaster struck as Jansen found himself in the clear down the left-hand side with acres of space in front of him. Jansen played the ball into the box where a couple of deflections laid it into the path of Dunn. Dunn moved the ball from right foot to left foot past Hendry and fired his shot under Banks from inside the six-yard box; 2-0 down with 15 minutes remaining, Bolton looked defeated.

Six minutes later, the defeat was confirmed when Craig Hignett picked up the ball and launched it towards Jansen, who had beaten the offside flag and zipped past Hendry on the edge of the box. Jansen was one-on-one with Banks and dummied to shoot which caused Banks to dive so all Jansen had to do was scoop it over his arms to make it 3-0. It was hard to be angry with Banks as in fact, it could have been a cricket score at that point and he had helped avoid that. Hendry and Bergsson had been embarrassed on that day and many Bolton fans looked at the age of the backline as a cause of concern due to the youth and pace of Duff and Jansen. How right they were. Some supporters voted with their feet after the third goal as the stadium started to empty. Jansen's 14th goal of the season in the 81st minute had been too much for them to handle.

Ricketts pulled one back in the 84th minute to make it 3-1 with his 17th of the season but that consolation was short-lived as Blackburn regained their three-goal lead with a strike from Hignett in the 89th minute. With probably the best goal of the game, Hignett struck a sweet free kick into Banks's top corner to confirm an awful day for Bolton but a moment that would catapult Blackburn's season. Bolton had been humbled and would only go on to win one of their next seven matches. In the replay for the fifth round of the FA Cup, Blackburn would again prevail at the Reebok with a 3-0 success. Blackburn were back in the race and by the end of March, when Bolton drew at home with 11th-placed Wimbledon, Rovers had leapfrogged them into second place.

The dismal afternoon gave the bragging rights to Blackburn and those Bolton fans who lived on the border of the town in areas such as Edgworth, Bromley Cross, Abbey Village and Egerton were often mocked by their local neighbours. However, on that day there was one shining light.

Michael Ricketts was born in Birmingham and had come through the youth system at Walsall; by the age of 18 he had made the first-team and would score 15 goals in 90 games for the Saddlers before he made the journey to join Bolton. The pacy yet strong striker had been labelled as the First Division Emile Heskey by the fans and the comparisons in their playing style was clear. The season before signing, he had impressed Allardyce in both the matches against Bolton for Walsall and had done enough, including goals in both matches in 1999/2000 to convince the board to part with £400,000. Ricketts had caused

Bergsson and Fish a lot of trouble and Sam felt the £400,000 fee would prove to be a bargain. After the departure of Guðjohnsen to Chelsea, a lot of expectation was placed on the shoulders of Ricketts who would make the majority of his contributions in that season from the bench. However, by the time Blackburn had battered Bolton in February, Ricketts had scored 17 goals. Ricketts was a handful for many defences in the First Division and would go on to do the same in the Premier League further down the line.

However, issues arose around his attitude and motivation. Frustrated by his new role as a 'supersub', Ricketts would often display a moody demeanour on the pitch, bench and around the Euxton training ground and when a move to Tottenham fell through at the last minute in 2002, he struggled to hide his dismay. He had built up a strong relationship with youngster Kevin Nolan and the pair motivated each other to get to the top of their game and although Nolan would have the better career of the two, Ricketts' contribution during the 2000/01 season would go on to create a goal record that would take 20 years to be broken by Eoin Doyle in 2021. Ricketts' lightning pace, powerful striking and excellent heading ability ensured Bolton had enough firepower to remain in the top three for the majority of the season. A favourite of the fans, Ricketts would go on to score 46 goals before a £3.5m move to Middlesbrough in 2003 ended his Bolton career, one which included a call-up to the England squad to play the Netherlands where he would play alongside Sol Campbell, Rio Ferdinand, David Beckham, Paul Scholes and Steven Gerrard in a 1-1 draw. However, many would argue that Ricketts would never be the same player again after this as his form dipped dramatically. His 22 goals by the end of the 2000/01 season eventually helped Bolton but it would be his next two goals which would cement his place in club folklore.

However, as the First Division season began to come to a close, by mid-April, Bolton found themselves six points behind Blackburn whose impressive run had seen them join Fulham in the top two. By the time Bolton recorded a 1-0 win away at Barnsley on 28 April with a goal from Ricketts, Blackburn had confirmed their promotion with a 3-1 win over Portsmouth at Ewood Park. The East Lancashire club celebrated into the night and knew that they and Fulham would be joining the Premier League elite the next season. But for Sam and Bolton it was that dreaded word again – play-offs.

5

Cardiff calling

AS BOLTON'S place in the play-off places had been confirmed for weeks, Sam decided to use the last game of the season to make some changes in the first-team squad and give some of the more reliable heads some time off before the semi-finals. He fielded a team with either first or second senior appearances from Leam Richardson (21), Jeff Smith (20), Emanuele Morini (19), Chris Downey (18) and Nicky Hunt (17). They were sporting the following season's strip, a more modest Reebok kit with a plain white core and black slits across the shoulders. Many were hoping this new modern style would be showing itself in the Premier League come August. Bolton drew 1-1 with Sheffield United thanks to a 90th-minute equaliser from Dean Holden, who was returning from injury, and preparation continued for a two-legged play-off bout with West Bromwich Albion.

West Brom had finished sixth in the First Division under manager Gary Megson and had beaten Bolton once that season at the Reebok, 1-0. The West Midlands club were on the rise and were looking to reach the Premier League for the first time and gain bragging rights over their rivals Wolves. Of course, Allardyce, a Wolves fan in his youth, loved nothing more than to help ensure those rights remained at Molineux. Albion striker Lee Hughes was making the headlines with 21 league goals that season and was gaining the attention of many Premier League clubs, as was his strike partner Jason Roberts. Making up other parts of the team were former Bolton players Richard Sneekes and play-off warrior Bob Taylor who Allardyce had sold to West Brom the season prior after he had scored 21 goals over a two-year period. However, Taylor was an icon at The Hawthorns, and either side of his Bolton tenure he played for West Brom for a combined nine years, scoring 129 goals for the Baggies in all competitions.

In a change from previous seasons, Bolton would go into the play-offs as the favourites after taking third place and just missing out on automatic promotion, finishing 13 points ahead of West Brom. When they met in the first leg at The Hawthorns on 13 May, Wanderers lined up in a yellow strip due to a kit clash between the two clubs and wore the away shirt from two seasons previous. There was great excitement at The Hawthorns as 18,167 entered the ground for West Brom's big day, one of three they were hoping for. West Brom had never played in the Premier League and were one of the favourites for relegation at the start of the season so many were expecting a rollover Bolton victory.

Bolton lined up with a much-changed team from the one who had drawn with Sheffield United and welcomed back Matt Clarke in goal as part of a strong line-up of Guðni Bergsson, Robbie Elliott, Simon Charlton, Colin Hendry, Anthony Barness, Gareth Farrelly, Bo Hansen, Dean Holdsworth, Ricardo Gardner and a start for Michael Ricketts. The Baggies showed off a strike force of Roberts and Hughes and it was they who would cause a frantic start to the first leg.

Allardyce admitted that the play-offs had always been a jinx to him and they were also seeming that way to Bolton after the heartbreak at Wembley against Watford and the drama of the previous year's semi-final defeat to Ipswich, adding to that the two semi-final defeats in the League Cup and FA Cup in 1999/2000. However, it seemed that Sam's hypothesis of a jinx was true as the game kicked off in the Midlands.

The Hawthorns mirrored a building site as the Midlands club were re-structuring the main stand which, unfortunately for them, was being directly filmed by the Sky Sports cameras. However, it was Bolton who were being demolished at the start, not the stadium. As the West Brom defence had dealt with a Bolton cross easily, Neil Clement launched a massive long ball towards Hughes, who started a rapid foot race with Hendry. Hughes cleverly used his body to put Hendry off balance and as the Scot slipped to the ground, the star striker was free and running into the box with the ball at his feet and only Clarke to beat. As Hughes struck a sweet right-footed strike, it sailed past Clarke and slammed against the bar. The Bolton fans behind that goal were anxious and this was a sign of things to come as Barness managed to scoop it away. However, Bolton had not learned and after another long ball from the back, rapid striker Roberts beat Bergsson to it on the edge of the box and slid it past Clarke, in for the injured Jääskeläinen, to make it 1-0 Baggies on the stroke of half-time.

Ten minutes into the second half, another blow hit the Wanderers as West Brom started where they left off. With balls flying into the box and each one seeming to fall at the feet of a home player, Bolton were pegged inside their own penalty area. The ball fell to Roberts on the edge of the box after some good work down the wing, and he drove forward before going down under the trailing leg of Hendry. It was a 50/50 that could have gone either way but Hendry had been playing with fire by diving in. Referee David Laws pointed to the spot and West Brom had a penalty. Up stepped Hughes to put the Baggies further ahead, in front of the home fans, and with a confident run-up he smashed it past Clarke to make it 2-0. The game and promotion was slipping through Bolton's hands and the supporters who had travelled to the Midlands were making themselves heard as boos started to come from the away end. Surely not another semi-final heartbreak?

The Bolton defence had been having a horrible time and Hendry in particular was struggling after receiving a booking. Thinking of the issues of red cards from the previous season, Allardyce decided to make a change and brought him off. Allardyce changed from a 3-5-2 to a 4-3-3 in the hope that Hansen and Gardner would expose the three West Brom central defenders. He also brought on Per Frandsen, and with the change in formation, new life seemed to come into the team. Ricketts was a man possessed, harassing and bullying the West Brom defence, but as the game got to the 80th minute it was still 2-0 West Brom and Allardyce knew if the score remained the same, the home side would go into the second leg to frustrate his men and defend for their lives.

On 81 minutes, a quick one-two between Ricketts and Farrelly found Ricketts inside the penalty area on the left, but just as the striker was about to play it across into the danger area, a great tackle by Des Lyttle put the ball out for a corner. The big men from the back came forward in an attempt to salvage something from this torrid game. For 81 minutes, West Brom had held Bolton's number and played amazingly. Yet this was all about to change. A corner swung into the box from Irish international Farrelly and was heading for the right of the six-yard box. There, skipper Bergsson, sandwiched in between two defenders, rose highest and claimed a firm header which looped over the arms of keeper Russell Hoult and bounced off the bar and into the net; 2-1 and game on.

Ricketts grabbed the ball from the net and sprinted to the other half to get the game rolling. The last eight minutes were like a basketball match as Bolton rushed forward to gain the equaliser, but West Brom would try and counter. It was end-to-end as Elliott picked the ball up inside his own half and drove forward. As he twisted and turned, Farrelly took over and started to play down the right-hand side. He looked up and saw the run of Bo Hansen and with the outside of his boot played a perfectly timed ball that beat the defence and with one touch, Hansen knocked it past the backline and was in the box running at speed with the ball. All Hansen had to do was look and shoot but he took a touch and just as he was about to strike, a leg from Lyttle tripped him up. Albeit a soft foul, it was a foul and although Hansen made the most of it, Bolton had a penalty in the 88th minute. Eight minutes prior they had been 2-0 down and now they were looking at the chance to take a draw back to the Reebok.

Substitute Frandsen stepped up in front of the Bolton fans and, after a long run-up, swung his right leg towards the ball and placed it in the bottom right-hand corner before running to the supporters who only 15 minutes ago had started to boo him and his team-mates. There were no more boos, just elation; 2-2. The home crowd was flat and they had been deflated by Bolton's comeback.

The final whistle went and the Wanderers saw themselves extremely lucky to be going back to the Reebok with a draw. Allardyce made his feelings known in the dressing room but also looked to motivate the team ahead of the big match at home five days later. He told the media that if his side 'were as bad in the second leg as they were today then they could forget going to the play-off final'. Megson, on the other hand, was crushed as he saw the Bolton fans elated. This would not be the last time Megson would have issues with Wanderers supporters as he would go on to have a toxic relationship with them during his time as manager in the late 2000s.

Five days later, the Reebok Stadium welcomed 23,515 fans for the second leg – the highest attendance of the season. There was still a lot of tension but when Bergsson scored after just ten minutes, there was no stopping Sam Allardyce's upwardly mobile Whites.

Bolton still needed a magnificent performance from Colin Hendry at the heart of the defence – the Scotland international making up for a poor display in the first game – but when Anthony Barness set up Ricardo Gardner for the second goal on 63 minutes it was all over bar the shouting. All that remained was for Michael Ricketts to make it three in the 90th minute with his 23rd goal of the season and the bandwagon headed for Cardiff's Millennium Stadium – used while Wembley was being rebuilt – and a match that chairman Phil Gartside reckoned was worth £40m to the winners. It had finished 3-0 on the night and 5-2 on aggregate. The Wanderers had made it to the final where they would face local rivals Preston North End.

One player who was keen to exorcise the ghosts of play-off misery was 22-year-old Jamaican winger Ricardo Gardner. Gardner had been originally signed by Colin Todd in the summer of 1998 from Jamaican side Harbour View at the age of 18. His youthful looks and raw pace would earn him the nickname 'Bibi' by both fans and team-mates alike. A quiet yet self-assured young man, Gardner showed great bravery to move to Bolton at such an early age. Gardner had caught Todd's eye in the World Cup of 1998 where Jamaica went out in the group stages with defeats to Croatia and Argentina, but a win against Japan in their final game gave them some pride to take back home to the Caribbean. After this tournament, Bolton would pay £1m for his services, quite a fee for a First Division side to splash on an unknown quantity. However, Todd's faith would prove to be magic and Gardner became one of the most-loved players in Bolton history.

In his first league appearance for Bolton, Gardner came on as substitute and scored the winner in a 3-2 victory over West Brom in 1998; he would go on to play not only in the First Division but also the Premier League and the UEFA Cup including a famous strike in a 2-2 draw with Bayern Munich. Over his tenure at the Wanderers, Gardner was used as a left midfielder, winger, striker and a central midfielder but where he played his best football was at left-back under Sam Allardyce. Allardyce used Gardner's raw pace, skill and creativity to turn him into a defender who could bomb up and down the wing with his unparalleled fitness and ability. Gardner, initially wary of big names coming to the team during the Premier League years, used this as motivation to extend his game in a new position. He would deputise as vice-captain on many occasions as well as being made captain of Jamaica in 2005. Gardner would go on to play 425 games for Bolton in a 14-year period before his release and retirement in 2012; he was also named player of the year in 2006 after his transition to left-back.

However, in the build-up to the play-off final in 2001, Gardner was returning from an injury that had kept him out the majority of the season after suffering a nasty cruciate ligament problem which would go on to haunt him at different times in his career. He had made it back into the team for the last few games and after his goal in the second leg of the semi-final, he was excited to get on the pitch at the Millennium Stadium and get Bolton back to the big time. Gardner was on that pitch in 1999 for the defeat to Watford at Wembley and the ghosts of that day were driving him forward to put in a big performance.

Preston were similar to West Brom in that they had not been expected to be in the promotion hunt at the start of the season. But, the great work of David Moyes, who would go on to manage Everton, West Ham and Manchester United, was key to this success. Moyes had taken Preston from Second Division champions to the cusp of the Premier League in the space of 18 months and the Lancashire club had finished behind Bolton in fourth. Many were backing Preston to do the unthinkable and gain back-to-back promotions and upset the Wanderers.

Preston's rise had been down to their lethal front line of Jon Macken, David Healy and American Brian McBride, and Allardyce knew that if Wanderers were to progress to the Premier League, they needed to keep those three quiet on 28 May, the traditional bank holiday Monday date for the play-off final. Allardyce felt there was nothing to fear going into the final as Bolton had recorded a pair of 2-0 victories over Preston in the regular season but felt the fragility of the players' mindsets could be an issue after so much semi-final and final heartbreak over the last three years. Sam used the aid of Mike Forde, his sports psychologist, in abundance during the week ahead leading to the final. Forde would be vital and ensured that the players were focussed on the task but also relaxed enough to ensure no distractions would get into their heads. As with many occasions in football, outside distractions, especially in the build-up to the final, were there. However, Sam put the distractions side of the build-up on his staff rather than his players and made his staff deal with requests for tickets, family accommodations for the final and ensured that the family of players were there the night before and they all had a ticket well in advance.

Additionally, Sam asked a favour from the man who had met him at Burnden Park all those years ago and the man who lived and breathed Bolton Wanderers, the Lion of Vienna, Sir Nat Lofthouse. Lofthouse, who was no stranger to cup heartbreak and redemption, was asked to speak to the players about what this game meant to the club but also his own experiences of cup despair and glory. Sir Nat had been in the team in 1953 which lost the infamous Stanley Matthews FA Cup Final to Blackpool but also was an example of redemption as in 1958, he scored two goals at Wembley as Bolton beat Manchester United 2-0 to lift the FA Cup. Lofthouse was club president in 2001 and entered the dressing room and simply told the players, 'Do well for Bolton, cocker. You'll be all right, cocker. Don't worry, cocker.' Allardyce would state that the northern term of endearment 'cocker' was used a lot by Lofthouse as he struggled to remember a lot of the players' names, especially those from foreign isles.

The day before the final, the squad and backroom staff went to the Millennium Stadium to watch the Second Division play-off final between Reading and Millwall so the players could get a feel for the atmosphere before their own match. However, Allardyce was concerned over the pitch as the First Division showdown was the last final in three days and the playing surface had taken some hammering over that weekend. On the morning of the final Allardyce caught a glimpse of Moyes, who looked quite nervous. Moyes, a relative newcomer to management, had actually been signed by Allardyce at Preston and was still technically on the books as a player in 2001 too. After seeing his counterpart's nerves, Allardyce spoke to his backroom team and stated that he knew they would win. This was disseminated to the players who were told to just play their normal way and to ensure they played the game, not the occasion.

After the success of the semi-finals Allardyce again chose to go with a 4-3-3 or a 4-5-1 in defence, a formation that would become his go-to in years to come. The players were up for it but Michael Ricketts was obviously annoyed as he was named on the bench and Dean Holdsworth got the starting nod. However, as had been shown so many times that season, Allardyce had a plan for Ricketts who was informed his time on the bench would be short-lived. Some 54,328 fans piled into the Millennium Stadium and by 3pm, when referee Uriah Rennie blew for kick-off, the stands were a sea of white from both sets of supporters. Bolton were in their away strip of light blue as Sky Sports pundit Ray Wilkins spoke of their recent record of falling at the final hurdle, and how he felt Preston would win as the Trotters would struggle with the expectation and mental strength needed. He also recalled the fact of how teams who finished third often didn't make the Premier League.

In the crowd, Lofthouse cheered as the game kicked off with midfielders Kevin Nolan, Per Frandsen and Gareth Farrelly exchanging passes before Farrelly played it to Guðni Bergsson who hit the ball long towards Nolan, playing his first final at 18 years of age. An early chance from Jon Macken scared the Bolton defence as he headed straight at Matt Clarke and the game was tight until the 17th minute.

Holdsworth held the ball up well to gain a free kick as Simon Charlton floated a pass into the box from deep. The ball was headed out by the Preston defence and pinballed to the edge of the box where it was met by Farrelly. Farrelly who had scored the goal for Everton to keep them up when Bolton went down in 1998, made up for his transgressions as he shot hard and low from the edge of the box through a melee of players and into the left-hand side of the net past goalkeeper David Lucas to make it 1-0. Half the stadium, Lofthouse and Allardyce included, erupted as Bolton had settled the nerves early on. Farrelly had shown a touch of quality that helped him gain international recognition for the Republic of Ireland. It was by no means his greatest finish but that didn't matter.

'Wanderers, Wanderers, Wanderers!' The Bolton fans were in full voice, could this be the time? By no means his greatest finish but it didn't matter. The game continued in a tight fashion as Bolton went into the changing rooms at half-time 1-0 up, with supporters dreaming of Old Trafford, Anfield and Highbury away. The second half started and Allardyce's team carried on dominating and really could and should have been two or three up by the hour mark. As the half progressed Clarke had stopped Healy from equalising with a great save; Moyes held his head in his hands.

As promised, Allardyce brought on Ricketts with 20 minutes to go to try and seal the final – it took them almost all of those 20 minutes to do so. Ricketts was working well with Gardner and causing the Preston defence all manner of issues. In the 90th minute he received the ball just inside the Preston half and decided to drive at goal. Ricketts used his raw pace to storm past the challenges of anyone who came near him, got inside the box and rounded Lucas, and with an open goal slid the ball over the line to make it 2-0. Bolton were going to the big time; the Trotters were back.

The drama wasn't over and just as the supporters finished celebrating Ricketts' goal, they were up again. Gardner picked up the ball and began to drive down the left, then brushed off three tackles before smashing his shot across Lucas and into the net and sprinting down the touchline in front of the Bolton fans to cement promotion. The whistle blew and half the stadium erupted and by the time Bergsson and Sam lifted the play-off final trophy, it was party time. The club had booked a function room in the Angel Hotel in Cardiff and a proper knees-up ensued. Sam returned to Bolton that night after his friends had booked an executive coach. Champagne and cigars followed and the celebrations continued at the Reebok long into the night. Bolton had done it. From that heartbreak at Stamford Bridge in 1998 and all the heartbreak along the way to this magic moment in Wales. They were back, and for Sam Allardyce, who just 18 months prior was Notts County manager in the Second Division, he was now in the Premier League ready to start a legacy and an impact that would for ever be remembered as he could now rub shoulders and take on the likes of Messrs Wenger, Houllier and Ferguson.

6

Back in the big time

SAM ALLARDYCE had achieved a career milestone by becoming a Premier League manager and was ready to take the top flight by storm and show the rest of the league and many naysayers that Bolton were there to stay. Although the obvious next step was to ensure that Wanderers achieved Premier League survival for the first time in their history, there was also a deep desire for Allardyce to test his modern methods of psychology, nutrition and data analysis against the big boys. Many pundits stated that Bolton were the favourites to make an instant return to the First Division and some had written them off before a ball was kicked in the 2001/02 Premier League season.

BBC pundit and former Liverpool star Mark Lawrenson was a key critic of Bolton's chances in the big league and stated that they had no chance of survival. Lawrenson was a regular on the BBC show *Football Focus* and stated many times how little faith he had for Bolton's cause and was put under the sword, well the razor, by four supporters who would appear alongside him. Lawrenson was given a put up or shut up ultimatum and was told to put his money where his mouth was. He accepted a challenge and stated that if Bolton were to survive and confirm their place in the Premier League by the end of the season then he would shave off his trademark moustache. This 'cutting' prediction was an inspiration to many fans and also to those within the club, none more so than Sam Allardyce. Weirdly enough, Sam had shaved his own moustache in the build-up to his first season in the Premier League and was also hoping to be the man behind the razor come May 2002.

In all fairness to Lawrenson, he said that he was happy to raise money for Bolton Hospice to support the cause further if Bolton did stay up, and if they were relegated, the funds would go to a Merseyside-based charity. Two of the four fans who appeared on the show, Simon Maddrell and Gary Parkinson, spoke to the media about their glee at the potential of proving one of the big names wrong and stated that they felt Lawrenson and the football 'experts' should have afforded Sam and his team more respect. Extra motivation indeed but Allardyce and his squad didn't need any more. They had their own.

Out of the three teams that came up from the First Division in 2001, Bolton were certainly the paupers. The summer budget was not what many would expect from a Premier League club and Sam had to act smart to recruit players from around the world as he felt the premium on English players was far too much. After the drama of Cardiff, Sam gave himself two weeks off but in reality, he never stopped preparing for the upcoming season. Eddie Davies was made full owner and this ended a period of uncertainty of having multiple shareholders. Davies, by his own admission, didn't expect Bolton to return to the big time so soon and was unprepared for the finance needed to compete in the top league so a big budget would not be handed to Sam. He would have to use his relationships across football and his extensive scouting network built by Jack Chapman to add to his team. The chances of relegation far reduce the longer you manage to stay in the league and Sam and Phil Gartside wanted to ensure that Bolton remained in the Premier League before they could build to the next step. Sam managed to use some of the Lifeline lottery scheme money to help make some changes at the training ground which he felt would give his team a competitive edge where they couldn't compete in the transfer market. Lifeline was created by the club in the 1980s during financial hardship and still exists to this day. In fact, many players and staff, including Allardyce, are still paying members today.

Sam's team looked around England to try and build up the squad but felt that their valuation of English players did not match with those of the selling clubs. The manager was wary of promoted clubs in the past who had struggled with big-money signings on long-term contracts and the team at the Reebok felt that consistency and sustainability was key should the worst happen and Bolton get relegated. They decided to look abroad for their summer signings and Sam received offers from multiple agents with free transfer offers as well as opportunities to take players on loan. Sam tried to sell Bolton as a stepping stone for younger players to reach the bigger clubs and also a way back into the top league for older players who may have lost their way.

One player he saw as someone who could support the ageing defence was French defender Bruno N'Gotty. Sam had tried multiple times to sign the former AC Milan centre-back from Marseille but he was unable to sell project Bolton to N'Gotty. Initially at least. However, Sam was able to sign Senegalese defender Djibril Diawara on loan from Torino in Italy. Diawara was keen to get into the Premier League and upon signing informed Sam he wanted to play central midfield despite never playing there before. He and Sam would argue about this and eventually, Diawara would lose and his loan was ended before the new year after nine appearances.

Sam would look to recruit from his trusted Scandinavia as he had in the past and signed Silkeborg striker Henrik Pedersen for £650,000. The Dane had scored 25 goals for the Danish outfit the previous season and Bolton would fight off competition from Borussia Dortmund for his signature. Although not an instant hit, Pedersen would go on to be fondly remembered by Bolton fans in years to come, especially with his famous 'peacock' celebration. Fellow Danes Bo Hansen and Per Frandsen were tasked with helping Pedersen settle in BL6.

Before the season kicked off Bolton would also land Gillingham midfielder Nicky Southall on a free, before signing unproven Japanese striker Akinori Nishizawa on loan from Cerezo Osaka. The 'Man from Japan' would be a hit in the club shop with Nishizawa shirts being sold in their droves. However, he would never play a league game for the club as he was deemed not good enough before being sent back to Japan in December.

All in all, it was a very underwhelming summer of incomings for the club. Yet, despite sharks circling around Michael Ricketts and Kevin Nolan, Bolton were able to keep the majority of their first-team squad other than losing Geordie Robbie Elliott at the end of his contract, to Newcastle United. Sam tried to keep Elliott at the Reebok but a return to his boyhood club was impossible to turn down. By the time Bolton were ready to kick off in their first game away at Leicester City, they lined up with nine of the 11 players having started the play-off final earlier in the year. Were they ready for the big time? The pundits and sceptics certainly didn't think so. Many around the football world had ignored Bolton in the First Division but now many would be doing their homework and realised Sam's work behind the scenes and his creation of the 'team behind the team' had something many others didn't. Many long in the tooth would criticise this and refuse to adapt, especially in the media and even in the stands. Sam didn't care, he knew he was on the start of something special.

Bolton would go to Filbert Street to face Leicester City on 18 August 2001, a beautiful summer's day. Leicester would be moving to their new stadium in the next few years so many Bolton fans took the opportunity to travel for what they worried could be their last chance to visit Filbert Street. Leicester themselves had been on quite a journey and just one year prior had played in their second League Cup Final in the space of two years. Former manager Martin O'Neill had built a dynasty at Leicester but since he left for Celtic, the buzz wasn't there any more. Leicester had recently lost England striker Emile Heskey and were playing Dean Sturridge and Ade Akinbiyi in front of a midfield including former England player Dennis Wise. Weirdly enough, Wise had played in Bolton's last Premier League fixture, when the Whites' hearts were broken at Chelsea in 1998. Foxes manager Peter Taylor was hoping to build on the work by O'Neill and give Leicester a stable and successful season.

The game kicked off to a rapturous atmosphere from the travelling fans. Bolton, in their home strip of white shirts, dark navy shorts and white socks, played against the blue-white-blue of Leicester. Early in the first half, both teams looked strong with Bolton surprising many with their quick passing play and speed down the wings. On 15 minutes, Per Frandsen picked up the ball and drove past the challenge of Muzzy Izzet to end up on the right wing. He got into a foot race with Robbie Savage as he knocked the ball forward and just before Savage was able to tackle, he swung a right-footed cross towards the penalty spot. The ball reached Kevin Nolan who had to leap with every sinew to get a connection with his head. Totally unmarked, the 19-year-old Liverpudlian made a great connection with the ball as it looped up and dipped past keeper Tim Flowers into the top-right corner. Flowers, who had formerly played for local rivals Blackburn Rovers, could have done a lot better but was caught off his line and flat-footed as Nolan had surprised many by heading the ball rather than taking a touch. The young midfielder ran away in glee with his arms aloft towards the away supporters.

What a start. Bolton were full of energy and Leicester looked shocked. Seventeen minutes later, it happened again. The ball was picked up in space by Ricardo Gardner who, with the outside of his boot, played a pass through in front of Michael Ricketts who tussled with Callum Davidson. Davidson and Ricketts had a battle of strength which Ricketts won with ease. As Davidson was on the floor shouting at the referee, Ricketts was through with a sight of goal. Inside the box, Ricketts took one touch and had one look then unleashed a thunderous strike past Flowers and into the same corner that Nolan had scored in. Ricketts trotted away with a dance and shuffle and his team-mates ran towards him; little old Bolton, relegation favourites, were 2-0 up away after 33 minutes in their opening game. What a start, and even in Sam's wildest dreams he didn't see this start happening. As the score came through on *Football Focus*, Lawrenson would start to go very quiet and maybe feel a few twitches in the moustache. Bolton continued to push as Leicester began to lose confidence. This wasn't supposed to happen, the Foxes were supposed to welcome Bolton to the Premier League with a thumping.

In the 41st minute, Bolton scored again. A free kick in the Leicester half was taken by Per Frandsen. Frandsen chipped the ball over the wall as the makings of a move from the training ground started to take place. The ball landed to Guðni Bergsson, who cleverly flicked it past the oncoming Leicester defenders for Nolan, once again unmarked, who smashed a volley underneath Flowers to make it 3-0. Even Sam looked stunned this time. It wasn't even half-time.

And yet, there was more; just as the Leicester team were getting back into position a fourth goal hit them. Bolton got another free kick on the edge of the box. As the Leicester players tried to position themselves to avoid the same move that caused the third goal, Frandsen saw a gap in the edge of the wall. He smashed the ball with his laces low and hard past the wall and into the bottom right-hand corner to make it 4-0 in the 45th minute. The whistle blew, a source of mercy from referee Rob Styles as Bolton went into the changing rooms elated. Allardyce had not prepared for this eventuality and simply said, 'Err … keep it going?' as his players came in for their break.

As the second half progressed, the game seemed to have died and Sam brought on two of his new signings, to see how they fared. Pedersen and Southall arrived with 20 minutes to go and were later joined on the pitch by 35-year-old Ian Marshall. The game was all but over by the time Frandsen added a fifth. In the 83rd minute, he was over the ball again about to hit a free kick. However, instead of chipping it as he did for Nolan's second goal or driving it hard and low as he did to make it 4-0 he decided to curl his shot. The ball bent around the wall and into the top-right corner. Five bloody nil. As the whistle blew for full time there was a chorus of boos from Leicester fans that was being drowned out by cheers and singing of the 2,000 travelling supporters. The Wanderers were top of the Premier League and were making many 'experts' question their judgement. Mr Lawrenson's moustache was particularly more twitchy than usual. However, this match gave Sam quite a conundrum. In fact it would be known as quite the 'mouthful'.

As supporters and associates alike celebrated long into the night, Sam and his backroom team knew that this amazing result brought a 'tasty' consequence. Never one to shy from new and exciting methods, Sam had created an incentive programme through the help of his backroom staff. One of Mike Forde's methods to motivate the players came in some challenges laid down to create a sense of competition around the changing room. One of them was suggested by Dean Holdsworth who had played for the famous Crazy Gang of Wimbledon in the late 80s and early 90s. This team was famous for the extreme and his suggestion from the old days did not disappoint.

Many say that the way to a man's heart is through his stomach and this certainly seemed the case at Bolton Wanderers in 2001. The gauntlet was thrown down at the start of the season that anytime the team lost by three goals or more then the players involved would have to eat sheep's testicles and eyeballs. However, if they won by three or more goals, then Allardyce, Forde, Phil Brown and the rest of the backroom staff would have to do the same. Straight after the 5-0 demolition of Leicester, chairman Phil Gartside reminded the changing room of this and was elated to see the reactions of the players who were keen for this to be done immediately. Before Sam knew it, Gartside had booked a Turkish restaurant in Manchester who were more than happy to oblige with this request. *I'm a Celebrity...Get Me Out of Here!* would debut in 2002, but Bolton had to create their own bushtucker trial to create some incentives for the playing staff. As Sam and his backroom team sat down for their 'meal', the whole playing squad joined in as did some of the local media. The team spirit was evident as many could see the bond created by Allardyce and his team was as strong as ever. In a 2003 Christmas DVD named *More Own Goals and Gaffs*, comedian Rory McGrath created a feature where fans across the country could revel in the strange and marvellous ways at Bolton. McGrath laughed at this method and would state that this was 'the closest Bolton would ever get to Europe'. How little did he know what the future would hold.

Three days later Bolton played in the Premier League again with a 1-0 win over Middlesbrough at the Reebok thanks to a 39th-minute strike from Michael Ricketts. Two games, two wins, two clean sheets and still top of the Premier League. A crowd of 20,747 went to the Reebok on that August Tuesday night, and over 27,000 would fill the Reebok and make their way down Burnden Way for the next game. It would be shown on Sky Sports' *Monday Night Football* as they welcomed the multiple cup winners of 2001 and four times European champions, Liverpool, on 27 August.

Over the recent months, Liverpool had won the FA Cup, League Cup, UEFA Cup, UEFA Super Cup and the FA Charity Shield. Gérard Houllier's Reds, spearheaded by Ballon D'or winner Michael Owen and £11m man Emile Heskey, were looking to give Bolton some top-flight comeuppance when they arrived in BL6. The team was also littered with stars such as impressive youngster Steven

Gerrard, club icon Robbie Fowler and German playmaker Dietmar Hamann. This was what Sam was waiting for, a true giant to pit his wits against and show the league and the country what Bolton were capable of. Allardyce himself would admit that a draw would be an amazing result as many fully expected Liverpool to embarrass his team. With all this in mind, Bolton were still top of the league with Liverpool languishing in 13th after gaining only three points in their first two games. Liverpool would go on to finish second that season, seven points behind title winners Arsenal and three points ahead of rivals Manchester United. However, a tough start to the campaign would see the Anfield club sit in sixth by October.

The Reebok had its first sell-out of the season for the visit of Houllier and his team with many of the Scouse persuasion putting on fake Bolton accents to gain entry and sitting on their hands in the home end. Sam's men were on the crest of a wave and he and Phil Brown felt that no changes to the team that had got Bolton to the top of the league were needed as he once again went with Hansen and Ricketts up front, much to the dismay of Dean Holdsworth. Liverpool's attacking options were pure football icons with Owen and Fowler starting in attack, and Heskey eagerly awaiting from the bench. Sander Westerveld started in goal with a myriad of stars in front of him including Gerrard, Jamie Carragher and Gary McAllister.

Sam welcomed Houllier to the Reebok with a handshake as the cameras panned over to the dugouts before the game was kicked off by Kevin Nolan's short pass to Per Frandsen. Many of the youth of the town were enjoying their last week of the summer holidays before a return to school the week after, and were looking forward to bragging to their friends over seeing England stars Owen, Fowler and Gerrard in the flesh.

Bolton started the fastest and Ricketts was proving to be a handful for the Liverpool defence, in particular, Swiss international Stéphane Henchoz. The ball stopped at the feet of Nolan, on the edge of the box, before he laid it to his midfield partner Per Frandsen who fizzed a shot over the bar early on to show Bolton's attacking intent. Nolan was slick with his passing and was energetic as ever, particularly keen to impress against his boyhood club after his release from Anfield as a youngster.

The game was fairly even by the time it reached 25 minutes as both sides had some efforts on goal but nothing with substance as the ball was stuck in midfield. Many felt Bolton had done well, but that it was only a matter of time before Liverpool took control as Fowler and Owen looked particularly sharp in the box. Sam's game plan was evident from the start: bully and use their strength as much as they could but once the ball was in the final third, use skill and quality to test the defence. Referee Graham Poll was paying particular focus on Ricketts who was continuing to cause the Liverpool backline issues with his physicality. On 26 minutes, Nolan picked the ball up outside of the box after some good work from Ricketts, and tried to curl the ball towards goal but the ball took a deflection from Sami Hyypiä and went out for a corner to Bolton. The Reebok's noise levels went up a few decibels as Ricardo Gardner went over to take the corner. The box was rammed, especially the six-yard area as Bolton tried to test the resolve of Westerveld. With Liverpool defenders focussing on the six-yard box, Bo Hansen sprinted towards Gardner who played a quick one-two with the Dane before crossing into the penalty area. The ball had a bit too much distance on it but was found by veteran all-rounder Paul Warhurst. The number six, sporting his long hair, headed from the left-hand side of the box towards that crowded six-yard area. It looped over the head of Henchoz who turned around to see Ricketts waiting. From four yards out, Ricketts guided the ball with his head past Westerveld and into the back of the net; 1-0 Bolton as the Reebok erupted and the Liverpool defenders started to point fingers at each other.

While Carragher and Hyypiä showed their anger, Ricketts wheeled away and performed a knee slide to the North Stand. Nolan and Frandsen embraced with Ricketts and Bolton looked good value for the lead, despite the shock from everyone without a local accent in the crowd. It had been awful marking from the Liverpool backline but Wanderers didn't care and the clever play from Warhurst had given Ricketts the opportunity for his third goal in three games, and on a night when England fans were looking at Fowler, Owen and Heskey to show if they could be the next Three Lions heroes, it was instead Ricketts who was giving England manager Sven-Göran Eriksson food for thought. The Horwich night sky grew darker and the Reebok floodlights went into full effect, showing the magic and mystique of the landmark stadium.

Bolton played it safe and tried to keep hold of the ball. However, chances from Danny Murphy and Fowler scared the home fans as Liverpool were getting closer. On the stroke of half-time the ball found its way to Gerrard on the edge of the box, where he found some space and looked to bend in a pass to find Owen. The midfielder whipped the ball in but it missed everyone and went out. At this moment, Graham Poll blew the whistle and Bolton went into half-time 1-0 up. The Sky Sports pundits deliberated. Were Bolton good? Were Liverpool bad? In reality, Bolton had taken their chances whereas Liverpool had been sloppy in attack and struggled with Bolton's aerial attack.

The teams came out for the second half sporting new shirts as, due to the heat and the effort they had put in, their first-half shirts were drenched with sweat by the time they had gone for their break. Liverpool made one change, replacing Markus Babbel with summer signing and free-kick expert John Arne Riise. Ten minutes into the second half, Liverpool, and in particular Owen had come close. Bolton were looking stretched and Sam felt some fresh legs were needed as he brought off goalscorer Ricketts for Holdsworth. Holdsworth had been frustrated not to start yet and was given 35 minutes to stake his claim. Bergsson was proving to be a rock in the defence. At 36, the Icelandic veteran had kept Owen and Fowler fairly quiet, so much so that Houllier brought Fowler off on 63 minutes for Emile Heskey.

Almost instantly, Liverpool looked a different team as Heskey seemed to test the mettle of Mike Whitlow and Simon Charlton on the left-hand side. Three minutes after coming on, Heskey, a future Reebok player himself, would break Bolton hearts. Liverpool had taken control of the midfield battle and were starting to gain confidence. Balls between Hamann and Gerrard stretched the Bolton midfield and gaps were showing which Liverpool were looking to exploit. On 65 minutes, the Liverpool backline were gaining into the Bolton half and after a long clearance from Hyypiä, Jussi Jääskeläinen came out of his box to kick the ball out for a throw-in deep in Bolton's half. The throw-in from Henchoz found its way back to Hamann in midfield who looked up and played a ball towards the box to McAllister that slid through four Bolton players. McAllister took one touch and played it across the box to the unmarked Heskey. Heskey didn't need a touch as he placed his shot straight past Jääskeläinen into the bottom-right corner before running past the Bolton supporters in glee then celebrating with his team-mates. This was the moment the home fans were dreading as many feared that Liverpool would now make an example of Bolton and open the floodgates. This was the first goal they had conceded all season and Liverpool had ripped their entire midfield and defence apart with two passes.

Bolton made some changes in midfield as they saw the centre of their team being stretched and felt they needed some fresher legs. On came Gareth Farrelly for Frandsen and then Kevin Nolan came off for summer signing Djibril Diawara for his debut. Despite being signed as a defender, it seemed Sam had caved and played the Senegalese man in midfield. Then, on 73 minutes, the ball was played by Heskey towards Owen who, with a quick turn of pace, knocked it past Bergsson and was through on goal. The 21-year-old was in a foot race with 36-year-old Bergsson. However, before Owen could gain control, Bergsson found some pace and matched Owen. He kept up with him and eventually shepherded Owen away from goal, towards the by-line and caused the England international to kick it out for a throw-in. This was celebrated like a goal by the home supporters and gave them – and the team – a glimpse of hope. Owen, one week away from scoring a hat-trick away at Germany in a 5-1 win for England, was humbled by Bergsson and Bolton in front of the cameras. Bolton were big time and Owen looked defeated.

On 85 minutes, a block from Anthony Barness caused Liverpool a corner deep into the dying embers of the game. At 1-1 both teams knew that a goal now would most likely win it as McAllister stepped up to take the corner. The ball came in but after a few bobbles, it was eventually booted out by Warhurst far into the Liverpool half straight to Westerveld. Every time Liverpool came into their half it was a heart-in-mouth moment for the home fans. Bolton were five minutes away from keeping their unbeaten record for the season and a famous result against one of Europe's biggest clubs.

On 88 minutes, after a miss from Hamann, Jääskeläinen had a goal kick that made its way to Gardner on the left wing, just inside the Liverpool half. Gardner played the ball to Holdsworth who was hugging the touchline with no one in the box or in his reach to pass to. At a pedestrian pace, Holdsworth kept possession and cut inside toward the centre of the pitch about 35 yards from goal. Suddenly, he looked up and saw he was in acres of space. The Liverpool players were waiting for Holdsworth to try and pass to Diawara who was bombing into the box. Holdsworth saw the space as an opportunity to have a go and try and get back into the team. Holdsworth hit the ball with a slice, totally mis-kicking the ball, and his tame hit spun towards the middle of the Liverpool goal. Westerveld set himself and dived on the ball. Holdsworth looked away but he heard an almighty cheer: the ball had bounced underneath the Dutchman and into the back of the net; 2-1 Bolton in the last minute.

Holdsworth ran off with his arm in the air, not so modestly claiming full intention. It didn't matter; the former Wimbledon man had exorcised the ghosts of the miss at Wembley in 2000 and had given Bolton one of the most famous results in their history. Bolton Wanderers 2 Liverpool 1. Westerveld was later dropped to the bench for his blunder as Liverpool signed Jerzy Dudek and Chris Kirkland as their new stoppers. Upon the final whistle, the

Reebok erupted. The Sky Sports cameras were shaking as they showed a calm Sam Allardyce shake hands with a furious Gérard Houllier and his assistant Phil Thompson. Future Bolton number two and manager Sammy Lee congratulated Sam as Houllier rushed down the tunnel. Holdsworth was followed by the cameras as he looked upon his adoring fans with a feeling of redemption. Bolton were still top of the league and went into the international break ready for more.

This result impressed many over the football world, none more so than Sam's main summer target, Bruno N'Gotty, who on 7 September had a change of heart and agreed to join on loan from Marseille which would eventually become permanent in January for £500,000. The first of Bolton's elite League of Nations world XI was in the changing room as N'Gotty was handed the number two shirt and would watch from the stands as Bolton would get another great result at another European giant of times gone by, Leeds United. Bolton drew 0-0 at Elland Road to stay at the top of the league before a 4-2 win over Walsall in the League Cup, where new signings Pedersen and Nishizawa would both open their accounts. Bolton would eventually lose top spot due to a 1-0 home defeat to Southampton but two draws away from home, firstly 1-1 at Blackburn Rovers and the same score at Arsenal, meant they ended September with 12 points. Sam had envisaged that 40 points would be enough to keep Bolton safe. After only seven games, they had over a quarter of that already. Not too bad this Premier League, Sam thought, as Champions League winner N'Gotty signed for the club, and it was evident that the days of old were starting to change for the Wanderers. N'Gotty was a commanding defender but for the first part of his Bolton career he played very much as a right-back in a back four. His debut in September against Blackburn at Ewood Park came off the bench as a late change for Pedersen. The game would be remembered for another new signing, Rod Wallace, joining late in the window on loan from Glasgow Rangers, scoring on his debut. Although it ended in a draw, it was another example of Bolton's mettle failing to waver.

By mid-October, Bolton had slipped to eighth in the league after two back-to-back defeats against north-east opposition at home. They had lost 2-0 to Sunderland and suffered a thumping 4-0 home defeat to Newcastle which saw Jussi Jääskeläinen sent off for handling outside the box and also saw striker Bo Hansen spend some time in goal. Allardyce had rarely used a substitute goalkeeper and felt he couldn't trust Steve Banks in the top flight. In late October he would sign the veteran Kevin Poole on a free transfer from Birmingham City.

With Bolton in eighth and on the end of a run that had seen no win in six Premier League matches, many around the nation felt that their bubble had burst, and by the 20th October, many felt it would be totally obliterated when they travelled to Old Trafford to face reigning champions Manchester United. Many had seen this as the biggest game of the season for the fans and the squad prepared with a relaxing team-building session in the Lake District much to their shock. Allardyce and Phil Brown had planned to relax the players and change their routine to be ready to expect the unexpected as they checked the squad into the Low Wood Bay Hotel on the shoreline of Lake Windermere ready for some team-building exercises. The squad and staff spent three days of raft-building, paintballing, 'toilet racing' and orienteering to bring the boys together ahead of their toughest test of the season. Bo Hansen in particular moaned about this and spoke openly about his disappointment to Brown of being away from the training pitch ahead of a trip to Old Trafford, but by the end of day three he was waxing lyrical about the trip and was even looking ahead at booking his own trip there. Upon their return to Bolton, Sam decided to give the players two days off which left no preparation and no analysis ahead of the game. Many within the club questioned and demonstrated their opposition to this decision and many felt that Sam had made a massive mistake. However, history would show that, once again, Sam had shown a stroke of genius.

Bolton and Manchester United in recent times had been privy to a one-sided rivalry as many Whites supporters would look towards the elite Manchester club with disdain and, some could even argue if they were being honest, jealousy. Some fans had not forgiven both United and the country for their treatment of Nat Lofthouse and his team after the 1958 FA Cup win. Manchester United were the nation's darlings in 1958 following the Munich air disaster and the whole nation, other than Bolton, were desperate for the Red Devils to win, a concept that seems quite alien in modern times. On its way back to Bolton with the cup, the team bus was vandalised by United supporters as it passed through Salford, and a rivalry was born. Although United would class Liverpool and Manchester City as their main rivals, there was no denying that there was an extra bite when the two played each other. As only 13 miles separated Bolton town centre and Old Trafford, many of the 'plastic reds', as they were coined by Bolton fans, often lived in the town. United were a global machine compared to the Wanderers and had won three Premier League titles in three years and two years earlier had won an unprecedented treble of the Premier League, FA Cup and Champions

League – a feat that helped Scottish manager Alex Ferguson become Sir Alex. Bolton had already beaten one giant in Liverpool and had gained a point from Arsenal so were certainly not feeling any fear. But, after a run of six without a win and scoring one goal in three matches, adding to their lack of preparation, there was some apprehension as the Trotters travelled via Salford to Sir Matt Busby Way in October 2001.

The teams came out of the corner tunnel at Old Trafford as the refreshed and recently bonded team made their way on to the pitch and looked around they saw 67,559 fans fill the stadium. Bolton hadn't even played in front of this many in their play-off final so to be welcomed by a crowd like this in a regular league game was an experience for many of the players, who had never played above the First Division. However, Sam had made it clear, just as he did at Cardiff in May, that his squad should 'play the game, not the occasion' as he knew that United were there for the taking after a midweek Champions League loss to Deportivo La Coruña. Adding to this, United were missing England captain David Beckham and club captain Roy Keane, and had benched Welsh wizard Ryan Giggs and Bury-born but Bolton-living England right-back Gary Neville. Bolton had made some changes of their own and started with N'Gotty as well as moving Warhurst from defence into midfield.

Allardyce took his seat in the away dugout and looked to his right and saw a true legend of the game opposite him. This was what Sam had waited for, a moment to test himself against the very best football had to offer. Allardyce and Ferguson would go on to be close friends in the years to come but it was by no means a friendly affair between two of England's most historical clubs. The Bolton fans were in fine voice as over 5,000 of them travelled to Old

Trafford. They had earmarked this match as a must-do when the fixtures were released in the summer and many had arrived early to savour their big day out against one of their – in their eyes, at least – biggest rivals. A group of young supporters were standing in the away end with the phrase 'I 8 UNITED' on the back of their Bolton shirts to show their distaste for the Red Devils, and also their refusal to follow a team purely based on glory. Graham Barber blew his whistle and the game kicked off.

United's French goalkeeper Fabien Barthez had tussled with Ricketts a couple of times in the first ten minutes as he had come out wide from his box to cut out some through passes towards the striker. The World Cup winner was ever a fan of the flamboyant, much to the disapproval of Ferguson, and would often get caught out during his United career. However, so far, he had dealt with Bolton's balls to Ricketts very well. United's midfield three of Paul Scholes, Juan Sebastián Verón and Nicky Butt were starting to stretch the game and pull the Bolton players into all sorts of positions. Even without Beckham and Giggs on the pitch, United looked dangerous.

A ball from Butt was picked up by Andy Cole who was tackled from behind by captain Guðni Bergsson. Cole had manipulated the situation well with his back to goal and had forced Bergsson into a needless foul right in front of the referee. On 25 minutes, United had a free kick in what many would call 'Beckham territory'. However, he was not in the squad, and neither was his second-in-command on dead balls, Denis Irwin. However, up stepped Argentine midfielder Verón with the ball around 25 yards from goal. Verón had signed from Lazio in the summer for a British transfer record deal of £28.1m on a five-year deal. When you compare that to Bolton's £500,000 for N'Gotty during the same time, the gulf between the clubs was evident. Verón stood over the ball and took two steps back. Jääskeläinen directed his wall and screamed at them to stay strong and sharp. As the whistle blew, Verón took a run-up and swept his right foot through the ball and over the wall. The pace on his shot caught Jääskeläinen out and as he dived, it was too late as the ball nestled into the top-right hand corner of the goal. 'Who needs David Beckham?' stated the commentary team as Verón wheeled away to the celebrating United fans. Business as usual many believed and another defeat for Bolton seemed on the cards.

United grew more confident after the goal and began to test Jääskeläinen as well as pressuring the Bolton defence, and shots from Scholes and Dwight Yorke came close to making it 2-0. Bolton needed to show their grit and resilience and after a ten-minute onslaught they started to work their way back into the game before, on 35 minutes, the unthinkable happened. After some great battling work from Gardner, who seemed to be playing some kind of free role, he passed to N'Gotty on the halfway line; the Frenchman controlled and moved into the United half. Seeing a run from Ricketts, he floated the ball towards the penalty area from the right-hand side over to the left corner of the box. Ricketts had peeled away from United defender David May and managed to head the ball towards the edge of the area. It found Kevin Nolan who let the ball bounce once before swinging a sweet right-footed half-volley past Wes Brown in defence and fizzing beyond the diving Barthez to stun the Stretford End into silence and sent the away fans into ecstasy. The boyhood Liverpool fan cupped his ear to the United crowd before celebrating with close friend Ricketts. The combination of N'Gotty, Ricketts and Nolan had turned the game on its head. Sam stayed a picture of calm on the bench and the action restarted.

United were obviously furious as Verón's strike was palmed away by Jääskeläinen into the path of Ole Gunnar Solskjær who put the ball into an empty net but was deemed offside. Moments later, United were close again and Bolton were begging for half-time. Scholes received the ball on the edge of the box and his left-footed strike was saved amazingly by Jääskeläinen diving to his left. As the ball bounced off the Finn's palm it fell into the path of Cole, who was one-on-one with an out-of-position Jääskeläinen inside the six-yard box. Cole took one swipe with the side of his foot but Jääskeläinen jumped across his goal and blocked the shot with his forearms, pushing it out for a corner. Cole, Scholes and Ferguson had their heads in their hands and couldn't believe they had not scored. As for Bolton, all you could hear was screams of 'Jussi, Jussi, Jussi!' from the away end and the team jumped to congratulate Jääskeläinen. Sam stood in the away dugout, tapping his knees and biting his nails as the whistle blew for half-time.

The game continued in the same fashion after the break as United began to dominate and Bolton defended well thanks to a solid structure and patient play. On a counterattack, Per Frandsen broke into the box and was brought down by Verón. Many felt it was an obvious penalty, including those in the commentary box, but the referee waved away the protests. Jääskeläinen proved again to be imperious as he came for every ball and claimed some tricky crosses and shots in the second half. Another player proving to be a handful was Gardner who seemed to have both Phil Neville and Mikaël Silvestre quite fearful. The game plan continued to be to get the ball to Ricketts as often as possible and as far up the pitch as possible where he would try to hold it up and keep it away from the United midfield where Verón and Scholes were taking shot after shot to try and restore their team's lead. As the game entered the last ten minutes this game plan paid off, and how.

After a period of pressure from the Red Devils in the last ten minutes which saw Cole once again come close and Giggs enter the pitch, the ball was won by Ricketts inside the United box. Ricketts had received a long clearance from the back and had won his tussle with Wes Brown. Ricketts had gambled and as the ball bounced off him away from Brown, the striker took two touches and looked up before placing his shot into the top corner to make it 2-1 to Bolton in the 85th minute. The away end erupted and a wry smile was upon Sam's face. As United pushed for an equaliser, they became more and more frustrated and made rash decisions much to the joy of Bolton as Solskjær came close with a ball across the box. However, as Jääskeläinen cleared, the referee blew and Ricketts was a hero. Sam had done the unthinkable and won at the reigning champions. He told ITV, 'Other than watching my children being born, there is no better feeling. It is my best result as a manager.'

In the space of three months, Bolton had gone to sixth in the Premier League, drawn with Arsenal, beaten Liverpool and then saw off United in their own backyard. No one saw this coming, even Sam. Many rumours circling around Michael Ricketts' future at Bolton started to appear in the media with Tottenham eventually having a bid rejected in the January. Ricketts would gain his England cap the following month due to his 12 goals in 21 games for Bolton to that point.

However, a slump would hit and Bolton would win only one of their next 15 games after Old Trafford and by February 2002, they had fallen to 17th, one place above the relegation zone and had found themselves in a scrap despite their amazing start. Sam realised that more quality was needed, and once again he looked to his scout Jack Chapman to search overseas.

7

Le God

ON 2 February, Bolton dropped into the bottom three with a 3-2 away defeat to Newcastle United after a run of form which had produced only one win since that victory at Old Trafford in October. Since that day, Bolton had fallen from sixth to 18th and were in serious fear of letting their amazing start to the season be in vain if they did not start to get results soon. A 1-0 home win over West Ham United would take them out of the drop zone the next game but from then until the end of the season, Bolton were in a relegation dogfight. Their previous two ventures in the top flight had resulted in relegation so the hierarchy were keen to ensure Bolton's Premier League status for another season at least.

In one of the games, before the new year, Bolton had hosted Leicester City in a hotly contested 2-2 draw earned thanks to a last-minute equaliser, but they had two men sent off thanks to referee Mike Reilly and some work of the 'dark arts' from Robbie Savage. The Foxes were keen to avenge the opening-day humbling from Bolton and had made life hard for their hosts. Savage, in particular, worked hard to push the willpower of the Wanderers with his theatrical diving and antics which saw Warhurst and

Holdsworth dismissed. During this game, Sam Allardyce had volunteered to wear a heart monitor for a television documentary on *Tonight with Trevor McDonald*, as did the Leicester manager Dave Bassett. The resulting data was frightening and showed that Allardyce's blood pressure and heart rate hit dangerous levels during the match. At one point, he recorded 160 beats per minute which was four times his resting rate. The hypothesis was that Allardyce was putting his heart on the line for his profession and through a 90-minute match, was reaching the same heart rate levels as a long-distance runner or a vigorous gym work-out.

Earlier in the season, Liverpool manager Gérard Houllier had suffered heart problems so many in the media and the football world were growing worried about the condition of managers due to the pressure they were under. Sam was aware of this as well and noticed how much more stressed he felt when Bolton were at the wrong end of the table. In the new year, Sam set on starting to solve this problem in the transfer market. After Ricketts' England call-up in February, Sam felt that the striker had grown something of an ego and felt he was untouchable. Prior to his England cap, Ricketts was in outstanding form and caused the likes of Sol Campbell, Sami Hyypiä and Marcel Desailly all manner of problems. After his underwhelming international appearance where was substituted at half-time against the Netherlands, he didn't score again for Bolton that season. His body fat was constantly tested and viewed as too high as he was often seen eating sweets and takeaways after matches. On a bus to an away fixture, Sam snapped as he saw Ricketts eating sweets and lost it. He gave Ricketts some home truths about his performances after his England cap which fell on deaf ears.

With Ricketts' goals gone dry, Sam looked to the continent to get Bolton back on a roll. He secured the future of Bruno N'Gotty by finalising the £500,000 deal with Marseille in late January and continued to use his European scouting network to build his team due to the massive premium still seen on English players. One player he set his sights on was yet another Dane: Hamburg midfielder Stig Tøfting arrived for £250,000 after falling out of favour in Germany. Denmark had qualified for the upcoming 2002 World Cup in Japan and Korea and Tøfting wanted to secure his place in the squad by playing regular football; the attraction of the Premier League was also a major factor. The Danish hard man was an enigma and team-mate Nicky Hunt would refer to him as a 'nutter' as the motorcycle-riding Hell's Angel was famous for his wild parties at his apartment in Eagley Mills on Blackburn Road, Astley Bridge. His Bolton career was stop-start and riddled with injury and though Tøfting would do enough to secure his place on the Denmark squad that summer, his tournament would be marred with issues as during a celebratory drinking session back in his home country, Tøfting assaulted the owner and served four months in jail.

Sam also knew he needed goals, so in came German international Fredi Bobic on loan from German giants Borussia Dortmund until the end of the season. Bobic, born in Yugoslavia but migrated to Germany as an infant, was recognised in 1996 as one of Europe's most clinical strikers and had helped Germany win Euro 96 at Wembley. However, by 2002, he had fallen out of favour with the national team and at Dortmund and similar to many Bolton targets during this time, he was looking for regular football to get back into the World Cup fold. Adding to this, Wanderers signed Frenchman Mario Espartero from Metz on loan and the month after would sign Greek defender Kostas Konstantinidis on loan from Hertha Berlin. Both of the latter signings would fail to make an impact, and leaving was striker Ian Marshall on a free to Blackpool. Yet the club was about to pull off potentially its most iconic transfer in its history.

Enter, Youri Djorkaeff.

As alluded to earlier, many players were looking to give themselves a healthy chance of playing at the World Cup with regular football. Many players who had lost their starting places at club level had found themselves on the periphery of their national teams. At 33, Frenchman Djorkaeff was very much in that boat. He was aware that this could be his last tournament and wanted one last go at the big time. The mercurial midfielder had started his career at French club Grenoble before a move to Monaco, via a stint at Strasbourg, saw Djorkaeff hit the world stage. After helping Monaco win the Coupe de France in 1991 and scoring 14 goals in two years, Djorkaeff gained his first cap for France. His amazing form saw a move to Paris Saint-Germain in 1995 before a spectacular move to Inter Milan saw him reach the UEFA Cup Final in his first season, then win the competition the following year. After the emergence of Brazilian sensation Ronaldo, Djorkaeff found appearances hard to come by and moved to German side Kaiserslautern, all while still staying with the France squad as Les Bleus won the 1998 World Cup and Euro 2000.

However, by 2002, Djorkaeff had fallen out with the hierarchy at Kaiserslautern over their standards in training and felt that he and his team-mates could be working under better technical professionals. At this point, his agent put out feelers to teams in the top tiers of the main leagues in

Europe about the Frenchman's availability. Of course, one of the people contacted was Sam Allardyce. Chairman Phil Gartside told Sam he had no chance of getting Djorkaeff to join Bolton as the manager flew to Germany for talks. Sam had impressed Youri by flying to meet him as most clubs would demand it be the other way around. This showed the desire that Sam showed to not only convince Djorkaeff to come, but to build Bolton into something different.

Sam showed Djorkaeff the medical and statistical headway Bolton had made, along with images of the modern Reebok Stadium. Sam admitted to Djorkaeff about Bolton's league position and their recent history of being a First Division club but he also added that his team and backroom staff were fighters and innovators, and said Djorkaeff would only improve the team and if he performed, he would find his way into the World Cup squad. It was a win-win for all parties. Bolton would get a World Cup winner and Djorkaeff would get games and a free place at the De Vere Whites Hotel until the newly acquired player liaison team could find him a house in Manchester. Djorkaeff was sold and before even stepping foot in Bolton he told Sam, 'If I can help you, you can help me.' Djorkaeff would deal with his contract at Kaiserslautern and after issues with image rights and becoming Bolton's highest wage-earner in their history, Djorkaeff was a Trotter as he arrived on a free transfer on 13 February 2002 on a short-term deal with a view to potentially renew after the World Cup.

Almost instantly, Djorkaeff brought a level of football intelligence that had never been seen at Bolton before. This was someone who had done it and won it at the highest level, shared a midfield with Zinedine Zidane, played alongside Thierry Henry and lifted a World Cup. The days of –

with all respect – Ian Marshall and Allan Johnston were a thing of the past as Bolton added Djorkaeff to their ever-growing League of Nations. Djorkaeff would be pivotal for Bolton's future and would also convince future legends Jay-Jay Okocha, Iván Campo and Stelios Giannakopoulos to come to the club. 'Le God' was a hit with supporters and over a two-and-a-half-year stint, he would score 21 goals in 87 games including nine goals at the age of 36. Djorkaeff is seen as the catalyst for a steep change in Bolton's fortunes and although he never played in Europe in the famous white shirt, he was as integral to that achievement as anyone else. Djorkaeff would go on to play in the MLS for New York Red Bulls after a three-game stint at Blackburn before retiring. Djorkaeff still watches out for Bolton's results and mentions them regularly on his social media feed.

After Djorkaeff's signing, he was handed the number 13 shirt with his favoured number six already taken by Paul Warhurst. The club shop sold out of 'Le God' T-shirts almost instantly as Djorkaeff started with a strong string of performances. However, as Bolton travelled to London for a late-March fixture with Charlton Athletic, they lay in the relegation zone. Two moments of Djorkaeff magic at The Valley opened up a 2-0 lead, and the eventual 2-1 win moved the Trotters up from 18th to 16th. The away following sang 'We are staying up, we are staying up!' before starting their new chant of 'Youri, Youri, Youri!' as they bowed down to the Frenchman at every corner or set piece.

'Le God' was a legend in Lancashire and put on another clinic in the next game as Bolton won 3-2 at home to Aston Villa thanks to an own goal from Mark Delaney, a first for Bobic and Kevin Nolan grabbing his eighth of the season in front of almost 25,000 fans to move the team up to 15th. Sam's men would lose their next game away to Everton but would then face fellow relegation strugglers Ipswich Town. Their former play-off semi-final foes were coming to the Reebok and whoever lost would be in the relegation zone with four games remaining.

Ipswich had become a different club from the one that faced Bolton in those two successive years of play-off semis and had worked hard to establish themselves the season prior. After beating Bolton over two legs in 2000, they defeated Barnsley at Wembley to become a top-flight club once again. Back in the Premier League – having previously been relegated in 1995 – they had defied the odds to finish fifth and qualify for the UEFA Cup after spending most of the season in third place. This feat for a newly promoted team was outstanding and showed the amazing job that George Burley had done. In 2001/02, Ipswich had fought on both domestic and European fronts and would be knocked out of the UEFA Cup by Inter Milan. Despite a 1-0 victory at Portman Road in the first leg, Ipswich were battered 4-1 in the return at the San Siro to bow out in the third round. However, this European campaign had taken its toll on Ipswich's league form and coming into their game with Bolton they sat 18th and three points behind the Trotters after scoring only five goals in eight games, a run which saw them pick up five defeats. Ipswich knew in order to remain a Premier League club, they needed a good result at the Reebok Stadium as three of their four remaining games involved Arsenal, Manchester United and Liverpool. Adding to this, Bolton had already picked up three points from Ipswich that season after a 2-1 winin November. u8

As 25,817 fans entered the stadium, there was a tense feeling in the air with Bolton feeling that a win would give them a huge chance of survival but a defeat would throw the fight wide open. Sam would call this match their 'biggest game of the season' and a 'relegation showdown'. He had decided to start with a front duo of Rod Wallace and Fredi Bobic, both loan players and both with something to prove. Michael Ricketts' dip in form and Dean Holdsworth's lack of games had given the pair the chance to take their chances with Djorkaeff playing behind them dictating the play. Only a handful of the players who knocked Bolton out of the play-offs two years prior remained in the Ipswich 11 but they had some serious quality in the form of Nigerian international Finidi George and Matt Holland. Holland, who had a knack for goals against Bolton, would feature for the Republic of Ireland later that year in the 2002 World Cup.

Bolton set the early pace and after a scramble in the Ipswich box, the ball was bouncing around the edge with players trying to get their heads on it. After two minutes, Bolton held the upper hand and the ball soon fell to Kevin Nolan at the edge of the box, where the youngster hit a strike which lacked pace but was heading towards the goal from 35 yards out. However, the ball was trapped by Bobic on the penalty spot. Bobic then spun around to face the goal while keeping control of the ball. With the Ipswich keeper Andy Marshall steaming towards the German, Bobic looked up and passed the ball underneath Marshall to make it 1-0 after two minutes and send the Reebok rocking. Simon Charlton grabbed Bobic in celebration but also gave a tongue-in-cheek look to the striker about trapping Nolan's shot. The barrel-chested Allardyce celebrated from his seat in the stands with his radio headset to Phil Brown on the bench applied to his ear as he sent down the next set of instructions.

Almost instantly, the visitors had a chance to equalise as George sent in a cross from the right into the path of

Argentinian Sixto Peralta who controlled the ball but was stopped from shooting due to a last-ditch tackle from right-back Anthony Barness. By 30 minutes, it was 2-0 to Bolton and Ipswich feared that their season was crumbling in front of their eyes. A long ball came into the box from Djorkaeff and it seemed like an easy catch for Marshall. However, Wallace used his pace to cut in and get to it first before taking it around Marshall to shoot towards goal. Marshall saved but the ball broke back to Bobic who scored his second of the game, performing a diving header to the left side of the goal. Marshall got a touch but it fumbled past his hand and into the net. Many strikers would have taken a touch or tried to smash it but Bobic used his experience and intelligence to notice the keeper being in trouble to nod it away from him.

The supporters were still sitting back down but Bolton were not finished, and five minutes later they were on the attack again. Marshall received an easy backpass and sliced his kick, only going as far as the edge of the box to Bobic who headed it and followed it to the right wing. Bobic lifted the ball into the box and as it sailed past the Ipswich defence and over Marshall, Wallace had sprinted over to the back post and he headed it back across the six-yard line where Djorkaeff was waiting to pass into an empty net. It had been an awful five minutes for Ipswich, in particular Marshall but an amazing first half for Bolton who were 3-0 up after 35 minutes. 'Le God' celebrated by jumping over the advertising boards and ran towards the Bolton fans with his fists clenched.

What a start, and still Bolton were not done with the Tractor Boys and their own survival and Ipswich's demise was nearly confirmed three minutes later. A right-wing corner was swung in by Gardner with his left foot. As the ball entered the box, Bobic ran towards the edge of the six-yard line and flicked it on with his head over Marshall and into the opposite corner. Ipswich midfielder Fabian Wilnis attempted to head it out but ended up helping it into the net. Bolton were 4-0 up after 38 minutes, Bobic had a hat-trick and Allardyce's team, barring a mathematical anomaly, were near enough safe by half-time.

They went into the break with the crowd on fire. The stadium had a carnival atmosphere at half-time as renditions of 'We are staying up!' were being sung loudly from the stands. All this while many Ipswich fans left their seats and decided to get an early start on the road back to East Anglia. The second half was a non-event until Ipswich scored to make it 4-1 in the last minute where Jamie Clapham netted a screamer from 30 yards into the top corner. However, the final whistle blew and Allardyce, who had now come down to the bench, and Bobic embraced.

Fredi Bobic only played 16 games for Bolton in all and returned to the Bundesliga in the summer. Yet he would for ever be remembered in Reebok Stadium legend as the man who scored Bolton's first Premier League hat-trick and, with the help of Djorkaeff, Gardner, Nolan and Bergsson, kept the club in the Premier League. Sam, Phil and the rest of the backroom staff got ready for another helping of sheep's testicles to celebrate the victory and survival. Bolton would lose their remaining three games that season but it didn't matter: they had done enough that day against Ipswich. Ipswich, along with Derby County and Leicester City, would be relegated as Bolton finished 16th and finished on Sam's magic 40 points.

Sam had made history and managed to keep Bolton in the Premier League at the first time of asking, and on a shoestring budget too. Tøfting and Djorkaeff would play in the World Cup that summer but Bobic would miss out for eventual runners-up Germany. However, his omission from the squad was not the only 'cut' in that summer as Bolton fans and Sam had not forgotten the bet and prediction made by pundit Mark Lawrenson at the start of the campaign. Lawrenson would sit down in the barber's chair and have his trademark moustache shaved and admitted he had underappreciated the work Sam had done. Sam and the team had shown that budgets and large transfer fees were nothing to their use of 'measured spirit'.

Back in Horwich, Sam was starting to look to build for the following season and would again try to strengthen his team by exploring away from the English leagues and towards players who were after a fresh start away from other nations.

One of them turned out to be so good, they named him twice.

8

Lightning strikes twice but the rain pours

YOURI DJORKAEFF and Stig Tøfting's World Cup campaigns were not successful as France and Denmark were both knocked out before the quarter-finals. Japanese loan signing Akinori Nishizawa made one appearance but by then had left Bolton and former player Claus Jensen joined Tøfting by being knocked out 3-0 by England in the last 16, when future Wanderers striker Emile Heskey scored. However, Sam Allardyce did not have the luxury of enjoying the World Cup that summer as he sent his scouts away to look for the next Djorkaeff and Bruno N'Gotty. As Djorkaeff signed a new two-year deal that summer, the Bolton hierarchy were hoping that the influence of 'Le God' would attract more high-profile eyes to BL6. As England played their final group game against Nigeria, many supporters in Bolton paid extra attention to the Nigerian number ten. Wanderers had been heavily linked to the Paris Saint-Germain midfielder Jay-Jay Okocha, who was available on a free transfer.

Sam had started initial conversations with Okocha, who did not have an agent at this time, yet the manager was worried that after a good World Cup run, more established eyes would notice the Nigerian's skill and usurp Bolton's attempts. He had also tried to sign another player from PSG that summer – Sylvain Distin. The cultured and calm French defender had impressed on a season-long loan at Newcastle the season earlier but as the Magpies decided to sign Jonathan Woodgate from Leeds United, they decided not to make Distin's move permanent. Additionally, Sam was trying to create strong links with the French club to use for the future as he also put in an enquiry about young full-back Bernard Mendy. Sam was waiting to hear back on the PSG trio as the World Cup continued and England were knocked out in the quarter-finals thanks to a 2-1 defeat to eventual winners Brazil.

Leaving the club would be former stalwart Paul Warhurst on a free, this potentially being a sign of the strides in calibre of player Bolton had acquired and targeted since their promotion in 2001. Dean Holden would finally depart for Oldham Athletic on a free, youth player David Norris joined Plymouth Argyle for £38,000, and Bo Hansen ended a three-year stint at the Reebok by signing for Midtjylland in his native Denmark on a free transfer. Later in the window, former fans' favourite Dean Holdsworth would join Coventry City on loan before making it permanent later in the season. In terms of retention, Sam had convinced captain Guðni Bergsson to sign a one-year extension. At 38, the Icelandic defender was ready to retire and start a career back home in Scandinavia as a lawyer but Allardyce wanted to squeeze one last year out of him to help Bolton consolidate their Premier League status.

After the World Cup, Allardyce flew to Paris's Charles de Gaulle Airport to meet with Okocha, alongside chairman Phil Gartside and club secretary and historian

Simon Marland. They met at the terminal, Allardyce briefing Okocha on project Bolton and even showing him a message from Youri Djorkaeff in an attempt to use the prestige of the Frenchman to convince the midfielder to join. Aged 28, Okocha was not in the dying embers of his career but a player closer to his prime. A messiah figure in his home country of Nigeria, Okocha had joined PSG for £14m from Fenerbahçe three years earlier and had served as a mentor for Ronaldinho during his time in France. Okocha and Allardyce spoke of their vision and the features that made Bolton different from other clubs, with their focus on spirit and the analytical side of the game. Okocha was convinced that he would be able to prolong his career and if needs be, use Bolton as a stepping stone to get back to the Champions League arena. Okocha seemed sold and informed the Bolton trio that he would meet them at the Reebok to sign the deal the next day. They offered to fly Okocha back on their trip but the Nigerian refused and said he would drive from Paris to Bolton the next day. Allardyce and Gartside's hearts fell as they thought that Okocha was going to ring them later that day to tell them the deal was off, or simply just not turn up. By this point they had already been let down by Distin who decided to join Manchester City instead.

Gartside, Marland and Allardyce returned to Manchester Airport deflated and after heading home, arrived at the Reebok Stadium the next day. They waited for the phone call or to be stood up but as Gartside looked out of his office he saw a French licence plate parking up outside the stadium and out of the car stepped Okocha. He signed a two-year deal that day and Allardyce and Bolton had a new number ten and another marquee international signing.

He and Djorkaeff were by far the highest earners at the club and Gartside worried that it would cause division in the ranks, yet this was not the case as the pair made sure their contribution on the pitch more than justified their wages. Following Okocha from PSG was Bernard Mendy who joined on a season-long loan. The 21-year-old was looking to get some games and was known for his pace and power down the right. Additionally, Bolton signed Huddersfield Town striker Delroy Facey, Turkish midfielder Bülent Akın and Tottenham Hotspur striker Chris Armstrong. All of the latter signed on free transfers as Sam didn't spend a penny on fees during the summer of 2002.

Sam was also hoping that Michael Ricketts would seem like a new signing. A major dip in form had occurred after his England cap in the February and Sam was looking to give Ricketts a chance at redemption in the new season. Bolton looked to build on their success of 2001/02 and adopted a 4-5-1 formation for the first game of the new campaign away at Fulham. N'Gotty had moved to central defence to support Bergsson with loan signing Mendy in at right-back. Okocha joined Kevin Nolan and Per Frandsen in midfield with Ricketts leading the line as Djorkaeff and Ricardo Gardner lined up either side of him. After Djorkaeff was fouled in the box in the first few moments of the match, Ricketts started the season perfectly with a goal from the spot after four minutes to make it 1-0 and score the first goal in the 2002/03 Premier League season. However, their joy was short-lived as goals from Louis Saha, Sylvain Legwinski (two) and Steve Marlet assured a 4-1 win for Fulham at their temporary home of Loftus Road while work was being done at Craven Cottage. Bolton would be defeated in their next game, at home to Charlton Athletic, before a Reebok Stadium victory over Aston Villa thanks to another Ricketts penalty gave them a lift before a return to Old Trafford in September to face Manchester United.

Prior to that match, Sam had been worried about Bolton's leaking defence and decided to shuffle again by bringing Anthony Barness and Mike Whitlow back in for some old-fashioned British steel. Mendy and Okocha were injured by this point and Akın wasn't making the grade; the manager would later state that he was 'hopeless'.

Akın wouldn't last very long at Bolton after a training ground bust-up with Mendy caused by a 50/50 challenge gone wrong. Akın felt that Mendy was trying to hurt him intentionally in a tackle and a fight ensued. Kevin Nolan, years later, noted how they both refused to stop fighting and were constantly held back. After several blows, they both were ushered into Sam's office where they refused to bury the hatchet. It is unknown whether Sam allowed the next part or whether it was beyond his control but the two then started to fight again in the manager's office with Mendy believed to be the winner by Nolan's accounts of the event. Apparently, at one point there was a karate kick from Akın and Mendy chased him around the Euxton car park until physio Faz Page, a former nightclub doorman, held on to Mendy as Akın drove off to his Bromley Cross apartment. Akın was seen as the least of the losses to the squad and was sent back to Turkey before being released in the summer. He made one Premier League appearance and played in one League Cup tie, being sent off in a defeat to local rivals Bury at Gigg Lane.

With a waning squad, Sam sent his feelers out again and offered trials for over 75 players but to no avail.

Yet, before the game at Old Trafford, Champions League-winning Spanish defender Iván Campo was made available for loan by Real Madrid. Sam had flexed his muscles in the transfer window and put in a loan offer for the shaggy-haired centre-back. Many laughed at the club's chances of getting a Real Madrid player but once Sam spoke with Campo he was able to, yet again, sell project Bolton to a serial winner. Campo spoke with his Madrid team-mate Steve McManaman about Bolton and his thoughts on the move. Similar to Djorkaeff, Campo had lost his place in the team and was keen for regular games and McManaman, the man who had destroyed Bolton in the 1995 League Cup Final in his Liverpool days, promoted Wanderers to Campo and told him it would be a great move for him to get some games and also experience the Premier League. Prior to the United game, Campo signed on a season-long loan from Real Madrid to join the increasing League of Nations at Bolton. Sam had been warned against Campo by some in the game after some discipline, weight and mentality issues in the past but the boss knew that with his mix of man management and medical support, he would be able to calm Campo down and get him playing. Within a few months, Campo-style wigs were flying off the club shop shelves.

Campo was named on the bench as Bolton travelled to Old Trafford for a night fixture on 11 September 2002. United's team had more star power than the 11 that had lost to Bolton the previous season as they included Ruud van Nistelrooy, David Beckham, Ryan Giggs, Juan Sebastián Verón, Nicky Butt and Rio Ferdinand. However, despite the collection of stars, lightning struck twice.

A half-volley by Kevin Nolan gave Bolton a 1-0 lead with 15 minutes to go as he took the ball from Beckham and drove it past Fabien Barthez in front of the travelling fans. Campo got his debut when he was brought on in the dying minutes to shore up the defence as Bolton recorded another victory at Old Trafford to go 13th in the Premier League. After the euphoria of this result, a visit from Liverpool was next for Bolton but there was no repeat of the previous season's victory as the Reds ran out 3-2 winners with Campo getting a goal on his second appearance. A defeat at Arsenal followed as Bolton's start to the season saw only two wins in six before another series of defeats and draws saw the team teeter between 20th and 19th in the Premier League by the time December arrived. In reality, the result at Old Trafford had sugar-coated an awful start and although many supporters revelled in the result it was little consolation for a potential relegation. Sales of the VHS of the 1-0 win sold well in the club shop but this did not hide the murmurings from the support around the dip in results.

Adding to Sam's woes, despite a strong start, Campo was proving to have a few mistakes in him at central defence and some of the fans were starting to turn on him during games as he was seen as unpredictable and unreliable. Mendy and Okocha had seen large spells out of the team and Kevin Nolan was out of the team due to poor form. Bolton also were struggling to keep the Reebok a fortress as they couldn't buy a win at home, going six home games without one by the time December arrived. One man who was proving to be Mr Consistent though was Youri Djorkaeff, who was still scoring the odd goal and providing assists where he could, recording four goals by Christmas 2002. Michael Ricketts' form was showing inconsistency but he had scored six goals by the same time.

By the festive period, Bolton were struggling as Newcastle United arrived at the Reebok Stadium for the Boxing Day game in front of 27,314 fans. They had recorded just one win in 14 and were 19th in the Premier League after 17 games in contrast to Sir Bobby Robson's Newcastle who were fourth and had the same points as Manchester United when they came to Horwich for the 1pm post-Christmas match. As with many Boxing Day games, there was a bumper crowd as the Reebok was at almost full capacity. Bolton fans would flock home from different areas of the country and the globe for the Christmas period and what better way to celebrate a family occasion during the festive period than watching their team?

Newcastle had been fighting on many fronts by the time December 2002 came but would eventually be knocked out of the Champions League later that season in the second group stage after being placed into the proverbial 'group of death' which included Inter Milan, Barcelona and Bayer Leverkusen. Desperate for another stab at Europe's elite competition, Newcastle wanted to stay in the top four and came to the Reebok on the back of four games unbeaten where star strikers Alan Shearer and Craig Bellamy had scored four goals between them.

However, much to the surprise of many, Bellamy was dropped to the bench for the game as Robson went with Shola Ameobi to partner Shearer in a 4-4-2 formation. Sam also surprised many by showing faith in Henrik Pedersen as a starter of late. The Danish striker had been signed the previous season but failed to make an impact and had been sent out on loan back to Silkeborg towards the back end of the season. However, he had returned fitter and sharper and grabbed a double in a 4-2 win over Leeds in November. Pedersen was a strong worker and gave 100 per cent for the team. He was not the prolific striker that Sam thought he had signed in 2001 but he was turning into a vital component.

Another promising sign was the return of Okocha, yet Mendy was still out. Okocha started in midfield with

Gardner, Djorkaeff and Frandsen as Bolton looked to get a result to pull them back out of the bottom three; five minutes in, he showed the fans why they had missed him so much. Gardner received a pass on the edge of the box after some strong work from Ricketts as he shielded the ball from the Newcastle defence. Ricketts had started to regain some of the form that saw him receive plaudits the previous season and seemed to enjoy playing with Okocha. However, as he supported Gardner, the Jamaican ran across the edge of the box with the ball and saw Okocha unmarked on the edge of the D. A simple pass to Okocha teed the ball up perfectly for the Nigerian who struck his shot with ferocity and pace as it thrusted from his right boot into the top-left corner leaving the diving Shay Given absolutely no chance. The fans roared as James Brown's 'I Feel Good' came from the stadium speakers signifying a goal for the home team.

Some sloppy defending three minutes later gave Newcastle an equaliser as Shearer scored from close range, but a further minute on, Bolton hit back to end a frantic first ten minutes. They had a free kick on the edge of the box and many felt Djorkaeff or Okocha would attempt a strike on goal. However, Gardner ushered them away and felt his crafty left foot could do some business. Many would have used the opportunity to get the ball in the box to try and create a chance. Not for Gardner, who looked up and swung a glorious left-footed strike, bending and curling away from goal then into the top-left corner past Given. Gardner ran to the bench and was congratulated by the subs and then by the gleeful Simon Charlton.

After this chaotic start, both sides decided to slow things down and started to move into a calm, passing way of playing. With the game coming towards half-time, Frandsen had the ball midway inside the Newcastle half.

With many expecting him to play it back to the defence, Frandsen used the bounce of the ball to his advantage and scooped a looping cross into the Geordie box. Smartly, Ricketts had stayed in line with defenders Gary Caldwell and Andy O'Brien as the ball was hit by Frandsen. Ricketts then peeled away and as the ball came into the box, he rose like a salmon and beat O'Brien in the air from the edge of the six-yard line to make it 3-1 as the referee blew for half-time.

As the half-time Golden Gamble lottery was drawn, that chant came back again – 'We are staying up!' – as the fans knew that three points would put Bolton out of the drop zone. Ricketts seemed to be rejuvenated and with a spring in his step and was starting to play with a smile on his face again. At the start of the second half, both teams had chances as Bolton looked to see out their lead and Newcastle tried to get back into the game. Future Wanderers midfielder Gary Speed was trying to launch many an attack, and a couple of times he put Shearer in but Jussi Jääskeläinen was a match for the former England captain. Speed received the ball again on 63 minutes and was looking to go past Okocha near the halfway line. Okocha made life difficult for Speed and wouldn't let him pass and caused the Newcastle man to turn around and pass the ball back to his defence.

However, Speed's backpass was cleverly intercepted by Ricketts who drove past O'Brien and moved towards the box with the ball. Given came rushing out of his goal to try and stop Ricketts but the striker calmly put the ball on to his right foot and from the edge of the box, he placed a curling shot into the net. Ricketts peeled away and ran towards the north-west corner of the stadium with his arm raised as he celebrated putting his team 4-1 up. This was the Ricketts who had got Bolton promoted, who had earned an England cap, who enjoyed his football and made Sam Allardyce a happy, happy man. Sam, looking to see the game out, brought on Kevin Nolan to add more steel to the midfield. However, two late goals from Ameobi in the 71st minute and Shearer again in the 80th made it a tense end to the match with Shearer getting his 350th career goal. Pedersen, after a warrior-like performance, came off to be replaced with Delroy Facey. Newcastle pushed but their efforts were not enough as referee Uriah Rennie blew his whistle and the home supporters erupted to celebrate a massive three points which helped Bolton move up to 17th in the league and out of the relegation zone as 2003 was approaching.

After Ricketts' upturn in form, just as they did the previous January, the rumours of a transfer started to circulate. Ricketts had been keen to leave the season prior as he was close to an £8m move to Tottenham Hotspur but Bolton blocked it. Many supporters felt that Ricketts' goals could keep Bolton up again and the Birmingham-born striker was a fans' favourite, especially with the younger group. Ricketts and Nolan were the guests for the Junior Whites' Christmas party in mid-December and Nolan relished in the festivities by getting involved with the games and signing autographs for the young supporters. Ricketts, the Junior Whites' favourite, seemed different though and seemed keen to leave as soon as possible. When invited to a game of penalties, he refused due to the newness of his trainers; the host, Ian Cheeseman, told the fans that Sam wouldn't allow Ricketts to kick the ball due to a niggling injury so the event could save face.

The year before, Phil Gartside had slapped a not for sale sign on Ricketts and the chairman had said the same for the transfer window of January 2003 as Spurs came in again for the striker. The winter transfer window had been great for Sam the year previous thanks to the acquisitions of Youri Djorkaeff and Fredi Bobic but Sam was struggling to replicate that success and there was no money in the budget to sign anyone. Sam invited French pair Pierre-Yves André and Florent Laville on trial with the opportunity of a deal if terms could be met and a fee – well, hopefully a free – could be reached with Bolton's limited resources. The thought of selling Ricketts was not something that Sam was happy about but the funds created could be used to strengthen elsewhere, especially defence as Iván Campo had moved from a potentially calamitous central defender, unable to cope with the pace of Premier League strikers, to a calm and dictating defensive midfielder, but this left a gap in defence. Sam was also looking for a long-term defensive replacement for Guðni Bergsson who would retire in the summer, and Laville was seen as a possibility for that if he impressed during his trial.

However, Bolton were in a worse position and with fewer points than the same time the previous year and supporters were aware that if the team was to go backwards and return to the First Division, then the likes of Okocha, Djorkaeff and Ricketts would go anyway.

As the final day of the transfer window approached, Bolton had turned down a £2m bid from Tottenham for Ricketts but received a bid from Teesside club Middlesbrough late in the day, of £2.5m down and an additional £1m in future appearances. Allardyce and Gartside deliberated the pros and cons and eventually felt that the fee was acceptable and that it would also help the manager bring in some fresh blood such as Laville. By 11pm, Ricketts had agreed terms at the Riverside and was a Boro player. Many young supporters woke up the morning after to hear of the sale of their favourite player – the first Wanderer to play for England in over 30 years.

With the available funds and the last embers of the window showing, Laville was signed on loan until the end of the season from Lyon as well as strikers Pierre-Yves André from Nantes and Salva Ballesta from Valencia. The three were presented to the crowd ahead of the home game against Birmingham City on 1 February 2003. Bolton won 4-2 with Pedersen scoring and Okocha being named man of the match. Pedersen was happy to try and replace Ricketts' goals and Okocha was happy to move into the Junior Whites' favourite role. Sam, however, knew a massive dose of that 'measured spirit' was needed for Bolton to reach or surpass 40 points this time as they needed a strong run to ensure that they avoided the last relegation place and West Ham would take it instead, with Sunderland and West Brom both already seeming doomed with 12 games remaining.

9

So good they named him twice

AUGUSTINE AZUKA Okocha was born in 1973 in the city of Enugu in Nigeria. The name Jay-Jay came from his older brother James who passed it down to his sibling. As a youngster, Jay-Jay would play football on the streets with almost anything he could find and remarked in an interview with BBC Sport that he would use 'anything that was round, if it was a ball it was a bonus'. He started his career with local team Enugu Rangers before a fortuitous trip to West Germany turned out to be life-changing. Okocha visited in 1990, a country deep in World Cup fever, to visit childhood friend Binebi Numa who had signed for third-tier side Borussia Neunkirchen. Okocha joined in for a training session and impressed the higher-ups enough to offer him a contract at the age of 17. After two years with Neunkirchen, Okocha moved across Germany to sign for Eintracht Frankfurt in the Bundesliga where he would gain global fame for an unbelievable 1993 goal against Karlsruher SC where he dribbled the ball around four defenders and away from goalkeeper Oliver Kahn in a league game. It won various goal of the year awards but by the end of the 1996 season, Frankfurt were relegated and Okocha moved to Turkey where he would adopt the Turkish name Muhammed Yavuz when signing for Fenerbahçe for £1m.

His time in Turkey was a success and combined with a glittering career for Nigeria, he impressed French giants Paris Saint-Germain enough to join them for 14m Francs. However, after helping tutor Ronaldinho and helping the French club pick up the 2001 Intertoto Cup, he was on his way to Charles de Gaulle airport to meet with Sam Allardyce, Simon Marland and Phil Gartside in 2002.

Okocha's start at Bolton had not been ideal as injury had halted a promising beginning. Yet by the time that Bolton hosted Tottenham on *Monday Night Football* in March 2003, Okocha was showing his quality and having all manner of Premier League clubs hoping Bolton would get relegated so they could try and sign him on a cut-price deal in the summer. Okocha had scored four league goals by 24 March as Bolton had the chance to go two points clear of West Ham, who had recorded a victory over doomed Sunderland on the Saturday which put Wanderers into the bottom three heading into their game against Tottenham, the Hammers moving a point clear. Okocha had scored the weekend previous in a 2-0 win away at Sunderland and was the name on the end of every fan's lips as they entered the match ready for the 8pm kick-off.

Littered with Campo wigs, 'Le God' flags and 'So good they named him twice' T-shirts, the Bolton faithful were doing all they could to make the stadium a cauldron.

Tottenham were in ninth and looking to move up to seventh with a win. They had improved massively from the team that had drawn at the Reebok the previous year as former England manager Glenn Hoddle boasted a luxury of international players including Gustavo Poyet, Robbie Keane, Ledley King, Kasey Keller and Champions League winner Teddy Sheringham. Sheringham had played for England against Okocha's Nigeria in the 2002 World Cup in Japan the previous summer and was still a potent threat in his older years. As the lights shone down on the pitch, a feeling of optimism and also opportunity was in the air as Bolton knew a win in this match and then another at home the following Saturday against Manchester City would do wonders for their survival chances.

For one of the first times all season, Bolton were at full strength as they started with a team of Jääskeläinen, Mendy, Bergsson, Laville, N'Gotty, Gardner, Campo, Frandsen, Djorkaeff, Okocha and Pedersen. Pedersen was proving to be a handful for defences and Bolton were showing no signs of missing Ricketts. Campo was in the midst of a renaissance in his new position of defensive midfielder, showing his cultured class on the ball and sometimes a shot at the theatrical. Okocha, however, was the one unlocking defences. His silky skills and numerous stepovers had already embarrassed Roy Keane and Paul Scholes earlier in the season and his performances were a level above anything anyone had seen at the Reebok before.

The match kicked off to a rapturous ovation from the home fans as Bolton and Tottenham began to push each other for an opening goal. The visitors seemed to be trying to get an early goal as within the first 20 minutes, Simon Davies, Gus Poyet and Robbie Keane all tested Jääskeläinen. However, Ben Thatcher was substituted on 21 minutes after picking up a knock and Irish defender/striker Gary Doherty was brought on. Djorkaeff, not to be outplayed by Okocha, was swinging dangerous balls into the box to try and connect with Pedersen but American keeper Kasey Keller was a match for the Bolton attack.

Both teams went in at half-time feeling they could nick a goal and take control.

However, a draw would mean that Bolton stayed in the bottom three and this wasn't good enough for them. They came out with added vigour and motivation as Sam moved down from the hospitality seats to join Phil Brown and his team on the bench. They pushed and pushed and on 57 minutes Djorkaeff seemed to find his compatriot Mendy with a looping ball. Mendy was chasing the ball as he approached the box but Keller came out to punch it away just as the French full-back looked to have taken it past the goalkeeper. It was great bravery from Keller as Mendy had beaten the Spurs defence. Five minutes later, Bolton had a corner which was met by N'Gotty whose header fell to Campo in the six-yard box. The Spaniard performed an acrobatic volley which looked to have hit the arms of Darren Anderton from very close range, but it would have been too harsh for the referee to point to the spot as Spurs cleared.

The game had already kicked into gear as Doherty came close for the visitors with a shot-cum-cross before Okocha went up to the other end and hit a long-range shot which was held by Keller. On 72 minutes, substitute Anthony Barness, in an unfamiliar left-back role, cut in from the left and hit a rasping shot across goal which was blocked well by Keller. The ball fell to Okocha who shockingly headed over the bar from five yards out. The Nigerian lay on the ground in shock as Bolton piled on the pressure. Three minutes later the stadium was on its feet again as a curling cross from Djorkaeff was met brilliantly in the air by Bergsson whose header beat Keller but rattled against the post. Bolton fans started to lose hope; they felt their team couldn't do more as they continued to dominate the second half but were unable to put the ball past Keller. The North

Stand was almost attempting to suck the ball into the net as most home supporters had conceded to having to stand for the rest of the game.

Djorkaeff laid the ball to January acquisition Pierre-Yves André whose curling strike was tipped over the bar by Keller, who was having the game of his life, and other than Okocha and Djorkaeff, was the man of the match that evening. The game passed to injury time and it seemed that Bolton would remain in the bottom three. A 0-0 wasn't enough to move them out with seven matches remaining, including a six-pointer against West Ham in three weeks. They pushed with one more attack as Djorkaeff picked up the ball on the edge of the box and skipped past Doherty, who attempted to slide to get the ball from the Frenchman, but ended up in tripping Djorkaeff up as Keller rushed out to claim possession.

The stadium held its breath as Graham Poll put his whistle to his lips and pointed to the penalty spot with one minute of injury time remaining. A penalty in the 93rd minute and up stepped Okocha. He put the ball down on the spot and looked directly into Keller's eyes. As Okocha started his stuttering run-up, many would have been forgiven for backing the American in this duel after his amazing performance. Okocha shot towards the right-hand side of the net but saw Keller diving the correct way. The pace on the ball meant that Keller was a millisecond too slow and the spot-kick hit the blue and white netting. The stadium turned into a cauldron of noise as Okocha ran to the corner with Djorkaeff and grabbed his right ankle and swung it back and forward in his now trademark celebration. There was no time for a Tottenham fightback as Poll blew his whistle for full time and Bolton had created magic on that night and gone two points clear of West

Ham in 17th. What a night; Okocha cemented his place in Bolton folklore.

That following Saturday, Okocha had another penalty against Manchester City but pulled the ball wide this time, yet Bolton still won 2-0 thanks to Pedersen and another man of the moment, Iván Campo. The goals were assisted by Okocha and Djorkaeff respectively. Bolton would pick up six points from a possible 12 as they went into the final game week. One of those results was a 1-0 home victory against West Ham thanks to another Okocha special where he ran from his own half to slam the ball past keeper David James into the top corner. It was nominated for the goal of the season award by ITV, who still held the rights for the main highlights broadcast with their Saturday evening show, *The Premiership*. Additionally, Okocha also helped Bolton draw 2-2 with Arsenal in April after another masterclass by himself and Djorkaeff. Djorkaeff was unplayable as Bolton came back from 2-0 down against the champions. Okocha again made the highlights reel on Sky Sports as he flicked and tricked his way around Ray Parlour and Patrick Vieira.

Going into the final game against Middlesbrough, Okocha was asked by Sky Sports presenter Chris Kamara why he was at Bolton and not Real Madrid with his skills and ability. He simply replied, 'Anywhere I find myself, I will play and I want to play for Bolton Wanderers.'

Bolton and West Ham went into the final round of fixtures both having beaten the usual 40-point mark and sitting level on 41 points each. Wanderers held a goal difference advantage of six but the teams knew that whoever went down would be labelled as the 'best team to ever get relegated'. West Ham were at Birmingham with Sam Allardyce ringing his old friend Steve Bruce to ensure that they would not take their foot off the gas as the Brummies had nothing to play for. Bolton welcomed Middlesbrough and faced the return of Michael Ricketts.

Sam had given the players and backroom team four days off in preparation for the game that would define Bolton's season. Many in the local media questioned his methods and wondered if he had felt the pressure and lost it. However, Sam felt the boys needed the pressure off so he and Phil Brown enjoyed a day at Chester races with their wives before returning to the club on Friday to go through some team shape ahead of the Saturday. It was clear to all inside and outside of the Reebok Stadium that this match would be huge for the history of Bolton Wanderers as if they stayed up, they would be able to build on their two years in the Premier League and start to become established and attract further stars. Yet relegation would most likely mean losing Okocha, Djorkaeff, Jääskeläinen and N'Gotty as well as having no chance of Mendy, Laville and Campo returning. Sam and his team had worked too hard to simply allow the team to regress to the First Division days and with all fairness and respect to the likes of Dean Holdsworth, Paul Warhurst, Gareth Farrelly and Michael Johansen, the club had moved on to another level of player calibre by May 2003.

Bolton were at full strength other than the omission of Florent Laville who was suspended following his red card against Arsenal. Allardyce was furious with referee Andy D'Urso who sent Laville off for two yellow cards after committing only two fouls all game against the Gunners. Laville had become a sense of calm and class in the heart of the defence, with Bolton utilising the width of Gardner and Mendy to operate with a back five. Laville showed a cultured side to the game and had worked very well with the support of N'Gotty and Bergsson. The idea would be that if

Bolton stayed up, Laville would join N'Gotty in a back four after the retirement of Bergsson coming up in the summer.

A crowd of 27,241 arrived in Horwich for the decider; Middlesbrough had nothing to play for but some end-of-season pride. West Ham travelled to Birmingham with legendary former player Trevor Brooking taking the helm as the Irons' caretaker manager. Many Bolton fans were prepared for both the best and the worst as just like that day at Stamford Bridge in 1998, they were armed with their radios in hope of listening to the West Ham match while watching their team. No doubt the West Ham supporters had a similar setup in the away end at St Andrew's.

As the game kicked off, Gardner and Mendy were proving to be troublesome for the Middlesbrough full-backs Franck Queudrue and Stuart Parnaby as they stretched the visiting defence, forcing mistakes and endless throw-ins from which Okocha would float the ball towards Pedersen. Gardner lost possession and it went out for the throw-in on nine minutes which was taken by Parnaby in line with the box from the left. He passed to Dutch midfielder George Boateng who took the ball and played it into midfield to former Manchester United tough tackler Jonathan Greening. Greening, with his trademark long hair, looked up as he turned only to feel the power of a Danish Viking push him away. Per Frandsen, the man Allardyce had brought back from Blackburn Rovers, outmuscled Greening and stole the ball. Frandsen then drove forward towards the Middlesbrough box. The closer he got, the more Bolton fans stood up from their seats. As he approached the D, low monotone shouts of 'Shoooooot!' came from the home crowd. Frandsen looked up and unleashed a venomous right-footed rocket from the edge of the box. The pace on the ball wrong-footed Australian keeper Mark Schwarzer who dived to his right but was unable to get a touch to the ball as it raced past him into the net. Bolton led 1-0 after ten minutes, a dream start. Frandsen ran to the East Stand with his arms out aloft and performed a knee slide into the corner flag before turning around and catching a jumping Bernard Mendy. News of the goal reached Birmingham as West Ham fans began to groan in the away end.

The rasping strike was a great moment for the 33-year-old who had been questioned about his ability to withstand the influence of Okocha, Djorkaeff and Campo in midfield in the evolving Bolton side. However, he had shown that an old favourite was just as important as the new shiny toys as he gave Bolton the advantage and an amazing chance of staying up. Middlesbrough arrived at the Reebok with the best defensive record outside of the top five that season, and sat in 11th. However, their away form was the issue that stopped them from gaining a European place as they had recorded only three wins on the road all season. As the game progressed into the 20th minute, Gardner was again causing issues for the Middlesbrough backline and as he got towards the box he was hacked down to the left of the box by Greening. The midfielder, having a torrid time, was booked for the challenge and Bolton had a free kick in a fantastic position.

Chants of 'Jay-Jay Oko-Cha' came from the stands as the fans knew there was only one man they wanted to take it. Hearing the crowd's calls, Djorkaeff stepped away from the ball and gave it to Okocha to kick as the Frenchman began to direct traffic in the box. Okocha stumbled towards the ball and curled a sweet, bending strike over the wall and into the same side of the goal that Frandsen had just 11 minutes earlier. The stadium erupted and Allardyce and Phil Gartside embraced in the hospitality seats. Okocha ran towards the bench and threw his shirt over his head to reveal a vest with the writing 'THANK YOU JESUS!' written on it. Okocha was thanking Jesus, the Bolton fans were thanking their saviour and messiah. Cheers could be heard from the other side of Middlebrook as Bolton went into half-time 2-0 up and West Ham were still drawing 0-0 in Birmingham. This gave Wanderers a two-point cushion over the Hammers with 45 minutes of the season to go.

Middlesbrough manager Steve McClaren was not impressed and decided to take off the hapless Greening for Brazilian Doriva, as well as removing Malcolm Christie for the pantomime villain for the day, Michael Ricketts. Ricketts' exit had left a sour taste in the mouths of many Bolton fans as they felt he acted as if he was above the Trotters after his England cap. They made this known and Ricketts was met with a chorus of boos as he entered the pitch. It of course passed the mind of everyone attached to Bolton that there was a chance that Ricketts could relegate the club. However, it was something many, Allardyce included, could not bear to think about.

Bolton looked to protect their lead in the second half as chances were few and far between. Jääskeläinen made a great save from a Juninho free kick but by the 60th minute, the match seemed to be fading out as Okocha and Djorkaeff showed off their skills. Just as it looked like Bolton would consolidate their lead with another Okocha strike which sailed over the bar, Middlesbrough began to make some good work in midfield. Juninho set Parnaby away down the right and he looked up before playing the ball across the box. Laville's replacement for the day, Mike Whitlow, had lost his man and ran towards Parnaby but was too late as he played it past the six-yard box. Bolton fans then felt their hearts drop as they saw the ball fall to Ricketts, who stepped in front of Bergsson and flicked it past Jääskeläinen in the middle of the goal. The fans were stunned, and no longer hearing boos, Ricketts cupped his ears to the stands in acknowledgment of the silence he had caused in BL6. Never simple with Bolton is it, as six minutes later, West Ham scored against Birmingham to go level on points. How quickly the tide had turned. As the Sky Sports camera panned to Sam in the stands, his face painted more than a thousand words ever could. Same old Bolton, never easy.

The game had now become a frantic bag of nerves as Middlesbrough pushed for an equaliser. However, the job became a little bit easier as Queudrue was sent off for two yellow cards. Within minutes of this, news came through of a Birmingham equaliser at St Andrew's and then two minutes later, the Reebok Stadium let out an almighty cheer. No one had scored there but the radio holders in the ground had made the rest of the crowd aware that Birmingham had gone 2-1 up against West Ham in the 90th minute. That chant came out yet again, 'We are staying, we are staying up!'

West Ham equalised in the last minute through Paolo Di Canio but by then the whistle had blown for full time at the Reebok. Players, fans, backroom staff, stewards and stadium staff grabbed each other in embrace as Bolton had done it again, this time in a Steve McQueen-esque fashion. As the players celebrated, Mendy jumped on the back of Allardyce as they did a lap of honour around the pitch, and the manager and his new star man Okocha did a Nigerian dance in the middle of the Reebok pitch, which they would replicate 19 years later in a charity match at the stadium, by then the Unibol, in 2022.

Captain Guðni Bergsson waved goodbye to his adopted home of Bolton after the game. Sam had managed to convince him the year earlier to delay his retirement and tried yet again, but Bergsson had made up his mind. Bergsson, who arrived under Bruce Rioch in 1995 from Tottenham Hotspur as a right-back, had shown to be an amazing servant for Bolton under Rioch, Colin Todd and Allardyce and had been there through ups and downs. His links to Bolton would never be diminished as he would be named godfather to Jimmy Phillips' son, Nathaniel. This young man would later be known better as Liverpool defender Nat Phillips. Bergsson left Bolton after making 270 league appearances in an eight-year period. He would be remembered as a legend in Iceland for his 19-year career for his country but in the little pocket of England that he called home, he was an adopted Boltonion and an icon to many across the town.

Bolton had secured their Premier League status for another season but this wasn't enough for Sam as behind the scenes, plans had already been put in place for this to be the launchpad moment. The Wanderers didn't want to just play against the Premier League elite, they wanted to be one of the elite.

Many say vision and leadership is to be able to look towards the future, not to see the organisation or the group for what it is, but for what it can become. None were more fixed to that mantra than Sam and his backroom staff. As Sam, Phil Brown and the team settled down for a relaxing summer, the work had already begun with the manager off to Greece alongside Jack Chapman to scout a new player in the Olympiakos v AEK Athens derby. Upon his return, he informed Phil Gartside that the club could now move to the next level and that in order for the vision to become a reality, they had to spend money on assets of their own rather than relying on the loan market as they had done with the likes of Bobic, Tøfting, Mendy, Laville and Campo. Mendy and Laville returned to France and Campo, for now, went back to Madrid. Sam tried to get all three to return and could only convince two of his loan stars to do so. However, the truth was that Jay-Jay Okocha was the name on everyone's lips and had become a legend at the Reebok after only one year. Little did they all know that, as the saying goes, this was only the beginning.

10

Bolton Galácticos

MEASURED SPIRIT – the term this book coins relating to Sam Allardyce and Bolton's approach to football during this period – is believed to be the symbiotic marrying of belief and leaving nothing to chance. The Bolton backroom team of this time certainly did that and made quantitative or 'measured' decisions to add to the undoubted family nature and spirit of the club. There may have been a lack of budget or financial power, but the club was unbeatable in terms of measured spirit. However, with this in mind, Sam and the team were no longer happy with just staying up after two close calls in 2001/02 and 2002/03 and felt it was now time to move on from the borrowing of players in the loan market to save them and wanted to build a team that would be full of Bolton-owned players who challenged higher up the table.

Allardyce flew back from Greece waxing lyrical about a right-winger named Stylianos Giannakopoulos, who would later be referred to as 'Stelios'. The Greek international was available on a free transfer and would be yet another addition to Sam's League of Nations on 28 May 2003. Sam wanted to get his work done early this year as he aimed to start the 2003/04 season strongly. With Stelios's attention to the right wing, it seemed that Sam may have had to move on from Bernard Mendy. Mendy had returned to his club and felt his best chance of playing for France in Euro 2004 was at Paris Saint-Germain, so ultimately he turned down a return to the Reebok which left a gap at right-back as well. Luckily, Sam felt confident enough in youngster Nicky Hunt's abilities and called him up to first-team training that summer. Mendy would play 33 games for PSG that season, but did not make France's Euro 2004 squad. However, Hunt would play 31 games for Bolton in the same time and also received a call-up to England's under-21 squad.

As Allardyce, Simon Marland and Phil Gartside gave up on Mendy, two other previous loan stars were constantly linked with Bolton that summer in Iván Campo and Florent Laville. Laville's deal was the easier of the two as the terms had more or less been agreed when he arrived on loan in January, and Bolton tied up a deal for around a believed £500,000 for the French defender who was expected to form a formidable partnership with his compatriot, Bruno N'Gotty, after the retirement of Guðni Bergsson and the release of Colin Hendry and Mike Whitlow. Campo, on the other hand, was proving harder to get over the line as questions of medicals, terms and his contract at Real Madrid started to complicate things.

A change, in keeping with the idea of becoming a more elite force, was a slight evolution to Bolton's home kit, moving from their traditional white shirts, navy shorts and white socks to an all-white kit. Many stated it looked like they had copied Leeds United, but Sam thought otherwise. Maybe it was a ploy to convince many high-end players such as Campo to sign on at the Reebok but Sam and many within the club labelled Bolton 'the Galácticos', a name stolen from the famous white-kitted Real Madrid team in the early 2000s. The manufacturer, Reebok, had created a plain yet crisp kit that had a light red thread along the shoulders and, especially in the summer, looked like it would fit in well at the Bernabéu.

As the transfer window rolled on, Sam was still desperate to replace Michael Ricketts' goals from the seasons prior and made a special effort to sign strikers. Henrik Pedersen was trusted but Sam knew he needed some more firepower to support the Dane and Delroy Facey who was no longer impressing. Salva Ballesta and Pierre-Yves André had not done enough to earn a permanent contract either as well as reserve striker Jonathan Walters who was not making the grade. Allardyce toyed with the idea of putting Youri Djorkaeff up front but felt he would lose the Frenchman's creativity.

The next summer signing was very much a low-key one, in fact it didn't even gather enough attention for a press conference, but what a signing it would become. Among the superstars of the Okochas and the Djorkaeffs, in came a forgotten English striker. Kevin Davies was 26 and only five years earlier had signed for Blackburn Rovers for £7.5m from Southampton. At that point it seemed he was destined to join Michael Owen in attack for England. Alas, it never happened and the strong frontman found himself a free agent in 2003. Davies started his career at Chesterfield after leaving boyhood club Sheffield United at 15. He had reached national fame with the Spireites, helping them reach the 1997 FA Cup semi-final, which included a hat-trick against Bolton along the way. This earned him a move to Southampton where he really impressed in just one season before getting his big-money transfer to Ewood Park. However, one season and just one goal later, Davies was back at St Mary's in exchange for Egil Østenstad. Still young, Davies struggled to find a first-team place on the south coast and despite scoring in Southampton's run to the FA Cup Final, he was left out of the squad at the Millennium Stadium and was released at the end of the season.

Davies was short on confidence after a tough few years and Sam saw taking him on as a low-stakes risk. Signed on a low-wage contract, Davies wanted to enjoy his football again and Sam promised him that if he followed his advice, he would do that. On a pre-season tour of Ireland, Allardyce told Davies some home truths about his weight and his confidence and informed the striker that this would be his last chance at Premier League football and it was up to him to trim down and fight for his place or let his career fizzle away. Within a few weeks, Davies's body fat was down to under ten per cent and he was being forged into a target man. Davies was known for his pace in his younger years, but Sam wasn't interested in that, he wanted to use him as a magnet to play the ball to, so he could bring players like Okocha, Djorkaeff and Nolan into dangerous positions to increase Bolton's chances of goals. Davies was given this sign of faith and wanted to repay Sam with performances. Allardyce wasn't too concerned with Davies's goals, he wanted to see commitment to bring others into the game to create more goalscorers across the pitch. At that time it was labelled as long ball; I think today when Liverpool do it through Virgil van Dijk, it's a 'controlled long-field pass'.

Adding to the signing of Davies was another striker in Mário Jardel, on a free deal from Sporting Lisbon, but it could grow to £1.5m based on certain appearances. Jardel arrived, similar to Davies, overweight but where Davies showed motivation to change, the Brazilian saw this as another stop on his world party tour. By 2003, Jardel had scored over 200 goals in Brazil, Portugal and Turkey and was named the European Golden Boot winner in 1999 and 2002. Many were shocked at Allardyce's ability to sign someone who only 18 months earlier was the most-wanted striker in Europe. However, when they saw Jardel's shape, they saw why. Jardel was severely out of condition, yet Sam and his team had made a record of salvaging broken careers and fancied another go. Jardel arrived and lived with new Manchester United winger Cristiano Ronaldo, who had also moved over from Sporting Lisbon. Many around Bolton saw Jardel in the David Lloyd gym, near Chorley New Road, however he frequented the steam room and jacuzzi more than the cardio machines.

Another striker who arrived at the Reebok for a medical was Tottenham's 29-year-old Ukrainian, Sergei Rebrov. Rebrov was keen to join Bolton and had managed to do a deal with Spurs to join on a free. However, this would go on until September when Rebrov eventually did not join due to issues with his work permit. He had struggled with Tottenham after his £11m move from Dynamo Kiev in 2000 and wanted an opportunity to show himself off. Alas, it didn't happen and Bolton moved on. Funnily enough that deal had almost happened a year earlier when Tottenham offered Rebrov to Bolton in a swap for Michael Ricketts.

The season was close to starting and Bolton had signed Florent Laville, Stelios Giannakopoulos, Kevin Davies and Mário Jardel. Sam signed AC Milan midfielder Ibrahim Ba, another fitness project, before finally agreeing terms with Iván Campo on a three-year deal. 'The Wig' had returned ready for pre-season to stock up the midfield. Just before the window closed, Bolton agreed a loan swap with Delroy Facey going to Burnley and Glen Little coming to the Reebok for a one-month loan. Sam's new-look 'Bolton Galácticos' looked ready to take on the world as they took the short journey for their first league game of the season against Manchester United at Old Trafford. They lined up in a 4-4-2 with some new changes. Nicky Hunt made his first Premier League start in defence with Florent Laville and Bruno N'Gotty in the middle and a newly converted Ricardo Gardner at left-back, a position he would become famous for. In midfield was Kevin Nolan – eager to kickstart his career after a poor showing in 2002/03 – Campo, Stelios and newly appointed captain Jay-Jay Okocha. Up front were Kevin Davies and Henrik Pedersen.

There had been much speculation over the summer regarding who would take over the armband from Guðni Bergsson and many predicted it could be Nolan or Gardner, yet Okocha was chosen and led his team out at Old Trafford against a depleted United side who had recently lost David Beckham to Real Madrid. However, they had a new, young number seven by the name of Cristiano Ronaldo, who we can all agree turned out all right. Making up the five on Bolton's bench were Kevin Poole, Anthony Barness, Per Frandsen, Youri Djorkaeff and days before his move to Burnley, Delroy Facey.

After a strong start, Bolton found themselves on the wrong side of a 4-0 thumping. Such a scoreline always looks bad but the second goal wasn't scored until the 70th minute and the debut of the young Ronaldo stole the day for many at Old Trafford. Sam's *Galácticos* were humbled and would go on to gain just two points and two goals from their first four games which included another 4-0 hammering away at newly promoted Portsmouth. Not the start Sam wanted and surely not another relegation fight? Just before the window shut, Bolton signed Brazilian centre-back

Emerson Thome to add some steel to the back. Thome had played for Chelsea, Sheffield Wednesday and Sunderland in the Premier League and brought experience to the ranks. N'Gotty had picked up a knock early on and Thome was seen as competition for him and Laville. However, disaster struck Laville as he ruptured his cruciate ligament in a home victory over Middlesbrough in September. Allardyce stated that the silky, composed Frenchman would be back in six months' time but in the end, Laville never played for Bolton again. The knee injury constantly haunted Laville and after that match he would retire four years later, a period of time where he managed only 37 appearances back home in France. Instantly, Thome, who had come in as cover on a one-year deal, became the main defender with N'Gotty.

Bolton beat Middlesbrough 2-0 and tried to build a charge yet were met with inconsistent results and performances. Jardel, or as he was being nicknamed in certain quarters, 'Lardel', was a huge frustration and despite three goals in the League Cup, including a great header away at Anfield, Sam had enough and cancelled his contract by December, before the appearance clause fees kicked in and, back he went to South America where he signed for Newell's Old Boys after a brief loan stint in Italy with Ancona.

By October, Bolton were sitting in 15th and hoping to look up and avoid another relegation scrap. However, a 6-2 defeat at Manchester City and a 1-0 home reverse at the hands of Birmingham City put them in 18th and back in the thick of it. Yet some scrappy results, including wins away at Tottenham and Leeds adding to a home victory over Everton, left Bolton 13th in the league as they travelled to Stamford Bridge to take on Roman Abramovich's 'Chelski' on 13 December 2003.

In the summer of 2003, Chelsea had transformed from the club that Bolton had faced in the past. They had been bought by Russian billionaire Abramovich for £140m, quickly flooding the club with cash injections and relentless spending in the transfer window to turn the west Londoners into an elite force in England and eventually Europe. Chelsea had spent over £110m that summer on transfers including Hernán Crespo, Adrian Mutu, Damien Duff, Claude Makélélé, Joe Cole, Juan Sebastián Verón and Geremi. Many had touted Chelsea to be title contenders and be at the start of a legacy that would change English football. As right as they were in many cases, it wouldn't be until the following season that they won the title, funnily enough, at the Reebok Stadium.

However, in December 2003, Chelsea were unbeaten at home under manager Claudio Ranieri and had only lost once all season, away at eventual title-winners Arsenal. Sitting at the top of the Premier League, Chelsea, as many others did, felt that it was a formality that Bolton would be beaten that day at Stamford Bridge in a game labelled 'The Roman Empire vs Sam's Shoestring'.

With the injury to Laville and a small knock to Thome, Sam decided to put journeyman left-back Simon Charlton at centre-back to pair with N'Gotty. There were some trepidations around this, not around Charlton's effort or ability but his legs against a rapid attack which included Crespo, Duff and Mutu. With Charlton included, Bolton played in a 4-5-1 formation with Campo playing between midfield and defence. This position would be known as the 'Makélélé role' in years to come after the Chelsea midfielder's great ability. Maybe after this game it should have been referred to as the 'Campo role'.

The match started off at a quiet and slow pace as Bolton looked to keep their structure early and Chelsea looked to take their time to get going. Charlton seemed to be doing quite well against the home front line and neither team came close in the early exchanges. Frank Lampard attempted a through ball to Jesper Grønkjær which was effectively dealt with by first-choice left-back Ricardo Gardner, then Davies came close to getting on the end of a Djorkaeff cross at the other end but was stopped by Wayne Bridge in defence. Davies had scored five goals by December and was proving to be a quality acquisition due to his hunger and his ability to bring others into the game.

Despite Chelsea starting to press, Bolton looked solid, although Crespo fired wide after some good work from Damien Duff on the left. And the tide began to turn as Crespo was starting to cause Charlton and N'Gotty some serious issues. Crespo had the ball in the net after 15 minutes but it was ruled out for a handball in the build-up, and Gardner had to stop Crespo and Lampard in the box as Chelsea's onslaught became relentless. Mutu then went close as he robbed Okocha of the ball and drove towards Jääskeläinen only to shoot wide. Again, Gardner had to save Bolton as on 22 minutes he was able to block a cross from Grønkjær which gave Chelsea a corner. Up came French World Cup winner Marcel Desailly from the back and young English centre-back John Terry for the corner which was swung into the box by Duff. Terry got a flick to the ball just inside the six-yard box which fizzed across the goal and fell to Crespo three yards out, the Argentine stooping low to head past Jääskeläinen and the blue part of London cheering what they assumed would be the first of many goals that afternoon. Terry and Crespo embraced to celebrate the striker's first goal in four games.

Many felt that the floodgates had been opened and it was only a matter of time before Chelsea got their next goal. Bolton came back fighting and some good work from Okocha ended in the Nigerian putting a great ball towards Davies who flicked it to Campo in the box, but Carlo Cudicini was equal to it and claimed possession before being knocked down by Nolan and the referee blew for a foul. As Cudicini dropped the ball, Campo kicked it in the net and flamboyantly pleaded his innocence but the decision had already been made. The game progressed with both sides having chances and Crespo continuing to cause Bolton problems.

Five minutes before half-time, Wanderers were awarded a free kick around 40 yards from the Chelsea goal on the right after Makélélé fouled Frandsen. Djorkaeff stepped up and signalled to Davies to expect the ball. As the Frenchman swung in a pitch-perfect delivery, it was nowhere near Davies but fell to the head of the unmarked N'Gotty who thrust his head towards the ball with raw power and it slammed past Cudicini to draw Bolton level. N'Gotty was dragged to the floor by Campo, who hugged him before Nolan then jumped on top of the two. Other than a small pocket in the away end, Stamford Bridge was silent and the two teams went in level at half-time as Sam made his way down from the stand to join his team in the dressing room. The goal was made by a beautiful ball from Djorkaeff and a fantastically finished header by N'Gotty. It was a goal made in France, for Bolton, and N'Gotty became the first opposition player to score at Stamford Bridge for three months.

As the second half started, Sam started to dream of a famous result; he had been a 21-year-old Bolton player the last time they had won at Chelsea, 28 years earlier, and hoped that piece of history could bring some luck to his team. It looked as if Okocha might test Cudicini early on but after he lined up his shot, he swung and totally missed the ball much to the amusement of the Chelsea crowd. Okocha laughed this off and began to support his team's defence as Mutu came close at the other end, but Jääskeläinen was equal to it. Stelios came on for Nolan on 62 minutes and played the ball to Frandsen who tested Cudicini from long range with a looping shot. As the game flowed on, Chelsea made some changes and introduced Jimmy Floyd Hasselbaink, Cole and Geremi. Chelsea pushed for a winner with strikes from Cole and Mutu but neither were a serious challenge for Jääskeläinen.

As the game started to come towards its end, Sam brought on Pedersen for Djorkaeff, noticing that the Frenchman's legs were starting to wane after a tough afternoon. Pedersen seemed to be brought on to shore things up, add some strength to the wing and confirm a hard-fought 1-1 draw. As the game reached 90 minutes, Okocha passed the ball down the left wing to Pedersen who looked to take it to the corner to play the clock down. Bolton were on the verge of a great result, a draw at the 'Roman Empire'. Pedersen was being marked and followed by Glen Johnson, one of the summer recruits from relegated West Ham. As Pedersen approached the corner flag he turned up the gears and burst past Johnson and started driving towards the goal; the Bolton fans stood to their feet, Sam and Phil Brown started to lean to improve their views. Pedersen was in the box with the ball at his feet and a clear, yet tight, sight on goal. As Pedersen got towards the six-yard box he looked up and saw Davies running into a great position. The Dane attempted to pass across the face of goal to Davies but the ball bounced off Terry. Cudicini had started to dive to his left, expecting it to go past Terry but instead it flicked off the future England captain and into the empty net. Once again, Stamford Bridge was stunned: 90th minute, 2-1 Bolton. The visiting players embraced as they celebrated Terry's own goal and what was a first Chelsea defeat at Stamford Bridge for ten months and what did you know? It was little old Bolton. The whistle blew and the Bolton fans felt a moment of redemption at the ground where they had seen their team relegated five years earlier.

This time around, the Chelsea fans felt no pity for Bolton as the Wanderers fans celebrated a famous victory in their backyard. Chelsea would go on to finish second that season and reach the semi-finals of the Champions League. One year later they parted ways with Claudio Ranieri and replaced him with Porto manager José Mourinho and won the 2005 League Cup as well as their first Premier League title before embarking on a legacy under Abramovich's ownership, winning 18 major trophies in less than 20 years.

That result brought Bolton up to tenth and from that day on, they never had to worry about a relegation fight under Sam Allardyce again. A week later, Henrik Pedersen was the hero again as Bolton held future champions and 'Invincibles' Arsenal to a 1-1 draw at the Reebok, the Dane scoring a screamer from the edge of the box in the 83rd minute past Jens Lehmann. The switch had flipped and something had changed: Bolton had turned a corner and Sam's legacy was cementing but still evolving.

Sam's use of data and science was now being looked at across football as many were looking towards Bolton as the flag-bearers in advancing the game. No longer the working-class club from a former Lancashire mining town with a heart of gold, Bolton were now seen as the modern frontrunners in contemporary science and using data and science to their best benefit. A Sky Sports special in January 2004 highlighted the use of yoga, meditation and therapy to gain that extra marginal gain from Sam's players. Kevin Davies openly spoke about how much tapping into the inner psyche of him had added an extra level of his game and in reality, it would add another nine years to his Premier League career.

Bolton stayed either tenth or 11th by the start of 2004 and after a 3-2 win at Liverpool in the League Cup and a 1-0 victory over Southampton in the quarter-final, they had a cup semi-final to look forward to against Aston Villa over two legs, and a chance for revenge for that tough day at Wembley in 2000.

Sam's return to Bolton in 1999. The legacy had begun.

Semi-final shocker. Dean Holdsworth can't believe his miss as the 2000 FA Cup semi-final goes to penalties.

Back in the big time! Sam and the team lift the 2001 play-off trophy aloft to the Bolton fans at the Millenium Stadium in Cardiff to celebrate a return to the Premiership.

Brothers in arms. Sam and Phil Brown worked tirelessly to create a state-of-the-art environment where players could thrive on and off the pitch.

What a start. Bolton celebrate one of their five goals against Leicester on day one of the 2001/02 season.

Survival celebrations on the final day of the 2002/03 season against Middlesbrough.

Nolan, Djorkaeff, Hunt and Davies celebrate making the 2004 Carling Cup Final. However, the team fell at the final hurdle and lost the match 2-1 at Cardiff.

Redemption! The two Kevins celebrate as Davies scores the winner in a 2-1 victory against Southampton, the team that had released him the summer before.

Youri Djorkaeff celebrates scoring against Leeds United. The World Cup winner would go on to be remembered as one of the most important signings in Bolton Wanderers' history.

Once a solid relationship, Sam and Phil Gartside's relationship would become fractured over the progressing years.

El Hadji Diouf celebrates scoring the goal that confirmed Bolton's place in the UEFA Cup with a strike against Portsmouth.

What an Arse(ne). Bolton always brought out the worst in the Arsenal manager as the Reebok caused constant despair for the north London club.

Stelios puts Bolton ahead at the Stade Velodrome in the UEFA Cup last 32 tie away at Marseille. Bolton would lose the tie 2-1 but had taken a European giant to the edge of defeat.

The signing of Nicolas Anelka was another signal of intent from Bolton. Here, the former Arsenal striker celebrates a famous strike in a 3-1 win against the Gunners.

In the wrong dugout. Sam Allardyce returned to Bolton with Newcastle United on the first day of the 2007/08 season. Sam's Newcastle would beat Sammy Lee's Bolton 3-1.

11
Back to Cardiff

BOLTON STARTED 2004 with a home defeat to Manchester United and then a run of four back-to-back wins, including a thrilling 4-3 success at Blackburn Rovers. After drawing 2-2 at home to their local rivals earlier in the season, Bolton arrived at Ewood Park with little to fear. However, despite a goal from Kevin Nolan after 12 seconds, they found themselves 3-1 down on the cusp of half-time before a moment of brilliance from Youri Djorkaeff gave them hope. The Frenchman saw keeper Brad Friedel off his line and performed an outrageous half-volley/scoop/flick/loop shot over the American from outside the box before the half-time break to pull a goal back. A goal from Stelios in the 73rd minute made it 3-3 before a scramble in the box forced the ball to Nolan who stabbed home from close range to win it in the 79th minute. After this was a 1-0 home victory over Portsmouth, revenge for the battering earlier in the season, before Bolton welcomed Aston Villa to BL6 for the first leg of the League Cup semi-final.

Prior to the semi-final, much had been made about the fact that Jay-Jay Okocha was yet to sign a new deal and both Sam Allardyce and the supporters wanted this done ASAP, especially as Okocha was due to fly out to Tunisia directly after the first leg to join up with the Nigeria squad for the Africa Cup of Nations. Okocha had captured the eyes and the imagination of the Premier League and strong rumours were circling that if he did not extend his Bolton deal, he would be closely watched by Arsenal in the run-up to his contract ending in the summer. Okocha was yet to score a league goal that season which surprised many. Despite his best efforts, he had only one League Cup goal to his name so far in 2003/04, a free kick against Liverpool, despite coming ridiculously close on several occasions – a prime example of this was where he hit the woodwork three times against Tottenham. However, Okocha had vowed to do what he could in the first leg so his absence in the second leg would not be as severe.

Bolton's League Cup journey had begun in September with a 3-1 win over Walsall and then a 2-0 victory against Gillingham in October and then winning at Liverpool and at home to Southampton cemented their place in the last four along with Villa, Arsenal and Middlesbrough. This was the furthest they had been in the tournament since that awful night at Prenton Park in 2000 against Tranmere Rovers and the first time they had been in a cup semi-final since the heartbreak of penalties at Wembley against Villa in the same year. However, this was a different team, almost a different club. If you compare the team that started in the first leg against Tranmere in 2000 to the one that would start against Villa in 2004, they were worlds apart and a serious indication and sign of the amount of progress Bolton had made since Sam's arrival. Then they were a mid-table First Division team, now they were a mid-table Premier League team with lofty ambitions of even more.

Against Tranmere in 2000 the line-up was: Banks, O'Kane, Ritchie, Bergsson, Whitlow, Passi, Hansen, Jensen, Gardner, Johansen, Guðjohnsen.

Four years later against Villa, this was the team: Jääskeläinen, Hunt, N'Gotty, Thome, Barness, Campo, Stelios, Djorkaeff, Okocha, Nolan, Davies.

A surprisingly low crowd of 16,302 bought tickets for the first leg, which took place on a cold January night. Maybe they felt they would save for the final or maybe even didn't feel the same romance as they did towards the FA Cup, which always seemed to get bigger numbers. However, those who did go made themselves heard and the anticipation of a potential cup final showed that no extra motivation was needed for the boys in the changing rooms. Screams of 'We are the one and only Wanderers!' circulated around the stadium as the home fans attempted to turn the Reebok into a cauldron of noise. As the teams came out, the cold conditions were evident as every Bolton player, bar the fearless Kevin Davies, wore long sleeves. Villa, in their claret and blue kit, ran to their supporters who had made the journey from the Midlands. The game kicked off and it was clear the fans were making an impact on the home team as Nolan picked up the ball within one minute and began to drive towards the Villa defence. Nolan, who had regained and potentially even eclipsed the form that originally got him in the team three years prior, was playing some amazing football that season and just as it looked like he may be about to go through on goal, he was brought down by a young Peter Whittingham, who would go on to plead his innocence with referee Paul Durkin.

The ball lay close to the edge of the box as Bolton's glittering League of Nations stood over it with Djorkaeff, Stelios, Campo and Okocha all fancying a go at goal. After deliberation, it was agreed that the Nigerian would take charge. Still only two minutes into the game, Stelios ran over the ball and caused some confusion in the wall as Okocha then took a placed swipe at the ball which dipped over the wall and back down before bouncing over the line past the hapless Thomas Sørensen. The Danish keeper didn't even move as Okocha made it 1-0 and ran towards the Bolton dugout. As he celebrated, he looked towards Sam Allardyce and Phil Gartside in the stands and motioned a hand signal that looked as if he was signing something. This was a signal to the board, management, players and fanbase that he was ready and very much intent on renewing his contract. With a huge smile on his face he was joined by Djorkaeff in the celebrations before Nolan got involved.

Villa were shell-shocked as manager David O'Leary let out his fury from the bench. However, just six minutes later it was 2-0. After a flick-on by Davies, Nolan went on a run similar to the one that caused the free kick earlier and started driving past the Villa midfield as he got closer to the box. Once again, he got the better of Whittingham as he then pushed further forward and took the ball past the stumbling Olof Mellberg before slotting in the bottom-left corner to turn the Reebok Stadium into chaos. Nolan was joined by his namesake Davies in a celebration as Bolton celebrated a very early – and healthy – advantage. Still only 22, Nolan was proving to be a leader on the pitch and a fantastic midfielder in a position filled with global talent.

Villa had experimented that day by putting striker Dion Dublin at centre-back as an attempt to nullify the aerial presence of Davies. However, Sam's team were picking at the gaps in defence with ease. As the Villa players were getting frustrated, the fouls began to appear and Dublin met Davies in the air but got none of the ball and could only bring him down in order to beat him. It was a free kick to Bolton on the halfway line and Bruno N'Gotty put the ball down and looked to float it into the box. Dublin trotted back into position as many Bolton players moved forward, ready to reenact a training ground move. With the game not even 20 minutes old, N'Gotty lifted the ball to the penalty area, where it reached the competing Davies and Dublin. Davies jumped above the former England man and managed to get a measured flick on the ball which looped towards Stelios with his back to goal just outside the six-yard box. The Greek star then performed an acrobatic overhead bicycle kick which beat Sørensen. What a moment, what a goal, what a lead: Bolton Wanderers 3-0 Aston Villa after 17 minutes. This was the stuff of fairytales as even Lofty the Lion, the loyal mascot, tried to join in the celebrations of Stelios, Djorkaeff and Nolan. Not even on the score sheet, Davies had been unplayable inside the first 20 minutes and had, in the words of David O'Leary, 'bullied the defence'. Cast out into obscurity by Southampton, the striker had found a home at Bolton and was becoming adored by the Reebok faithful.

Being 3-0 down within the first 20 minutes had angered and fired Villa up and two minutes later they pulled one back. Juan Pablo Ángel was having a great season and had started to be among the goals. In the 20th minute he showed his strength to ride the tackle of Okocha before coming face-to-face with Davies on the edge of the box. The Bolton man slid in and took the ball away from Ángel and it looked to be going out for a throw. Ángel, however, managed to keep it in and Davies slid in again but this time was embarrassed as the striker popped the ball between his legs. Davies's face said it all but Ángel ran past him then looked up and saw the run of his strike partner

Darius Vassell and attempted a cross into the box. However, he overhit it and as the ball came closer to the bar, Jussi Jääskeläinen was wrong-footed and it sailed over the Finn's diving effort and went into the back of the net for 3-1.

Reinvigorated Villa then tried to push for more and tested Jääskeläinen further with efforts from Gareth Barry and Vassell, but Allardyce and O'Leary seemed to call for calm as both sides began to slow the play down with half-time arriving. Although Bolton were delighted by the score and the start, it was obvious and inevitable that Villa would be fighting back to reduce the lead going into the second leg, and on 56 minutes they reduced the deficit. Some good work in midfield from Whittingham and Barry found Lee Hendrie on the right wing. Hendrie saw the run of Whittingham who shot inside the box but the strike was saved by Jääskeläinen and the ball then was pushed out to the left side of the box where it was met with a half-volley across goal by Barry, which found Vassell, who shot against Ángel. The Colombian seemed to be in an offside position but the ball bounced off Vassell, rebounded off Ángel then back to Vassell before deflecting off Ángel again and into the roof of the net. Bolton hands were raised waiting for the linesman's flag but it never came and Villa were very much back in the game and the tie at 3-2. Stelios in particular was incensed and referee Paul Durkin had to keep him away from the linesman despite captain Okocha's pleas with the Greek to let it go and carry on with the game. O'Leary almost got involved with Stelios until the issue fizzled out and the game carried on.

There was still over half an hour left in the first leg and Bolton's lead had been reduced to a single goal. Villa pressed to try and get on an even footing as Bolton tried to contain the onslaught. Allardyce, now down from the stands and stood next to Phil Brown in the dugout, strived for his players to fight for their advantage and not let their amazing work in the first half be for nothing. Pedersen was brought on for the fiery Stelios and Simon Charlton came on for Anthony Barness who had deputised in an unfamiliar left-back role due to the absence of the injured Gardner.

On 74 minutes, Bolton had a corner in front of the North Stand after some strong work from Davies again. Djorkaeff walked over to the right-hand flag and was met by a chorus of the 'Youri!' chant as fans bowed down to him. He swung the ball into the box and fellow Frenchman N'Gotty leapt above the Villa defence and, just as he had done at Chelsea a month earlier, thundered the ball into the back of the net. N'Gotty ran to Djorkaeff after making it 4-2, while the Villa team dropped their heads.

Villa looked dead on their knees and devoid of the confidence they had earlier shown. Again, Davies was bullying their defenders, beating Jlloyd Samuel and Mark Delaney to the ball in the air on the edge of the box, and it fell to Djorkaeff but was cleared to Charlton who played a pass to Okocha just outside the box, where the Nigerian fired the ball straight at Sørensen. Going into the last ten minutes, Bolton were 4-2 up and ready to celebrate an amazing first-leg victory. On 81 minutes, Charlton played a ball towards Davies who was being wrestled by the sweat-ridden Dublin on the edge of the box. Davies held it up but Paul Durkin claimed that Dublin had fouled him. Dublin looked shattered and if Davies was to empty his back pockets at the end of the evening, he would have found Dion Dublin alongside his car keys and wallet. The free kick was by the left corner of the box and looked prime for another Djorkaeff delivery as N'Gotty came forward from the back. Djorkaeff collected the ball but saw a glint in the eye of Jay-Jay Okocha, who put the ball down and looked at the two-man wall and also saw that keeper Sørensen was on the right-hand side of his goal. Okocha ran directly at the ball and unleashed a strike that moved forward then bent around the wall and then back towards goal and nailed itself into the top-left corner. It almost defied the laws of physics and took everyone, Sørensen included, by surprise. Okocha again ran towards the dugout, right arm aloft, and celebrated with his team-mates while doing his trademark leg-swivel celebration.

The game ended at 5-2 and Bolton fans were dreaming of a return to Cardiff and the Millennium Stadium. Allardyce was over the moon with his team and especially the two goals from Okocha. He stated afterward that he felt the Nigerian was the 'best player Bolton had ever had' – even better than Sir Nat Lofthouse. As Okocha left for Tunisia the next day to play for his country, he had done his bit and given Bolton a huge chance of making the final.

As the week progressed between the two legs, an air of recognition was starting to come from the football world towards Bolton. After their emphatic win, many started to dig deeper and look at the fine work Sam and his team had done to turn Bolton around since arriving at the club in 1999. On the BBC's *Match of the Day*, Gary Lineker spoke of his respect and appreciation for Allardyce's achievements and how Bolton were transforming from a yo-yo club to an established Premier League outfit who had become comfortable competing on multiple fronts. The change was evident as Bolton no longer needed to look below them and could look towards the future with prospect and confidence. They could now look back on their dark years of uncertainty. The days of having to sell

Per Frandsen to survive or having their star players such as Eiður Guðjohnsen and Claus Jensen prized away from them without a choice were long gone. Now a star-studded team full of international players were at Bolton who wanted to stay and were not only integral to the project, but *wanted* to be integral.

Sam knew this would grow if it was allowed to and around this time, he started to look further afield for his next big swoop – although he wanted to use a transfer fee rather than a free agent or loan deal. Sam went to Phil Gartside during this time with a proposal that would cost between an initial £6m to £8m but could eventually make the club easily over £30m in the future. It was unclear exactly when this conversation happened but it is believed sometime between 2003 and 2004 by many sources that Sam spoke with Gartside about the potential of signing former Real Madrid striker Samuel Eto'o, then a goal machine for Real Mallorca. The Cameroon forward was scoring for fun in La Liga and was still in his early 20s and looking for the next step in his career. Sam believed he could sign the future double Champions League winner for a more modest fee and would be able to then develop the striker and make a huge profit in the coming years, much like he had been able to do with Guðjohnsen previously. Allardyce tried to convince Gartside but it was to no avail as the chairman felt that it was not worth the gamble and said no to the deal. To Sam's annoyance, by the next summer, Eto'o joined Barcelona for £24m where he would win multiple La Liga trophies and a Champions League as well as winning another at Inter Milan later on. The four-time African Player of the Year went on to be a legend of world football but could easily have been a bargain for Bolton Wanderers.

Allardyce set his sights on another legend of the game, Dennis Bergkamp, who was coming to the end of his contract with Arsenal in the summer. The Dutch forward was 34 at the time and would agree a financial deal with Bolton but never signed on the dotted line unfortunately as he felt settled in London and didn't want to move north. He would eventually sign a new contract at Arsenal and stay until 2006 before retiring after scoring 120 goals for the Gunners since his 1995 arrival to Highbury under former Bolton boss Bruce Rioch. However, Sam was able to sign at least one striker in the 2004 winter window in the form of Atlético Madrid striker Javi Moreno, on loan until the summer. Moreno came to fame after scoring a double in the UEFA Cup Final of 2001 against Liverpool for former club Alavés, which the Spanish club would eventually lose 5-4. That final in Dortmund put Moreno on the map but he had failed to live up to the hype after moves to AC Milan and then Atlético. Moreno would play ten games for Bolton that season and fail to score. Adding to Moreno were former England defender Steve Howey on a free transfer from Leicester City, and Liverpool full-back John Otsemobor on loan to add more cover for the defence. As well as this, Sam signed Jamaican goalkeeper Donovan Ricketts as additional cover and took a punt on unknown Guatemalan striker Dwight Pezzarossi on loan from Comunicaciones. Howey, Otsemobor, Ricketts and Pezzarossi played a grand total of 14 games in their Bolton careers.

The second leg approached with many backing the Whites to do the job at Villa Park and start planning their trip to Wales. Many Wanderers fans, confident of an aggregate win, had already booked trains and hotels in Cardiff for the late-February final date. With one foot at the Millennium Stadium, Bolton would have to do without

Okocha who was helping the Super Eagles face off against South Africa just four days later in the Africa Cup of Nations, scoring in a 4-0 win. Nigeria would eventually get knocked out in the semi-finals by hosts Tunisia on penalties in mid-February, much to the disdain of Bolton fans. As much as they wanted the best for Okocha and his Nigeria team, they wanted him back much earlier than the semi-final stage. On that night in Birmingham on 27 January, they were Okocha-less but ready to defend their three-goal lead.

A crowd of 36,883 piled into Villa Park that night with home fans wanting to see their team pull off a famous comeback. The man tasked with filling Okocha's boots was the only Bolton player left in the team who had also played at Burnden Park, Per Frandsen. Wanderers were also missing another scorer from the first leg in Kevin Nolan which gave a rare opportunity to start for summer signing Ibrahim Ba. The former AC Milan man had not settled too well at Bolton since his move and had been restricted to cameos from the bench for the most part. Villa were also missing their scorer from the first leg as Juan Pablo Ángel was ruled out with injury. Additionally, despite the dominance of Kevin Davies, O'Leary still chose to keep Dion Dublin in the centre of defence.

Ten minutes in the game broke into life as Villa struck early to cause a ruck of nerves in the Bolton fans at Villa Park and those watching at home. German midfielder Thomas Hitzlsperger had been left out of the starting 11 in the first leg but had been thrust in for the second for his long-range ability. He stood over a free kick on the edge of the box with Youri Djorkaeff trying to distract him. With a sweet strike of his left foot, he dipped it over the wall and directly into the back of the net before Jääskeläinen could even react. Not the start Bolton wanted as just ten minutes in, Villa had pulled the aggregate back to 5-3. The hosts sprinted back to their half ready to restart as quickly as possible. The finish was magnificent and was almost identical to Okocha's first free kick in the game at the Reebok.

The half passed with Villa pressing and Bolton defending well. Emerson Thome and Bruno N'Gotty were very organised and showed great discipline. On the cusp of half-time, Mark Delaney knocked the ball forward from the right-back position and midfielder Gavin McCann chased after it unmarked as he broke from Iván Campo. Jääskeläinen came storming from his goal and turned a 50/50 into a 90/10 and smothered the ball. At this moment, McCann stuck out a boot but missed the ball and kicked Jääskeläinen in the chest much to the anger of the Bolton players as the Finn lay on the floor in pain. Thome approached McCann, both of them former Sunderland team-mates, with anger. McCann, pleading his innocence to the fiery Bolton players, began to walk away. He had already been booked and cries of 'Off, off, off!' came from the Bolton end. Young right-back Nicky Hunt came storming over much to the anger of McCann as referee Steve Bennett tried to calm down proceedings. Thome then came over again and McCann, directly in front of the view of Bennett, slapped the Brazilian in the face. Before the ref could even get the card out, McCann knew and walked off screaming and pointing at his former team-mate. Bennett showed the red card towards McCann to a roar of cheers by the Bolton faithful.

The tie just got a little bit easier and the Villa crowd began to quieten down, although when the whistle blew for half-time Bolton saw themselves lucky still to be winning overall. It was evident they were missing Okocha and Nolan and they made some changes as the game wore on with Pedersen, Barness and Javi Moreno entering the pitch. Villa brought on Peter Whittingham and the youngster almost had an instant impact as he tested Jääskeläinen from 20 yards but the ball flashed just wide of the keeper's glove and past the post. Davies almost made it 6-3 overall as he broke through the Villa defence but pulled his strike wide of the post.

O'Leary pushed his defenders forward as the game reached the latter stages. In the 88th minute the ball was bouncing around the Bolton box and fell to the feet of Villa left-back Jlloyd Samuel. Samuel would go on to sign for Bolton in 2007 and was thought of in high regard at Villa Park at this time. Samuel looked up from the left of the box and poked the ball towards goal, where it took a flick from a diving tackle by Campo and looped over Jääskeläinen to make it 5-4 on aggregate with two minutes to go. However, Bolton held their nerve and celebrated in the changing room with topless drinking and sprays of champagne. A flag carrying the branding of League Cup sponsors Carling saying 'We are going to Cardiff!' was paraded around the dressing room as the team celebrated a great achievement and Sam celebrated his first domestic cup final in management. They would face Middlesbrough in the 2004 League Cup Final, an opponent they had already beaten 2-0 earlier in the season and 2-1 at the end of the previous season.

Redemption had been gained for that awful two-legged affair against Tranmere in 2000 and revenge had also been gained against Villa for the semi-final defeat at Wembley in 2000. Allardyce celebrated by driving home to Bromley Cross and enjoying a glass of champagne and a fish finger and cheese sandwich with his wife, Lynne.

His sandwich taste may not have been the most continental but his team certainly was as Sam's League of Nations were now cup finalists as fans flocked to the ticket office to secure their place at the big day in Wales. However, a mix-up with the client reference system at the ticket office meant that many of the tickets had sold out before the loyal season ticket holders could buy them. After this, Bolton stopped postal applications for tickets and looked to move to a fully online and phone system.

The build-up to the game was quite calm as Sam took the players to Wales quite early, similar to the play-off final in 2001, and tried to create an air of calm around the team as he played down the enormity of this moment. The Trotters had not won a major trophy since 1958 and this was an opportunity for the supporters to celebrate some silverware to add to their new-look team. Middlesbrough were looking for the same as they were yet to win any major trophy in their 128-year history. The final was played on 29 February 2004 and Sam spoke to the media about how a win in Cardiff could help him sign more players of Okocha, Djorkaeff and Campo's international status. He also felt that this would help him convince Djorkaeff to sign a new deal – like Okocha, he was out of contract in the summer. Controversial Middlesbrough defender Danny Mills stated that he was happy to frustrate Bolton fans and was ready for any abuse he may receive. Both sets of supporters would be forgiven for thinking that it was their moment as there was no Goliath and the match was two Davids taking each other on.

Sam decided to drop Stelios to the bench and went with Per Frandsen on the right side of midfield much to the surprise of many. Boro set up with their own star man Juninho in midfield paired with Spain legend Gaizka

Mendieta. Similar to Bolton, the Teesside club were building their own League of Nations with a starting 11 representing Brazil, the Netherlands, Cameroon, Australia, France, Spain and England. Both clubs were very similar, two former First Division clubs, in the shadow of bigger local rivals, with young British managers ready to impress. Both sides also had been able to turn around the declining careers of former world stars as many likened Juninho to Okocha and Mendieta to Djorkaeff. No matter what, many felt the final would be tight.

The winner would play European football the season after in the UEFA Cup. This was a stage that neither team had played on before and would be an indication for both clubs that they were now fighting at a higher level. With the potential prospect of European football and an expanding fanbase reaching the Whites, many were excited. As Sam had been keen to test himself against the elite of the Premier League in the past, he was now keen to test himself on the continental stage and the winner of the League Cup would be facing up against the likes of Sevilla, Valencia, Benfica, Schalke, Lazio as well as other up-and-coming teams from around Europe. With this prospect exciting not only the supporters but also the backroom team, Allardyce spoke about his excitement in the build-up to the final with Phil Gartside. Sam and Phil had grown close during their time working together as both held a similar passion for Bolton Wanderers.

Gartside, originally from the nearby town of Leigh, was a Bolton fan and had helped rescue the club after taking over the helm from Gordon Hargreaves and helping bring in investor Eddie Davies. Gartside had seen the rise of the club and was viewed in high esteem in the national game as he also held a seat on the FA board. He may have caused some frustration with supporters due to the lack of transfer funds but his aim, certainly during Sam's tenure at least, was to create a sustainable club and build slowly which also aligned with his manager's values. Gartside had been the man who agreed to the signings of the likes of Okocha, Djorkaeff and Campo but was also the man who had turned down some potentially lucrative deals as well. Yet he and Sam had a strong working bond and would always sit together in the first halves of games as Sam watched from a high vantage point before moving to the dugout for the second halves.

During the conversation prior to the final, Phil spoke of his happiness but also fear over the outcome. He stated that as he knew the winner would reach the UEFA Cup, he felt Bolton were not ready financially and alluded to Sam that in all fairness, he was content with both potential results and wouldn't be mortified if Bolton didn't win as European football would be far too expensive for the club at this stage in their journey. After this, Sam never saw Gartside the same way and their relationship started to fracture as they began to show opposing philosophies on what 'success' meant.

Sam and his team entered the pitch to a sea of roaring white opposed to a sea of roaring red. He brought his grandson and namesake Sam on the pitch as the toddler wore a shirt with 'LITTLE BIG SAM 6' printed on the back. The Bolton team wore specially designed tracksuit jackets as they lined up ready to face Boro, with cup final embroidering underneath the BWFC badge in the all-white kit as they were led out by the returning Jay-Jay Okocha. Fireworks set off as the teams came out and prepared for the national anthem with Bolton preparing to kick towards the Middlesbrough fans in the first half.

Danny Mills received the ball early after Nolan looked to come close to a chance on goal. Mills, ready to frustrate Bolton, brought it forward from the right-back position and knocked it forward towards Joseph-Désiré Job but Emerson Thome leapt higher to beat him near the edge of the box. However, his header was misjudged and it only reached the forward run of Mendieta who took the ball in his stride and drove towards the penalty area with pace. The Spaniard played the ball to the left over to former Chelsea midfielder Bolo Zenden who had beaten Nicky Hunt in a foot race and was facing Per Frandsen in a one-on-one. Zenden got in front of Frandsen and played the ball across the face of goal where, as it swooped past Jääskeläinen and Thome, Job tucked it in the back of the empty net ahead of the approaching Simon Charlton to break Bolton hearts and stun the men in white inside two minutes. The Cameroonian ran to Juninho and celebrated as the Bolton half of the stadium stood in shock.

A moment later, Wanderers were on the attack as Djorkaeff tested Mark Schwarzer from a tight angle after a ball from Charlton. The Frenchman blasted the ball towards the top corner but the Australian goalkeeper pushed it over the bar for a corner which led to nothing and Schwarzer had a goal kick which he pumped forward.

A few moments later, Okocha was outmuscled by George Boateng in midfield and the ball fell to Mendieta who was starting to pull the strings. The game, still only six minutes old, was at a frantic pace as the former Barcelona man had the ball on the right. Mendieta played a pass across the floor past N'Gotty and Charlton which slowly came to Job on the edge of the box. Job held it up against Thome as the two edged towards the penalty area. He knocked the ball past Thome and crashed to the ground, while the Brazilian felt he got the ball before it fell to N'Gotty to clear. Before N'Gotty could raise his foot, referee Mike Riley, someone who had a difficult history in Bolton matches, blew his whistle and pointed at the penalty spot. Thome looked at Riley and laughed in disbelief. Campo, Okocha and Frandsen screamed in Riley's face. The decision looked very harsh at first but Thome's clumsiness gave Riley a choice as his legs did make contact with Job's. Within seconds, every outfield Bolton player was surrounding Riley but the man in green walked away from them all.

Zenden picked up the ball ready to take the penalty. The Bolton fans behind were doing all they could to put him off, starting to shout and moving their positioning behind the net. The Dutch winger ran up and just as he was about to shoot, he slipped in front of the ball and kicked it against his inside leg before his spot-kick bounced towards the goal. Jääskeläinen dived in expectation of a clean strike but the ball looped towards the middle of the net. The big Finn managed to get a boot to it but it spun off and into the goal. Many Bolton fans and players looked at Riley as Zenden had kicked the ball twice while taking the penalty which should have led to either a retake or a free kick to Allardyce's team. Riley started to trot back to the halfway line while Zenden and the sea of red celebrated a second goal.

Sam was seething; Bolton were 2-0 down after seven minutes and felt unduly robbed of their special day. No one expected this, this wasn't supposed to happen at all. Children in the stands were crying, fans were shocked and you couldn't hear a peep from the stands while the Middlesbrough supporters celebrated an amazing start. Bolton looked stunned and took over ten minutes to start playing football again. On 20 minutes, Nolan won the ball on the right byline and played it down the line to Davies who took it past Gareth Southgate on the right-hand side of the box. He gained half a yard of space and hit an attempted cross which he sliced and it bobbled towards the arms of Schwarzer who knelt down to pick it up. Davies started to turn around and heard cheers from the other side of the stadium – Bolton had scored. Davies's strike had flicked up over Schwarzer's shoulder and gone in, the stopper misjudging its flight only to see it bounce off his forearms and into the goal behind him. Djorkaeff ran into the net to pick it up and restart the game while Nolan grabbed Davies to congratulate him on a cup final goal. What a bizarre and bonkers start to the match and now all parts of the stadium could feel the nerves.

Seconds later, Frandsen hit the post with Bolton so close to an equaliser and bringing the final back into balance. Then it was the turn of Djorkaeff to come close as his half-volley bounced past the left-hand post and inches away from Nolan with Bolton pushing for that second goal. Then Djorkaeff was in another great spot and looked to have scored the equaliser but Schwarzer was on hand to stop the ball with a reflex diving save to his left. It just wasn't going in.

In the second half it was all Bolton once more. The Whites pushed and pushed and despite their best efforts and a massive shout for handball against Ugo Ehiogu, a player Allardyce had helped bring through at West Bromwich Albion in the late 1980s, it was in vain as the whistle blew and Bolton had fallen at the final hurdle and Middlesbrough won their first major piece of silverware in their history.

Sam and his team grieved their loss and let the Teesside club have their moment in the sun. It was a hard one to take for Sam, especially after the horror around the penalty and also the potential handball. Sam was fined for some derogatory comments towards Mike Riley but Bolton had to pick themselves up and use this defeat as motivation and another opportunity to prove the naysayers wrong as they looked to work on their great first half to the Premier League season and consolidate their place in the top ten. It hurt and it would for a while but Bolton still had the chance to reach Europe through their league position and no matter what, they would be able to achieve their highest Premier League finish since the competition's formation in 1992.

12

Moving forward and moving up

THE POST-CARDIFF hangover lingered over Bolton for a few weeks as many in a white shirt felt sorry for themselves and hard done to by the result of the League Cup Final. Sam Allardyce, still seething, received his FA charge and fine for his comments about referee Mike Riley in the aftermath of the final and would add that he felt Riley was a 'disgrace'. He was even more incensed when Riley admitted to him that he didn't even realise Bolo Zenden's penalty was a double kick but even if he did, he wouldn't have disallowed it as it wasn't intentional.

Bolton lost their next three games after the final, going down 2-0 at Birmingham City, 2-0 at home to Chelsea and 2-1 away to Arsenal. Prior to the showpiece they had lost 3-1 at home to neighbours Manchester City as well so including being beaten by Middlesbrough, this was five defeats in a row as the old Bolton were starting to creep back. The post-final games showed a mental fragility that Sam hadn't seen for a long time and it was evident the players needed an incentive and a pick-me-up after the heartbreak. In the past, the club had introduced the famed 'ballsy' eating challenge incentive which was shown in their 5-0 win over Leicester in 2001. Yet it was a different team and almost a different club than the one that had come up from the First Division then, so a different approach was needed.

For the first time, Sam ignored his sports science team's wishes and introduced another incentive programme which stated that for every game the players won for the rest of the season, they could have the week off from Monday to Thursday. The medical staff, angered by this decision, stated that this would cause stiffness and some unneeded injuries and fitness niggles ahead of each weekend fixture.

The sports science and medical staff presented data and evidence to Sam to suggest that this would eventually not work and would cause more issues, yet the boss stated that with six games remaining, mental fatigue was more important than physical fitness if they were to end the season on a high.

The first game of this initiative was a 2-1 away victory at Wolves thanks to a last-minute winner from Kevin Davies, moving Bolton up to 12th ahead of their remaining five fixtures. Next up were Tottenham at the Reebok and they were dealt with easily, Wanderers ending up 2-0 winners thanks to Iván Campo and Henrik Pedersen before they set off for a sunny away day on the south coast against Southampton.

Both clubs were happy with their seasons so far; barring a cup final defeat for Bolton, they had enjoyed relative success and were sitting in mid-table having comfortably avoided relegation months earlier. Paul Sturrock's strong Southampton team had plenty of experience but also young talent as they started with a front three of Latvian Marian Pahars, England player James Beattie and former Golden Boot winner Kevin Phillips. The game showed little in the means of deciding anyone's fate, but it was huge for one person at least: Kevin Davies.

Only nine months earlier, Davies had been deemed surplus to requirements at St Mary's and was released after his second spell with the club. Davies had been in every squad for Southampton's run to the FA Cup Final in 2003, but upon arriving at the Millennium Stadium he was informed by Gordon Strachan that he was not in the matchday squad and also that he would be released after the match. Davies had scored over 26 goals in two stints with the club and would be forgiven for feeling he deserved a bit more class and respect. Heavy in weight and low on confidence upon his arrival at Bolton, Davies turned into a man on a mission. It was clear that he was keen to reinvigorate his Premier League career but also find a home where he was once again scoring and creating goals, but also where he was happy. Davies settled into the village of Egerton with his family and would stay with Bolton until 2013 in a time where he would captain the club, score many crucial goals including away at Bayern Munich, and also gain an England cap – all while wearing the famous white kit. Davies would go on to be a legend of the club and would show his loyalty during the toughest times for Bolton after Sam's departure and uncertain times. He scored 85 goals in 407 games for the Whites but one of those goals, a header at St Mary's on 24 April 2004, would be one he would never forget.

The Bolton fans in the crowd were enjoying a scorching day on the south coast and for some, tops were off and sun cream was applied as they travelled the 240-mile journey to Hampshire. Due to a kit clash between Southampton's red and white stripes being too similar to both Bolton's home kit of white and their away kit of red, the Trotters wore their yellow away kit of the season prior as the short sleeves were on show and a few red sunburnt noses from Kevin Nolan and Nicky Hunt were seen on the field of play.

One minute in, the ball fell to Jay-Jay Okocha inside the Southampton half. He took one touch and unleashed a hell of a strike which flew past the defenders and keeper Antti Niemi but crashed against the bar and over for a goal kick from 35 yards. Okocha was still yet to score in the league that season and in fact, would not do so until the following campaign, despite hitting the woodwork more than any other Premier League player in 2003/04. The Nigerian turned around and smiled at Nolan as if to suggest 'What do I have to do?!' as he walked back into position. Twenty minutes later, the Saints gained the upper hand. Right-back Paul Telfer brought the ball forward and executed a huge diagonal crossfield ball over to the left to find Pahars. Pahars, once labelled the 'Latvian Michael Owen', had burst past Anthony Barness and managed to take the ball down at speed before taking it away from the defender and tipping it over the oncoming Jussi Jääskeläinen into the net. Bolton had been undone by a long ball which they should have been very prepared for. Barness had been beaten far too easily and Sam would ponder future options in the full-back position in the summer. Barness would be replaced at half-time by Hunt with the writing maybe on the wall for his time at the new-look Bolton. Prior to this, with half-time approaching, Davies had come close following a quick pass from Nolan but he could only shoot straight at Niemi from inside the box. It was evident that Davies was eager to impress and right some wrongs at St Mary's and was perhaps too hasty with his shot rather than taking his time to pick his spot.

Deep in the second half, Bolton had a throw-in from Okocha with the 'Yellow Whites' attacking towards the away fans. The throw caused an un-sanctioned and unplanned 'game' of head tennis before finding its way to Hunt on the edge of the box; the defender performed a cross/shot which deflected towards Davies who looped the ball into the box from the right-hand side towards the centre of the six-yard line. The ball looped and fell to Nolan who rose high to nod past Niemi into the back of the net for his eighth goal of the season and a ninth assist of the season for Davies, the pair celebrating in front of the travelling support.

Bolton had equalised with 14 minutes remaining and could have played the game out for a strong point on the road. However, with the incentive of another four days off, the players pushed for more. Moments later, Okocha received the ball on the right side and whipped in an inviting cross towards the box. It reached the six-yard area with pace, leaving the Southampton defenders ball-watching, then before they knew it the ball had reached their former team-mate Davies, who met it with a beautifully timed headed flick beyond the watching Niemi and into the top-left corner. He had done it, righted the wrong, gained redemption and made the score 2-1 to Bolton with ten minutes to go. Davies ran to the Bolton fans and grabbed the badge on his shirt before kissing it in front of the supporters. He was then met by his team-mates who knew what that goal meant to the Yorkshireman.

Davies had got his ninth goal of the season that day, a year on from a grand total of one goal at St Mary's the year before. With the kiss of the badge he found a place in the hearts of many Bolton fans and would have his own song created, one that had previously been reserved for another legend, John McGinlay. The cries of 'Super, super Kev, super Kevin Davies' could be heard loudly on that day and at every Bolton game until 2013 and beyond. Davies had gone from forgotten man to hero and despite the work of Okocha, Nolan, Campo, Bruno N'Gotty and Youri Djorkaeff, it was he who was named player of the year that season. In a squad of global superstars, Bolton had found their best gem yet in Davies. The script had been written that day on the south coast, by Davies himself it seemed, and the Trotters held on to gain three points, four days off and moved up to tenth place ahead of the remaining three games of the season.

Now four games undefeated and after three wins in their last four, Bolton were within touching distance of a top-seven finish. After coming in 17th the season before, staying in tenth and then progressing into the upper echelons of the Premier League would be a ridiculously strong sign of progression and a massive sign of the gains the club had made since Sam Allardyce and Phil Gartside arrived. The week after their win at St Mary's, Bolton beat Leeds United 4-1 at home to move up to seventh. That result relegated Leeds to what would be renamed as the Championship that summer, and their fans were seen on television crying their eyes out on Sky Sports after Djorkaeff's double alongside a Nolan goal and an own goal from veteran Ian Harte. It was a huge sign of the changing landscape of English football as Leeds, giants of the game with three top-flight titles to their name and a legacy spanning from the 1970s to their Champions League semi-final appearance of 2001, were being relegated to the second tier at the same time as Bolton, minnows of the Premier League, were gaining on the top seven. After that, Bolton put another iconic English club to the sword with a 2-1 win over Everton at Goodison

Park, again thanks to a double from Djorkaeff who was now on nine goals for the season at the age of 36. Despite his age, he looked as fit and as sharp as ever in the most elite league in Europe.

Before the last game of the season, a home fixture against Fulham, the national media had swarmed to Bolton amid some breaking news. Sam was close to what could be classed, if it came off, as his most outrageous and high-profile signing yet. Born in Recife, Brazil, and enjoying a career spanning different continents including periods at Palmeiras and Deportivo La Coruña, but more famously Barcelona and AC Milan, the player Bolton were in for was a name even bigger than Okocha, Djorkaeff and Campo combined. The attacking midfielder in question had scored over 70 goals in his time in Europe and boasted eight major trophies including a Champions League win the season before. His 35 goals for Brazil also put him on the world stage as well as his World Cup winners medal from 2002. His name? Rivaldo.

The former Barcelona man had, similarly to Djorkaeff in 2002, hit a stumbling block in his career and had struggled with form. He found himself being released by AC Milan in 2003 and had spent some time back in Brazil that season for Cruzeiro on a short-term deal but had made it clear a return to Europe and top-flight football was something he needed as he wanted to prolong his international career.

As the media flocked to Bolton's training ground at Euxton, chairman Phil Gartside marched into the press room stating that he was in possession of a fax in his pocket that confirmed that Rivaldo wanted to sign for Bolton. Aged 32 at the time, Rivaldo had met with Gartside, Allardyce and Simon Marland at the Lowry Hotel on Salford Quays with his agent to discuss 'project Bolton'. Despite offering himself to Manchester United and Arsenal in the earlier January, Rivaldo was seen as happy to join Bolton to gain his entry into the Premier League and had seen the examples of Djorkaeff and Okocha as perfect motivation to move to the Reebok. With a beaming smile on his face, Allardyce seemed confident he could get the deal over the line and felt he could put his arm around the shoulder of Rivaldo and bring back his glory years. Gartside and Allardyce felt if they could get Rivaldo to the stadium, the deal would be confirmed, but the closest they were able to get him to Horwich was Salford, as the believed plan was that the player would sign for Bolton but live in Manchester, most likely a penthouse apartment overlooking Salford Quays. As the week progressed, supporters grew in excitement and started to produce unofficial merchandise with Rivaldo's face on. A pub on Stitch-Me-Lane, the White Horse, was known to be selling pictures and T-shirts of Rivaldo dressed as Rodney Trotter while Sam was dressed as Del Boy from the famous sitcom, *Only Fools and Horses* – a quick joke at Sam's ability to wheel and deal and convince anyone to join Bolton.

As time passed, It became clear to Allardyce and Gartside that Bolton were not the only club after Rivaldo as he was also meeting representatives from Qatar SC who were able to offer him a much bigger financial deal than Bolton but at a much lower level of football. Wanderers were starting to grow impatient as there seemed to be radio silence on the issue but the fans continued to be hopeful. Rumours started to circulate on the final-day game against Fulham that the Brazilian would be presented to the crowd at half-time but this never materialised. The talks, when they did happen, appeared fractured as Rivaldo was requesting a deal similar to that on offer from Qatar. It was at that point that Bolton pulled out. The deal was off and eventually Rivaldo would join neither club, instead opting for a payday in Greece at Olympiakos where he stated he moved due to being able to still play in the Champions League. For one moment, the world was in awe of Bolton as they almost pulled off the deal of the century. The club moved on and looked at other options for the summer but were now at a higher level of scouting and refused to drop their now elite standards of looking for players at the highest level. As many looked at moves in, one confirmed exit took the attention on the final day of the season.

As Bolton started the game against Fulham in seventh, a goodbye was made to a club favourite, Per Frandsen. Frandsen had agreed to leave at the end of the campaign and in a gesture of goodwill, Allardyce had made him captain for his final appearance. Bolton would lose it 2-0 but Frandsen received a rapturous applause when being replaced by Campo in the second half. Two stints for the club, the only remaining player to have played at Burnden Park and a true legend of the club said farewell to the Bolton faithful. Frandsen would move to Wigan Athletic before a serious injury would end his career. Many would never forget his work in the First Division and his displays in the early days of Bolton's Premier League survival campaigns.

The Trotters finished eighth in 2003/04 after winning six of their last nine games to end up on 53 points, only one win away from coming fifth and potentially qualifying for Europe. What a transformation; Bolton now were an established Premier League club, cup finalists and shopping in the high-end section of the transfer window. For a club that had been used to shopping in charity shops, it was now moving up to searching for deals in Harrods.

The summer transfer window was a hectic one with multiple ins and outs. Adding to Frandsen's departure were exits for Simon Charlton to Norwich, Ibrahim Ba to Çaykur Rizespor in Turkey, Jeff Smith to Port Vale and Emerson Thome joined Frandsen at Wigan. Okocha had signed his new deal but Djorkaeff was yet to do so as negotiations were still ongoing. Youri, the man who was seen by many to start the revolution of high-quality signings, had ended the season in scintillating form and wanted more security from a deal at Bolton. The Frenchman had requested a two-year contract so he could finish his career and potentially retire at the Reebok. However, due to his age and the need to grow the squad, the board felt they could only offer him one year. This went on for the majority of the summer and Djorkaeff would later state that he was originally offered two years but this was changed later on. He stated that the contract was ready to sign but Phil Gartside came back from a holiday and changed it to a one-year deal late on in negotiations. Much to the misery of Allardyce and the fans, the two parties were never able to agree terms and Djorkaeff, 'Le God', left in the summer of 2004. Djorkaeff would join Blackburn on a short-term basis but only played three games before ending his career in New York by signing for MLS side MetroStars. The France and Bolton legend now works for UEFA and sits on the board of French club Lyon but will for ever be remembered as the man who started it all at the Reebok Stadium.

Allardyce also wanted strong competition for Jussi Jääskeläinen and agreed terms with young Polish goalkeeper Tomasz Kuszczak from Hertha Berlin. However, after verbally agreeing, Kuszczak returned to his hotel room at the De Vere Whites Hotel for the night but when Allardyce went to meet him for breakfast the next morning, he had gone. Club secretary Simon Marland received an almighty rollocking by Sam who had told him to get the contract signed the night before. Kuszczak had snuck out of the hotel early, then drove to West Bromwich Albion and signed there, joining a club who could promise him first-team football. Allardyce was incensed with Kuszczak, Marland but also goalkeeper coach Fred Barber. Barber was job sharing at West Brom and Sam felt he had made a mistake and let it slip to the Baggies about Kuszczak. After this, Barber signed full-time terms with Bolton and cut his link to West Brom.

With the loss of Frandsen and Djorkaeff, it was evident that more quality needed to enter the door, and also some older heads. Sam started this by confirming the signing of two former experienced Premier League strikers in Michael Bridges and Les Ferdinand. Adding to this was the signing of Tunisia defender Radhi Jaïdi who had been scouted by Jack Chapman during the Africa Cup of Nations. Bolton also brought in Blessing Kaku and Tal Ben Haim from the Israeli Premier League, Júlio César from Real Valladolid as well as an iconic signing in former Real Madrid and Spain captain Fernando Hierro. A friend of Campo, Hierro was interested in project Bolton and signed a one-year deal. Sam also had Barcelona striker Patrick Kluivert in the Reebok Stadium for talks and felt that the deal was more or less done, however upon leaving Bolton to discuss the move with his family, Kluivert and his agent received a call from Newcastle United and the Dutch striker moved to St James' Park the next day.

After this setback, Sam set his sights on Wolves striker Henri Camara. Wolves were very critical of Bolton for 'unsettling' their player after they rejected two £2m-plus bids for the Senegalese forward. Camara would publicly explain his desire to leave Wolves and for Bolton to be one of the options. He had scored a screamer against Bolton in the season prior and Sam was a keen admirer. After weeks of efforts and rejected bids, Wanderers gave up as Camara moved to Celtic on loan to have the chance to play in Europe.

Sam was growing annoyed as he had lost out on bringing in more striking options with Rivaldo, Kluivert and Camara all falling through his fingers. Adding to this, Croatian striker Dado Pršo had turned Bolton down for a move to Rangers. The large striker had verbally agreed to join Bolton but later stated the chance of Champions League football was too much of a pull to turn down. It seemed there was a common denominator in Bolton's failings to land a quality striker, the allure of European football. Yet Sam finally added some more quality to his strike force late in the window with the loan signing of Liverpool striker El Hadji Diouf. The man who lit up the 2002 World Cup alongside Camara for Senegal was causing issues at Anfield and had some public and not public spats with captain Steven Gerrard as well as being famous for his lack of professionalism after his £10m move from Lens. Sam knew that his talent and potential was there to see as Bolton agreed a deal to take Diouf to the Reebok for the season and pay part of his wages.

The club's best bit of business that summer was for Wales captain and Premier League stalwart Gary Speed. The 35-year-old midfielder was one of the fittest players in the league and had been sold to Bolton behind the back of Newcastle manager Sir Bobby Robson. Sam had to convince Gartside to pay for Speed as the two clubs eventually agreed on a £750,000 deal. Sam got his sports science team to analyse Speed's stats and despite being 35, he had the fitness of a 25-year-old. What a bargain. Speed would take over Djorkaeff's number six shirt and would be one of the vice-captains along with Kevin Nolan and Ricardo Gardner, behind Jay-Jay Okocha as Bolton looked to progress on to the next level of their journey.

The signings of Ferdinand, Hierro and Speed may have looked like Sam was buying players past their peak and in the senior section of their careers but the manager made it clear that he wasn't signing them for their legs – he had the likes of Gardner, Davies, Nolan, Hunt and Stelios who could do the running – he was signing them for their minds. However, it was quickly shown that Speed had both, the legs and the brain.

One man who arrived late to pre-season training, though, was Stelios. His national side Greece had shocked the footballing world by winning Euro 2004 in Portugal. The outsiders beat the hosts Portugal twice including in the final itself as well as defeating holders France on their way to lifting the trophy in Lisbon. As the Greek team lifted the trophy and celebrated their win, Stelios was met on the pitch by his son Dimitri who, instead of wearing a Greece kit, was wearing a Bolton Wanderers kit for all the world to see. The winger had shown his loyalty to his club on the world stage.

Back in Bolton, plans were being put in place to add to their amazing end to the previous season and to push beyond their eighth-placed finish. Many would laugh at such a suggestion but it was the vision of Allardyce and the methods of Phil Brown and Mike Forde that would push this into action. Forde had used visualisation with the players since being brought into the club but when the squad returned to prepare ahead of 2004/05, Forde introduced the 'Bolton Bible', a manifesto for the players to follow: a code of conduct and a set of challenges for the players to follow and implement into their daily values and lives. It was a gradual approach to motivation and included famous quotes, speeches from serial winners and eventually manifesting European qualification.

Forde placed a picture of the UEFA Cup in front of the players and asked Phil Gartside to present the vision to the players in the chairman's suite. It created an aura of belief among the players and was a stamp and message to everyone involved that this was the next step on the journey. Brown and Allardyce made it clear to the players, 'Why can't we make it? What is stopping us?' As long as there was belief and togetherness, the world was their oyster. The team were told that they finished three points off Europe the season before and were now better so it was logical that they could make history and qualify for European competition in 2004/05. There was a confident self-assurance building in the team, not cocky but confident and a belief based on the staple vision around measured spirit.

As the new season approached with a home fixture to Charlton Athletic, Sam was able to boast depth in his Bolton team for the first time in his tenure. After many players came to the end of their contracts the previous campaign, the manager was able to rebuild his squad in many positions as Gartside's clutch on the club's wallet started to loosen. However, despite a solid summer of incomings, Wanderers still only spent a total of £1m with only Speed and Ben Haim costing a fee from the nine first-team players brought in during the summer. A friend of Diouf's, fellow Senegal international Khalilou Fadiga would join later on a free transfer in September after losing his place in the Inter Milan squad following some concerns over his heart. Those fears would be realised when Fadiga collapsed during a pre-match warm-up before a League Cup tie.

The season started superbly for Bolton as they beat Charlton 4-1 thanks to a double from Henrik Pedersen and another brace from Jay-Jay Okocha, on his birthday. The captain hadn't scored at all in 2003/04 but managed to get two on his first game of the new campaign. New signings Speed, Júlio César, Ben Haim and Ferdinand would all feature that day but Bolton would lose their next game, away at Fulham, after which Sam introduced Jaïdi into the first-team for Júlio César at Southampton, where his team won 2-1 for the second successive season.

With two wins from three, Bolton sat in third as they welcomed Liverpool under new manager Rafa Benítez to the Reebok. Benítez was welcomed to English football in quite a robust way and admitted he had never seen players bully a team of his so much, noting how his players struggled to deal with Kevin Davies who scored in the 1-0 win for the hosts. A young Xabi Alonso and Luis García were making their debuts for Liverpool that day but they quickly crashed to earth as they realised they would not be afforded the time on the ball they had been in La Liga. Sami Hyypiä left the field early due to a broken nose and Liverpool looked second best to everything. Bolton would remain in the top seven for most of the season and by the time Graeme Souness's Newcastle arrived at BL6 in late October, Allardyce's men were fourth in the Premier League after only two losses in 12 matches, a run that included draws against Manchester United and Arsenal and wins against Liverpool and Tottenham.

The visit of Newcastle was an odd one for Allardyce. Around the same time Bolton had beaten Liverpool in August, Newcastle had decided to part ways with their long-time boss and football icon, Sir Bobby Robson, and were looking for a new manager. The rumours in the media stated that Sam was the number one choice. In fact the rumours were very true, he was. Sitting 16th in the table and showing an ageing team, Newcastle wanted Allardyce to take control and reinvigorate the squad at what was in all honesty a vastly bigger club than Bolton. Newcastle would average 52,000 supporters every week at St James' Park and had a considerably bigger transfer budget. Magpies chairman Freddy Shepherd offered to pay Bolton the £1.5m fee that was needed to release Sam. Newcastle may have been the bigger of the two clubs but Sam felt his squad was much better as he listed the two comparing starting 11s and felt Bolton's was far superior. The Newcastle squad was past its best and would need a huge rebuild that would take time in a part of the world where supporters are famously not patient.

Gartside gave Sam permission to speak to Newcastle but had asked him to stay and offered him a promise of a new and improved contract. Sam would turn down Newcastle based on his loyalty to Bolton and also appreciation of the opportunity he had been given by Gartside in 1999. Newcastle tried again in September and tried to persuade Sam by offering him a £25m January transfer budget but he wouldn't budge. Sam signed a new five-year contract at Bolton and Newcastle appointed Blackburn manager Graeme Souness instead.

With the arrival of Newcastle at Bolton in late October, the game had added bite for Allardyce who was keen to show he had made the right decision. The level of talks with Newcastle didn't make the public domain at the time so he wasn't proving anything to anyone, maybe more to himself. Bolton faced the Toon Army and sat in fourth place after a fantastic start which would see them remain in the top half of the table all season, other than for two weeks in December during some bad form. By this time, Sam seemed to have a settled first-team squad after some experimenting with new signings at the start of the season. A back four of Nicky Hunt, Radhi Jaïdi, Bruno N'Gotty and Ricardo Gardner in front of Jussi Jääskeläinen would stay that way for the remainder of the season with Tal Ben Haim coming in and out of the defence as well as Fernando Hierro coming in at times to show experience and steel before his mid-season move to midfield. The midfield was also settled as Gary Speed had replaced Per Frandsen and Youri Djorkaeff's work rate. Jay-Jay Okocha, Kevin Nolan and Iván Campo were still pulling the strings as Sam had an ever-changing front three which would always have Kevin Davies in the middle but be joined by either Henrik Pedersen, Stelios or El Hadji Diouf. On that day, Diouf and Stelios started either side of Davies.

Diouf had put in some great performances so far during his loan move but was yet to open his goalscoring account; he hadn't scored at all in 18 months after being frozen out by Liverpool. The marmite-like forward was an instant hit with the Bolton fans as he showed grit and a lack of fear which Whites followers respected and opposing supporters despised. Diouf would often frequent the bars of Bolton town centre and interact with fans, maybe too much for Sam's liking, but he could back it up and despite enjoying a drink in j2 nightclub on Nelson's Square on a weekend, he would never throw in the towel for Bolton and would balance his work and play perfectly, something he didn't really do under anyone but Sam. A few months into their time together, Diouf would refer to Sam as 'Dad' and had found a place he was respected, acknowledged, valued and most of all, loved.

Bolton were in the best form of their Premier League history and everything they touched seemed to either go in or test a keeper. New Newcastle manager Souness tried to play down the quality of Bolton's squad in the build-up as he stated that Sam's team were just a team of 'long ball merchants and physical bullies'. Sam decided to let the football do the talking as 27,196 fans arrived for the 4pm kick-off.

The game was nervy at the start as both sides tested each other out in a cagey first half. However, after half-time, Bolton came out firing and after 50 minutes, they had a throw-in deep in Newcastle's half. Okocha trotted over to pick up the ball and wiped it dry with the inside of his shirt. As he flung the ball into the box, it made its way over the defence towards Davies who flicked it into the air before Jaïdi rose high to head back across goal and past keeper Shay Given. Given rushed out and tried to punch the ball but ended up flooring Jaïdi instead. As Given missed the ball it looped towards the far post and Diouf bent down to perform a diving header in between Stephen Carr and Lee Bowyer to make it 1-0. Diouf ran to the fans and pulled his shirt over his head in celebration at finally breaking his long drought. Nolan grabbed the shirt and put it back over his head but referee Graham Poll had seen it and handed Diouf a yellow card for his celebration. Did he care? Doubt it.

The goal had saved Diouf as before that, he had been playing quite poorly and Pedersen was stripped and ready to enter the field in his place. Yet Diouf stayed on to put Bolton ahead and really rattled Souness's cage. A crowd chorus of 'Diouuuuuuuuuuuf!' came from the fans as they celebrated with their new hero. Bolton's midfield were dominant as

Newcastle had gone with three strikers and were losing the numbers game in the middle. However, almost instantly, they hit back with a bolt from the blue. A ball from the Newcastle defence looped into the Bolton half and N'Gotty headed it out but only as far as youngster Darren Ambrose who chested it down just beyond the halfway line. Ambrose rode the tackles of Speed and Nolan before striking the ball hard and true from 30 yards out and into the top corner. It came from absolutely nothing but was one of the best goals ever seen at the Reebok Stadium and unsurprisingly, the Diouf chants stopped.

The Sky Sports viewers now had a game on their hands as both teams went to blows for the three points. On 70 minutes, Bolton had one of their trademark N'Gotty free kicks from deep. The Frenchman floated the ball into the box to his usual target Davies who ducked to flick it behind him towards Diouf who managed to get a tiny flick on it but was shoved by two Newcastle defenders. The ball looped in the air in the direction of no one but Davies rushed towards it in what seemed to be a 50/50 with Given. Davies threw his body at the ball and slid it past Given with his right foot to find the net. Davies ran to the Bolton fans with his right arm aloft, almost like Alan Shearer, who had been on the pitch but without having any impact. The replays showed that Davies slid the ball through Given's legs. Allardyce, in the dugout, thrust his arms in the air in glee as his decision to stay at his beloved Bolton had proved to be correct.

The Wanderers held on and almost extended their lead through Davies and substitute Pedersen. But at the final whistle they were 2-1 winners, third in the Premier League and looking to ruin the traditional 'big six'. It was also a big moment for Gary Speed who had shown the club who let him go that his best days were by no means behind him and he was still ready to compete and play at the highest level. Bolton would finish seven places above Newcastle that season and 14 points ahead of them to show the progression they had made. They may not have been able to spend £25m a transfer window but they had something other clubs, including Newcastle, didn't have – measured spirit.

13

'Sha lala lala lala la Diouf! Diouf!' and 'He came from Real Madrid, he didn't cost a quid'

AS THE season progressed, Bolton were continuing to pull up trees and humble many footballing titans. They had taken points away from Arsenal, Manchester United, Liverpool, Tottenham and Newcastle and by the end of November they were sitting pretty in fifth after taking a share of the spoils at Stamford Bridge in a 2-2 thriller against Chelsea. Bolton were two goals down thanks to strikes from Damien Duff and Thiago but headers from Kevin Davies and Radhi Jaïdi completed a spirited fightback against the future champions. Up next at the Reebok was what seemed to be a seemingly routine three points ahead of them as Portsmouth visited BL6.

The south coast side arrived with the typical miserable Bolton weather in full force as 25,008 took shelter from the elements in the stadium and Sam Allardyce started with a front three of Stelios, Davies and El Hadji Diouf. This combination had provided seven goals between them by now with Stelios and Diouf keeping out Henrik Pedersen, who had scored the same amount by himself by that point.

Although in a rich vein of scoring form, Pedersen was always seen as a supersub or second fiddle to Diouf and Stelios and there was little to no chance of him dislodging Davies up front. The Dane was also being tested out as a makeshift left-back for rotation as he, Ricardo Gardner and Gary Speed were the only left-footed players at the club and would be rotated in the role to give some competition but also recovery for Gardner at times.

Bolton never got going against Portsmouth and went down 1-0 due to a goal from former Wigan captain Arjan De Zeeuw to end their run of form. The game would also be remembered for two things – the start of a run which led Bolton to go from fifth to 14th, and a disgusting incident where Diouf was caught spitting at an opposition player. Before arriving at Bolton, Diouf had been reprimanded for spitting at a young Celtic fan in a UEFA Cup game for Liverpool at Celtic Park. He was fined £5,000 for that offence.

Sam had brought the forward in and would try to use his charm and man management to try and turn Diouf away from the controversial incidents that had seemed to follow him during his tenure at Anfield. However, he could not forgive Diouf's actions on 27 November 2004. Diouf had got into a verbal altercation with De Zeeuw and as he walked away he was seen to spit in the face of the Dutch defender. De Zeeuw kept his cool and informed the referee and Portsmouth officials after the game. This was testimony to the Pompey man's integrity; he did later admit to the media that he felt like punching Diouf in the face at the time.

Upon realising what had happened, Allardyce and Phil Gartside were infuriated and disgusted. The boss stated that he and the club did not and would not condone such behaviour from its players and Diouf was fined two weeks' wages. Allardyce had contemplated sending him back to Liverpool but he decided to stand by his man. The FA would later ban Diouf for three games and impose their own fine on the Senegalese forward. Diouf would publicly apologise for the incident and admitted he had let himself, the club and its fans down. He also publicly apologised to De Zeeuw who chose not to take legal action against him. This incident brought a dark cloud over what had been an amazing start to the season for Bolton and one which was looking to bring European football to the club for the first time in their history. The gloom remained as the result was the start of a run of six losses in a row, Wanderers going seven without a win overall as they scored just four times in that sequence and conceded 12.

The winter months were harsh on the Whites as a hectic fixture build-up saw defeat pile on defeat. Bolton would become very uncharacteristic as the roof started to cave in on the famous defensive stability and resilience they had shown for the last 12 months. They would look defensively frail and weak in the tackle in 3-2 defeats at Everton and Norwich, despite being 2-1 up in both games. Then a series of 1-0 home defeats hit them hard with defeats to Manchester City and Blackburn adding to the Portsmouth result. A 2-0 loss at Manchester United on Boxing Day followed with Sam rotating his team by bringing Júlio César back in and starting Tal Ben Haim as well as youth team forward Ricardo Vaz Tê for his full debut.

Bolton couldn't seem to buy a goal, never mind a win and welcomed West Bromwich Albion on New Year's Day 2005 for what was potentially another home defeat. The Baggies were in a relegation dogfight and were desperate for the win and saw the faltering Bolton as a perfect chance to pick up a vital three away points. After 13 minutes, it seemed to be the same story for Bolton as Hungarian forward Zoltán Gera put West Brom 1-0 up from their first shot on target.

In goal for Bolton was 41-year-old Kevin Poole in place of Jussi Jääskeläinen. There were massive rumours that Jääskeläinen was on his way to Arsenal that January and his exclusion from the first matchday squad of the month did nothing to quash the talk. Sam would later state it was to rest the Finn but many felt that it was an indication that Jussi may be on his way. However, Poole, as experienced and hard-working as he was, was 41 and did not have the same reflexes or athleticism he would have done ten years prior and was caught wanting on a few occasions after being saved by his defence. Sam had gone back to his trusted defensive four with Nicky Hunt, Bruno N'Gotty, Radhi Jaïdi and Ricardo Gardner in front of Poole. Over the losing run, he had changed things round with some rotation, mainly in defence as Júlio César, Fernando Hierro and Tal Ben Haim had all played in central defence over the run but the defeats didn't seem to stop.

The Whites would push forward and do their best to recover from their early setback as the game progressed but the ball just wouldn't hit the net. In a crazy few minutes, West Brom's former Bolton goalkeeper Russell Hoult saved from Davies before Jay-Jay Okocha's rebound was cleared off the line by Darren Purse. It seemed like it would never come as Bolton pushed in the pouring rain. Minutes later, Kevin Nolan got on the end of a cross from Nicky Hunt but the number four headed wide. After the half-time interval, Diouf, back from his ban, tested Hoult who was able to turn the strike around the post.

As a seventh straight defeat seemed inevitable, Bolton began to step up with the game entering its final ten minutes. In the space of five minutes, Okocha hit the post and Nolan was denied a stonewall penalty when Purse handled his shot in the box. The Albion fans were starting to celebrate what would be a famous win for their season when Hunt began to drive forward into the box on 85 minutes. The full-back passed to Iván Campo, who returned the ball to Hunt who had then run into the box on the right-hand side. The England under-21 star received the ball and played it across the box where the waiting Diouf got in front of Purse and sliced it into the roof of the net. The man who had been the villain of the Reebok weeks earlier was a hero again as he scored the goal that turned the season around. After six straight defeats, Bolton had gained a point and had stopped the rot.

As the whistle blew for a 1-1 draw, Bolton celebrated like it was a win and fans started their new song based on the Tony Christie classic, 'Amarillo'. The tune had made a comeback in the charts after Bolton comedian Peter Kay's charity appeal. However, the home supporters had made their own version. Instead of 'And sweet Marie who waits for me', the fans would sing 'Sha lala lala lala la Diouf, Diouf! El Hadji Diouf will spit on you!'. It may have been poor taste and not the classiest of chants, but it did coincide with an upturn of form which would lead to Diouf scoring nine goals by the end of the season.

After that home draw, Bolton would encounter an outstanding run of form which would take them from 14th back up to the top six. This sequence would coincide with the emergence of a legend of world football into the midfield – Fernando Hierro. Signed in the summer, Hierro was originally brought in as cover for the defence and to be an experienced head in the dressing room. Yet initially, the former Real Madrid captain and Champions League winner had struggled to adapt to the pace of Premier League strikers and had been caught wanting in defence on occasions. This reminded Sam of a similar issue he originally had when he signed Iván Campo on loan in 2002 and decided to re-use the previous method by putting Hierro into defensive midfield. When Hierro had signed, Campo had told Sam that he was worried about losing his place in the team to the Spanish legend. It may have taken longer than expected, but Campo was right as Hierro began to start in defensive midfield at the expense of his former Real Madrid and Spain team-mate.

Three days after the draw with West Brom, Bolton would record a long-awaited win away at Birmingham, 2-1 thanks to goals from Diouf and Nolan. They would then win 3-1 away in the FA Cup against Ipswich before welcoming Arsenal to the Reebok and resuming their dominance over the Gunners with a 1-0 victory thanks to a first-half header from Stelios. Bolton were now undefeated in Arsenal's last three visits to the Reebok Stadium and had taken four points away from the Gunners that season. This was part of a period of dominance over Arsenal that would eat away at Arsène Wenger for many years.

The Wanderers gained revenge over Blackburn with a 1-0 win at Ewood Park and would then beat Oldham Athletic away 1-0 in the FA Cup as well as picking up a home 3-1 win over Tottenham and three points at Crystal Palace thanks to a 1-0 scoreline. A goalless draw away at bogey team Middlesbrough was next and Wanderers sat in sixth. Next up were Fulham in the FA Cup and another 1-0 win confirmed progress to the quarter-finals.

Against the Cottagers, Hierro was unplayable as his calm manner showed the class that had helped him forge such a distinguished career. With a push for Europe really going, Hierro's experience was vital. Hierro showed he was a class above and even in his late 30s he was by far the best passer of the ball at the club then and since. He rolled his sleeves up and got stuck in and became the most vital cog to the UEFA Cup push. Bolton had a history of rejuvenating the careers of forgotten legends such as Okocha, Bobic, Djorkaeff, Speed and Campo, and Hierro was no exception to this as Sam had worked his magic so by the time Easter arrived, the European drive wasn't a dream any more but a very real push. Adding to this, young Israeli defender Tal Ben Haim had started to forge his way into the first-team as Bolton started to take a new dynamic shape.

Yet they would lose the FA Cup quarter-final, 1-0 at home to Arsenal in a game marred by a red card for El Hadji Diouf after elbowing visiting goalkeeper Jens Lehmann in the face. Allardyce, growing tired of Diouf's antics, offered him one more chance as he stated that the forward had cost his team and the fans an FA Cup semi-final place – the Gunners went on to face Blackburn in Cardiff. Diouf would return after another ban to score the winner in a 2-1 success at Charlton.

In the January, Sam had signed another World Cup winner in Vincent Candela on loan from Roma. Candela was to plug the gap at left-back, allowing Gardner to go back into midfield, also adding more depth to the squad. The Frenchman was showing to be another inspired signing as he would become a vital figure in the team and support the switching wingers. It was getting to a point where Sam could really rotate for the first time in his spell at Bolton, and do so with quality and not fear about losing momentum. Amazingly, the depth was at such a point that when Norwich came to the Reebok Stadium on 19 March 2005, sitting on the bench were Okocha, Campo, Jaïdi and Pedersen.

With a rejuvenated side sitting in sixth, Sam could start to bring his wildest dreams into reality and start to focus on what was at one point a non-starter. When he had taken over in 1999, Bolton sat in the lower half of the First Division and were looking at a potential financial crisis which had led to the sale of valuable assets such as Per Frandsen before Sam arrived, and then the later departures of Mark Fish, Eiður Guðjohnsen and Claus Jensen. Bolton were known as a yo-yo club with a squad of journeymen picking up a wage with methods varying from the old-fashioned to the lazy. Sam helped build a state-of-the-art training facility in Euxton, fitting it out with all new medical and statistical analysis tools including his very own war room. Adding to this, his backroom staff, sometimes a bigger squad than his playing staff, were at the forefront of the modern game. In 2005, Sam was on the cusp of greatness and had a genuine chance to bring European nights to Horwich. After a 1-0 victory at home to Norwich thanks to a goal of the season contender from Stelios, Bolton sat fifth with six games to go. They were even in contention for a Champions League spot as they battled with Everton and Liverpool to see who could finish fourth.

Games like those against Norwich and the likes of Crystal Palace would have been part of Bolton's downfall in the past as they seemed to always have a giant-killing big result in them somewhere but would often falter against the clubs lower down in the league. Mike Forde stated that he and his team had researched the Whites' form against the top eight compared to the bottom eight and if they managed to pick up maximum points from the bottom eight, especially at home, this would show the cornerstones of a successful season. By successful, Forde meant qualifying for Europe in some form. Forde would call those games 'mentality games' where the players would show what they were made of mentally, a quality almost more important than football talent.

Prior to meeting Norwich, Allardyce, Forde and Phil Brown held player appraisals in the chairman's suite to add a sense of aura to proceedings. The players who had achieved previous glory, like Okocha, Stelios and Hierro, spoke about the importance of winning against the small teams as they were the games they simply had to win if they were going to achieve their goals. Stelios in particular was vital for the run-in with his invaluable discipline and experience of being a serial winner in Greece with Olympiakos and with his national team the summer before. After this Norwich game, Bolton found themselves two points behind Everton who were fourth and one point ahead of Liverpool. Bolton had a game in hand against Southampton and had a chance to go fourth but were held to a 1-1 draw by the Saints. After this Everton started to pull away from Bolton and Liverpool and near enough confirmed their fourth place. With four matches to go, Bolton could confirm their UEFA Cup spot with a win but were held away at Villa 1-1 and then lost 2-0 at home to Chelsea who won the Premier League title that day thanks to a double from Frank Lampard. Wanderers' modest team put up a good fight against José Mourinho's superstars but were unable to stop the Blue machine from picking up their first title in 50 years.

Despite these two results, Wanderers still sat in sixth but now Tottenham and Middlesbrough were closing in on them as both sides sat only three points behind Sam's men with two games to go.

Bolton travelled to Portsmouth for their last away game of the season knowing at least a point would confirm a place in the UEFA Cup. It was a big match for the Whites and also for Diouf who was facing up against the team he gained villain status against earlier in the season due to his spitting incident. Bolton had the chance to make history as never before had the club qualified for European competition and Sam was keen to get this done so they could celebrate in the season finale at home to Everton, who had also confirmed their Champions League place.

A crowd of 20,188 were in attendance at Fratton Park that sunny May afternoon as Bolton lined up with a 4-3-3 formation of Jääskeläinen in goal behind a back four of Candela at right-back, N'Gotty and Ben Haim centrally and Gardner back at left-back. The midfield consisted of the experienced Hierro behind Speed and Okocha, while Davies started up front with Diouf and Stelios either side. With every touch of the ball, Diouf was universally booed by the Pompey fans and Arjan De Zeeuw paid extra attention to the Senegal forward.

With Portsmouth's season near enough over and their safety already confirmed, it was evident that the game meant so much more to Bolton as they had the better of the first-half exchanges. Diouf, in great form, was relishing the hostile reaction from the Portsmouth crowd and if anything, they spurred him on to one of his best performances in a Bolton shirt. Diouf lived for these sorts of occasions and did all he could to rile up the home supporters to aid his own game.

With 11 minutes on the clock, Stelios played the ball back to Candela on the right-hand side of the Bolton box and the Frenchman dipped it forward towards the halfway line. The ball bounced and De Zeeuw went to clear but confusion between him and Cameroon midfielder Valéry Mézague caused the ball to bounce off De Zeeuw and into the path of Diouf. Diouf picked it up around ten yards outside the box and drove towards goal. A crescendo of boos filled Fratton Park as Diouf side-stepped and took the ball around Dejan Stefanović and got inside the box. Diouf then looked up and hit a sweet strike across the goal, past goalkeeper Jamie Ashdown and into the bottom corner. Just the start Bolton wanted and Diouf cupped his ear to the Portsmouth fans before stopping dead in his tracks and smiling at them. The abuse ensued as many in a blue shirt stood from their seats, shouted profanities, and performed hand gestures towards Diouf. Sam had toyed with leaving Diouf out of the side that day due to the occasion and the issues he knew he would face with the Portsmouth fans, but he was so glad he didn't as the divisive figure had put Bolton one up and in the driving seat for European qualification.

As the game went on, Portsmouth failed to produce anything of any substance other than a free kick from future Bolton player Gary O'Neil which was tipped over easily by Jääskeläinen. After the half-time break, Bolton continued to be in the driving seat as they looked comfortable and would constantly put Portsmouth under pressure, especially from set pieces. On 65 minutes the Whites came close to a second as substitute Kevin Nolan smashed a strike against the post from close range after an in-swinging free kick from Hierro. They pushed for a second goal but on 72 minutes, Pompey scored against the run of play. Another free kick from O'Neil was smashed towards goal, and through sheer luck it hit the face of striker Yakubu and bounced past Jääskeläinen. The Bolton fans looked nervous as Portsmouth pushed forward and Diouf began to get frustrated, and his famously short temper was proving an issue so Allardyce brought him off with ten minutes to go for Pedersen to ensure there were no further issues.

Bolton held on to their point as the final whistle blew and an almighty roar sounded from the away fans and the bench. What an achievement: Sam Allardyce and his team had brought Bolton from the footballing brink to qualifying for the UEFA Cup. From his humble beginnings as a schoolboy signing for the club with Nat Lofthouse to this moment in 2005 where he had taken his Wanderers to one of the elite levels of club football, what a journey. Phil Brown took the press conference after the game and waxed lyrical about the achievement. Brown stated that it was the best objective Bolton could have achieved that season, and they had done it. He also spoke about the club's desire to sign Diouf on permanent terms from Liverpool if they were to repeat their feat and even progress the feat in 2005/06, additionally stating of the desire to convince Hierro to sign another one-year contract. Bolton had made Europe and as they went into their last match, at home to fourth-placed Everton, they could relax and enjoy the fanfare.

Prior to the match, Hierro made his stance clear and despite numerous attempts by Sam, he decided to hang up his boots and call a day on his football career. Despite only being there for one season, many had grown fond of Hierro and his legacy will for ever be mentioned. There were even reports of young Bolton supporters crying in school the day it was announced. Allardyce would later state that he felt Hierro and England midfielder Paul Scholes were the best passers in Premier League history and that the Spaniard started to change Sam's approach to coaching and how to use runs in behind as long as you had the right passer. Hierro was special and many fans were gutted they didn't sign him a few years earlier and get more than just the one season out of him.

Alas, the stage was set for a fond farewell as Bolton faced Everton on a celebratory summer's day for both clubs. Despite being brought down to ten men following a red card to N'Gotty in the first half, Bolton won 3-2 thanks to goals from Jaïdi, Davies and Stelios. On 67 minutes, Hierro was brought off by Allardyce and the entire stadium rose to their feet to applaud him and give him the farewell he deserved. Several fans had travelled from Spain to see the last appearance of the great former national team captain and Bolton fans waved Spain flags to say their goodbyes. It was a special moment as Hierro came off the pitch to be met by his close friend Iván Campo for a hug, followed by an embrace from Allardyce. No Bolton fans then or now could thank Hierro enough for what he did for the club in his short time. He showed Wanderers what they could be, he showed them the quality, he showed them the true meaning of 'measured spirit'.

As the players and staff did their traditional lap of honour, the staff waved a flag around the pitch that said 'Creating History Together'. That is just what they had done. From the cold nights away at Tranmere, the heartbreak at Wembley and the shattered play-off dreams, Bolton had lift-off and were now a totally different club from before and were now not just a force in England but about to be one in Europe as they prepared for their very first continental campaign, one which would see them face the likes of Beşiktaş and Marseille.

Bolton finished the season sixth in the Premier League, behind fifth-placed Liverpool only on goal difference. Two weeks later, Liverpool would win the Champions League after a thrilling fightback in the final against AC Milan in

Istanbul. For little old Bolton to finish on the same points as a huge club like Liverpool was incredible. It is not until after this period of time that you truly appreciate what was done. Bolton had made it big time and the good times kept on rolling.

14

We're all going on a European tour!

WITH THOSE celebrations on the final day at the Reebok well and truly done with, Sam Allardyce began to plan for Bolton's first season in European football. His backroom team had studied Middlesbrough's foray into Europe the season before and noticed that their league form faltered as a result and they failed to win in any of their eight league games after playing in the UEFA Cup during the week. It was evident that a strong level of rotation was vital if they were to be successful on all fronts and they were keen to make sure that the romance of the UEFA Cup didn't distract or sacrifice the hard work they had done to establish themselves in the Premier League. They looked at the example of Ipswich in 2001/02 who were relegated the year after qualifying for the UEFA Cup due to an inability to rotate and contend on multiple fronts.

The amount of games would build up and Sam would need to bring in new faces and bring up players from the youth team to expand his squad to ensure that rotation was possible but he still had elite quality available. Additionally, Bruno N'Gotty and Jay-Jay Okocha were now 34 and 32 respectively and would not have the same legs and impact they did in seasons gone by, especially with huge fixture congestion. With the ageing Okocha and the loss of Fernando Hierro, many felt midfield was a key priority to strengthen. Yes, the likes of Kevin Nolan, Iván Campo and Gary Speed were still firing on all cylinders, but Bolton were only a couple of injuries away from having huge gaps in midfield.

With this in mind, Sam took the advice of chief scout Jack Chapman and decided to take a closer look at Israeli attacking midfielder Yossi Benayoun from Racing Santander. The creative player was a hot commodity in Europe and was being closely watched by multiple clubs including Liverpool, Newcastle, West Ham and Real Sociedad after 80 career goals by the age of 25. After a thorough report from Chapman, Bolton took the plunge on Benayoun and had a bid of £2.5m accepted by Racing Santander in July. According to Allardyce, Benayoun had verbally agreed to join Bolton and would even have the pen in his hand ready to sign before a last-minute change of heart saw the player leave the Reebok Stadium boardroom and head to London to sign for West Ham United for the same transfer fee.

Allardyce was angry with Benayoun about this and said that moving to West Ham for, presumably, more money showed a lack of ambition from the midfielder as he would be seen to take a relegation dogfight at West Ham over playing in the UEFA Cup with Bolton. Benayoun would hit back in the media and say that his decision was not based on finance but a preference for the Hammers' style of play, feeling wanted by manager Alan Pardew and a desire to live in London over the north-west. Benayoun would go on to have a successful career in the Premier League and would sign for Liverpool, Chelsea and Arsenal after his stint at West Ham, eventually playing for Sam when he returned to West Ham on loan from Chelsea in 2012. With the rejection from Benayoun still fresh and the season approaching Sam decided to look to his next target.

To avoid falling short on midfield legs, especially in defensive midfield, Sam opted to try and entice former Barcelona man Pep Guardiola to join the ever-evolving League of Nations at the Reebok. Guardiola had left Barcelona four years prior and had spent the last four years floating around Serie A in Italy with Roma and Brescia before a spell in Qatar with Doha side Al-Ahli had finished by the summer of 2005 and he was a free agent. The Catalonian was a similar player to Hierro and a magician with the ball, adding to his ability to dictate play. Guardiola also shared similarities with Hierro in terms of spending some time in the Middle East after leaving La Liga but still having ambitions of carrying on his career. Sam flew to Barcelona and met the 33-year-old in his Catalan apartment and tried to make a deal work during a two-hour negotiation and chat with the man who had previously gained 47 caps for Spain and had been captained by Hierro in the national side.

Alas, the deal never happened and Sam headed back to Bolton without the signature of Guardiola, who decided to move to Mexico and sign for Dorados before retiring only ten games later. Although Pep didn't come to the Premier League in 2005, he would arrive in England in 2016 as manager of Manchester City, and by 2024 he became the most successful manager in European history due to his stints at Barcelona and Bayern Munich as well as at the Etihad Stadium. As of the summer of 2024, Guardiola had guided teams to 12 domestic championships, 15 domestic cups, three Champions Leagues, four UEFA Super Cups and four FIFA Club World Cups. That's some going for a man who had also won 16 trophies as a player before this and was named in the Euro 2000 Team of the Tournament. Sam would also miss out on another Spanish target later that month as left-back Juanfran chose a season-long loan from Beşiktaş to Ajax over Bolton, again despite verbally agreeing a move.

After what seemed like constant transfer rejection, Sam acted swiftly to avoid more disappointment and worked hard to sign Senegalese defensive midfielder/defender Abdoulaye Faye on an initial loan deal from Lens which would become permanent later in the season. Faye, initially a last-minute signing for cover, was a monster of a man and had a non-stop engine on him which proved to be vital for Bolton in their busy calendar. Sam was thankful to land Faye after using the support of Bolton's Senegalese pair El Hadji Diouf and Khalilou Fadiga who helped sell the club to Faye during their time together with the national team. Bolton also signed former Southampton midfielder Fabrice Fernandes on a free transfer as well as bringing in veteran Mexican striker Jared Borgetti for £1m from Pachuca. Borgetti was a legend in Mexico and had scored over 230 goals in his country, with Sam hoping he had found an unknown diamond for a small fee. His finishing was natural but there were questions over his ability to adapt to the English game, especially as he didn't know a word of English, so Iván Campo was tasked with being his chaperone and translator.

Although, potentially Sam's best piece of business that summer was not signing a new player but retaining the services of a current one. Stelios had been impressing many in the Premier League and the top European leagues with his dazzling displays on the wing for Bolton and performances for Greece, and was the subject of a £1m bid from Liverpool which, due to a clause in his contract, was accepted. The reigning Champions League holders had activated the release clause in Stelios's contract and the Greek held multiple daily talks with manager Rafa Benítez about a move to Merseyside. These talks would go on for a few weeks with many around the club, Sam Allardyce included, worrying that Stelios was on his way out, and at a cut price as well. Bolton and Liverpool had built up a strong relationship over the years starting from the deal which brought Roger Hunt to Burnden Park in 1969, Jason McAteer going the other way in 1995, and Diouf to Bolton in 2004; the Reds were hoping to use that relationship to bring Stelios to Anfield.

However, after a long transfer saga, Stelios decided to stay at Bolton and turn down the allure of Champions League football as Sam managed to convince him to stay at BL6 and sign a brand-new three-year deal, one without a release clause too. Allardyce told the club's website, 'We have been working hard behind the scenes to get this agreed and I'm delighted that we can put all the speculation behind us. I was concerned earlier this week that we might have lost him but in the end he always wanted to stay loyal to me and the club. He is a terrific little player and a real match-winner.'

Before the season started, Sam met up with fellow former pros Bryan Robson, Peter Reid and Sammy Lee to finish his UEFA Pro Licence course at Warwick University. It was during a post-classroom drinking session where Sam was hit with double heartbreak in the space of two phone calls as he lost two vital cogs. In the first call, he had been told that his first-team coach, Neil McDonald was joining Crystal Palace to be Iain Dowie's assistant manager. McDonald had been with Sam since the very start of his tenure but felt he had no chance of progressing to assistant manager or beyond as long as Phil Brown was in that post at Bolton.

Before Sam could even start to look at other options he received another call from agent Scott McGarvey who informed him that Derby County wanted Brown as their new manager. This was something Sam couldn't stand in the way of and Brown was announced at Pride Park Stadium that summer. Sam was in a pickle and had two high-profile vacancies in his carefully created backroom staff ahead of their most important season yet. In a conversation with Peter Reid, the former Bolton midfielder suggested Liverpool number two and current England coach Sammy Lee. Lee, who had played for Bolton in a very short period in the early 90s, knew Wanderers fairly well and was eager to get back into club coaching. Sam and Sammy spoke about the potential of this, and after speaking with Phil Gartside, Lee became Bolton's new number two. Due to Lee's 5ft 3in stature, the new duo was coined Big Sam and Little Sam. Lee would share this job with his role coaching for the England national team so was able to arrive at Bolton on a cheaper wage than Brown. To replace McDonald, Sam spoke with Manchester United manager Sir Alex Ferguson and convinced him to allow one of his coaches, Ricky Sbragia, to join as first-team coach.

With a new-look backroom staff there was apprehension ahead of the new campaign, but also excitement as both new additions had extensive experience of working with elite teams in Liverpool, England and Manchester United as well as coaching teams known for playing on multiple fronts. The club had progressed and it was only right that the backroom staff, not just the playing staff, did too. Soon after this, Bolton confirmed their signing of the summer and broke their transfer record to bring back El Hadji Diouf for £4.5m on a permanent deal after an amazing season on loan. Bolton would then sign former Fulham defender Martin Djetou on a free to add extra defensive cover and former England goalkeeper Ian Walker on a free transfer to replace the retiring Kevin Poole, before signing yet another international superstar in the form of Japan's captain Hidetoshi Nakata.

Nakata wasn't just a signing for the pitch but also for the club shop as the store's orders to Japan exploded and 'Nakata 16' was the most-requested nameset. The man from Kofu was labelled the 'Asian David Beckham' as he was not only an outstanding footballer but a massive celebrity in his homeland. Nakata had come to fame when playing with the amazing Parma side of the mid-90s before joining Roma in 2000 where he won Serie A in his first season there. He had mainly played in Italy before joining Bolton on loan from Italian giants Fiorentina and similarly to others in the past, Nakata had lost his way and wanted regular football ahead of the 2006 World Cup, so saw Sam and the Whites as the perfect opportunity. In reality, Nakata would play a bit-part in the season and mainly appeared in UEFA Cup games and against lower-level opposition in the league before retiring the next summer at the age of just 29, after Japan crashed out of the World Cup in the group stage. He may not have lit the pitch up during his time at Bolton but his status certainly helped grow the club; it was a stroke of genius for the commercial side as many travelled from Japan just to catch a glimpse of Nakata, and it also spread Bolton's image around Japan and the Far East which was only beneficial for all.

Speaking of this Asian exposure, Bolton were invited to play in the 2005 Premier League Bangkok Trophy during the pre-season and travelled to Thailand for a tournament against Everton, Manchester City and the Thailand national team. They would win the tournament after beating Manchester City on penalties in the semi-final and then seeing off Thailand 1-0 in the final thanks to a Diouf penalty.

The new season started with Bolton sporting a brand-new kit. Keeping the all-white *Galáctico* style introduced in 2003, the new kit was a modern twist on this with a navy blue stripe on the sleeve and a printed shiny logo rather than the traditional embroidered crest. This was a shirt perfect for Europe and perfect for both a more modern Bolton and more trendy Reebok Stadium to gain further exposure across the world. Later on, they announced their new navy and silver away kit in a similar style. Both would be remembered as classics by Bolton fans for many years to come.

On the playing side, Iván Campo had lost his place the season before due to Fernando Hierro's emergence but would be given a show of faith by Sam in pre-season as he was handed the number eight shirt to replace his previous 16 and would be informed he would start the first game away at Aston Villa. Campo scored in a thrilling start to the match, which was 2-2 after ten minutes. The score would remain that until the final whistle as Bolton looked to make another strong start to the season and rotate on a more regular basis. It was evident that there was a slow phasing out of Bruno N'Gotty and Jay-Jay Okocha who were out of contract in the summer as Radhi Jaïdi, Tel Ben Haim and Abdoulaye Faye were favoured as central defenders and Kevin Nolan, Gary Speed and Campo were Sam's number one midfield trio. However, both still contributed greatly and were not forgotten by Sam or the supporters.

The start of the season saw Bolton sit in fifth after five games including that draw at Villa Park, a 2-1 win over West Ham and 2-0 against Newcastle, a 0-0 draw at home to Blackburn and a 1-0 loss at home to Everton. As much as the league was very much the priority, the new attraction of the UEFA Cup was not lost on the players and the fans as they prepared to play their two-legged first-round game to see whether they would make the group stages.

As fans dreamed of European away days, it was Gartside who had taken the first stop on Bolton's European tour travelling in September to Monaco for the draw for the first round of the UEFA Cup. Gartside sat there for this historic moment for the Whites with dignitaries from all of Europe's elite clubs. Bolton were mixing it with the big boys and Gartside was honoured to be there to represent his boyhood club in front of the UEFA bigwigs; he would later admit he didn't care who they were drawn against and felt nothing but immense pride. This would conflict with Allardyce's view that Gartside didn't want European football but with anything there are always three sides to a story: Sam's, Phil's and the truth.

The formalities and welcomes ensued as the draw was televised live and supervised by UEFA chief executive Lars-Christer Olsson. As Bolton hoped for a glamorous journey to Rome, Paris, Munich or Madrid, the draw was made and instead they would be heading to the Balkans to meet Bulgarian champions Lokomotiv Plovdiv; the first leg would be at home on 15 September and the return a fortnight later. Many supporters had only heard of Bulgaria on the politics section of the national news and were fairly familiar with the area of Sofia but the phrase in everyone's mouth was, 'Where the hell is Plovdiv?' Funnily enough, to many Bulgarians, Plovdiv was a major city but for Bolton fans it posed another happy coincidence as Plovdiv was a mere two-hour coach away from the beach resort of Sunny Beach. It was a popular holiday destination each summer so some fans combined the two occasions and decided to spend over a week in the Bulgarian sunshine ahead of the away leg.

However, Bolton's first European tie would, romantically, be at home. The Reebok Stadium was built in 1997 with the vision of being a kickstart to loftier ambitions for the club. European football was only a dream at that point, but in 2005 it was a reality as Bolton lined up for their first match in Europe with a changed team: Nakata, Pedersen, Okocha and N'Gotty were brought in with Davies and Nolan dropping to the bench.

Some 19,723 tickets were sold as just over 70 per cent of the stadium was at capacity for the midweek tie. Diouf would start in the middle of the three and deputise as the focal figure while Davies sat on the bench. Channel Five covered the game as Bolton lined up and shook hands with their Bulgarian opposition and from minute one, the plan from the away side was clear, try to foul Diouf and get a reaction from him with the hard-hitting Bulgarian champions aiming to frustrate and bully Bolton. Early on, the Whites had the better of the chances as Campo floated a cross into the box and Stelios went for the diving header but misjudged, the ball bouncing under him and being cleared for a corner. From the ensuing set piece, Nakata worked the ball into the box well but Jaïdi headed across goal and wide.

Despite the early dominance, Plovdiv began to grow into the game and some through balls would beat the defence but be intercepted by Jääskeläinen. With 28 minutes on the clock, Plovdiv silenced the Bolton fans. Right-back Vladimir Ivanov had started a darting run down his flank and beat both Gardner and Pedersen for speed after a smart one-two with Georgi Iliev. Ivanov then swung the ball into the box directly into the path of Boban Jančevski. The striker had beaten Nicky Hunt to the ball, and from the centre of the box he hit a first-time strike which smashed past Jääskeläinen and into the back of the net. The stadium was shocked and stunned, other than the delirious Plovdiv fans in the South Stand. Home supporters started to fear that their European dream would be over before it had truly started and their team pushed forward instantly as Nakata came close with a header before the referee blew the half-time whistle. Fans were hoping to see a name like Okocha, Diouf or Stelios become the first European scorer at the Reebok Stadium but that title would for ever be Jančevski's.

In the second half Bolton continued to drive forward in an attempt to even the score, Okocha fizzing the ball past the post twice before being replaced by Kevin Nolan. Allardyce had also moved Gardner back to left-back, taken off Pedersen and replaced him with Jared Borgetti who went into the central striker role and Diouf moved to the wing. With 20 minutes left, Bolton fans began to feel cagey and the songs started to stop as they were worried that all that hard work from the season before would be undone over the space of two games. To not make the group stage would have been an embarrassment after all the talk of a 'European tour' all summer.

Bolton had a goal kick which Jääskeläinen opted to quickly pass to Hunt on the edge of his own box but the game had started to become a farce with the Plovdiv players playing a time-wasting game, needing medical attention after every single tackle. On one occasion, Nolan had had enough of the theatrics and he refused to kick the ball out, instead playing it across to Hunt. Hunt, in the right-back position, was driving towards the halfway line when he looked up and saw a darting run on the left by Diouf. Into the Plovdiv half, Hunt hit a beautiful crossfield ball from right to left which slowly dipped into the box. Diouf followed its path and continued his run. As it reached the box, the former Liverpool forward dived head-first towards the ball and met it with a diving header from close to the penalty spot. Diouf's superman dive had been enough to meet the ball with perfection and guide it into the opposite corner to make the game 1-1. Diouf grabbed the ball instantly and ran back to his own half while cheering with a fist up towards the Bolton fans who had started to sing again. Back in the game and back in the tie.

After this, it was all Bolton as they pushed forward in numbers. Fabrice Fernandes had come on for Stelios and the midfielder was starting to show glimpses of the form that made him a fan favourite at Southampton by whipping balls into the box aiming for Borgetti. The Frenchman also came close with a strike from outside the penalty area which whistled the wrong side of the right-hand post. After this, Jaïdi again came close with a header which was saved by Stoyan Kolev as the game entered injury time.

A 1-1 draw would have been an amazing result for the Bulgarians due to the gulf between their league and the Premier League and would also have given them hope ahead of the second leg on home soil. With a matter of seconds left, Gardner played the ball to Fernandes, who took it with his back to goal on the edge of the box and spun around on the left-hand side. He dipped a cross towards the danger area and it was met by a flicked header from Nakata, the Japanese star ducking down to make contact. The ball evaded the entire Plovdiv defence and fell at the feet of Borgetti with no one around him and just the keeper to beat. He seemed to be in an offside position but on closer inspection, the full-backs were playing the Mexican onside. Borgetti took a great touch and looked up and with Kolev approaching him 12 yards out, he didn't think twice and smashed his shot across the goal and into the bottom-left corner to make it 2-1 in injury time. What a moment for Bolton, and for Borgetti, who opened his Wanderers account with potentially one of the most historic moments in the club's history. He may not have known much English but he certainly knew what a cheer sounded like, as 20,000 Bolton fans screamed for joy in celebration of their first taste of European glory.

Two weeks later, Bolton sat third in the Premier League after 1-0 victories over Manchester City and Portsmouth before they set off for their big European away day in Plovdiv. Many supporters would make their own way there but for those who didn't, the club had to hire three planes from Manchester Airport as plenty of fans opted for the special UEFA Cup packages adding to those Boltonions who decided on combining a holiday with the tie – a bit different than a minibus to Blackburn away.

For that week, the resort of Sunny Beach had become 'Little Bolton' with flags stating areas such as Hall-I'th'-Wood, Little Lever, Horwich, Bromley Cross and Astley Bridge among others littering the beaches and bars. People bumped into people they hadn't seen in years as it seemed everyone in Bolton who could make the journey did so, to say, 'I was there!' Officially, 1,500 visiting supporters bought tickets but the home end would also be full of Lancashire accents and St George's flags as Bolton fans took over. A couple of weeks prior to the match, the venue had been changed as Plovdiv's ground did not meet UEFA regulations, so it was switched to the Naftex Stadium in Burgas, even more towards the east coast, and coincidentally a mere 30-minute drive from Sunny Beach. Those who had decided to combine a holiday with the football were ecstatic, and some who were simply there on holiday and had no connection to Bolton also got tickets. It seemed the majority in the ground were either from Bolton or on holiday from the UK as Sam again went with a changed side and handed a debut to Ian Walker in goal and a first start for Irish academy graduate Joey O'Brien. Borgetti and Fernandes would also start due to their work in the first leg. Supporters including Bolton boxer Amir Khan and his family were in the stands full of joy and excitement and anyone who was anyone in Bolton was also living the dream in Bulgaria.

Despite another early scare, Bolton would go on to win 2-1 and go through 4-2 on aggregate. An own goal from Aleksandar Tunchev and a late winner from Kevin Nolan would confirm the tie as the players and fans celebrated long into the night after making the group stage. Bolton were drawn against a higher calibre of opposition with Zenit Saint Petersburg (Russia), Vitória de Guimarães (Portugal), Beşiktaş (Turkey) and Spanish giants Sevilla making up Group H. The European tour lived on and many Boltonions flocked to the travel agents to plan their next foray, whether it would be Turkey or Portugal, or both.

The 2005/06 season was oddly similar to 2004/05 with Bolton starting strong and staying in the top six for the vast majority of it. Despite a 2-1 loss at newly promoted neighbours Wigan and a thrashing by Chelsea, the Whites went seven games undefeated in league and cup as they picked up wins at home to West Brom, away at Charlton and at home to Spurs in the league as well as over West Ham in the League Cup and draws against Beşiktaş and Vitória de Guimarães which added to a win over Zenit Saint Petersburg in the UEFA Cup before a loss at Fulham at the end of November. They entered December in sixth place.

At the end of November, Sam made a very difficult decision and stripped Jay-Jay Okocha of the captaincy and handed it to 23-year-old Kevin Nolan. In and out of the team and into the last year of his contract, Okocha's performances had dipped and Sam wanted him to focus on his own game rather than the additional responsibilities of being captain. He made it clear that it was by no means an admission of Okocha's summer departure but felt he would benefit from not having the extra responsibility, and Sam also had an eye to the future by giving Nolan the armband. Gary Speed, Kevin Davies and Ricardo Gardner would act as vice-captains. This was a huge show of faith towards Nolan from Allardyce as although the midfielder was still very young, his game had progressed and was starting to be spoken about for a potential England call-up. His performance and screamer in the 1-0 victory over Tottenham, especially, was outstanding and caught many eyes across the football world with Liverpool apparently interested in taking him back to Merseyside, although nothing ever materialised. Additionally, it was reported that Sir Alex Ferguson was looking at taking Nolan to Old Trafford.

With a new captain and an ever-rotating squad, Bolton continued to progress on all fronts as they beat Leicester City to reach the quarter-finals of the League Cup thanks to goals from Borgetti and youngster Vaz Tê, but they would need to revert to full strength as a huge test would come next when Arsenal visited the Reebok Stadium in the annual fierce contest.

Arsène Wenger, it would be fair to say, hated his trips to Bolton and did not show much respect to the team or even the club in general. In 2003, Bolton had railroaded the Gunners' title push as they came back from two goals down to draw 2-2 late on to help hand the title to Manchester United. After that, Bolton had drawn 1-1 at home in 2003/04 and won 1-0 in 2004/05, as well as getting a point at Highbury in a 2-2 draw earlier in 2004/05 to compound Wenger's Bolton blues. Whites supporters were starting to refer to Arsenal as a soft touch, a team that could be easily intimidated, as the players would use their physicality and the 'Reebok Roar' to get under Arsenal's skin and pick up valuable points each season. By many means, Arsenal's squad was far superior to Bolton's in terms of honours, medals, skills, and most would say, footballing talent. World Cup winner and former PFA and FWA player of the year Thierry Henry spearheaded the attack with Robert Pires, Freddie Ljungberg, Gilberto Silva, Sol Campbell, Dennis Bergkamp, Lauren, a young Cesc Fàbregas and Robin van Persie also in the team. However, the Gunners were a wounded animal by late 2005 after losing captain Patrick Vieira in the summer and were now fighting for a top-four spot rather than the league title. Only three points separated Bolton and Arsenal before the match, with the north London outfit sat in third and Allardyce's men in seventh.

It was obvious to Sam that Arsenal detested coming to Bolton as Wenger often tried to create a pre-match villainous aura around the club to the media by creating a perception that they were bullies and cheats and all they did was commit fouls and hurt his players while his Gunners wanted to play 'nice, free-flowing football'. Sam also felt that the media bought into this, as did a few refs as Wenger would make comments that Bolton would 'kick lumps' out of his team and that they had 'no interest in playing football' which could not be further from the truth. It would be interesting for Wenger to explain this to the likes of Okocha, Djorkaeff, Hierro and Campo over the years wouldn't it? Bolton did not receive the credit for their scientific approach and their research into opposition teams. The rhetoric was usually about Arsenal dropping points rather than commending Bolton for gaining them which did nothing but infuriate Allardyce and make him want to prove everyone wrong even more. At one point, Wenger refused to shake hands with Allardyce. A great manager? Absolutely. A great loser? Never.

On that cold December afternoon in 2005, Arsenal arrived at the Reebok Stadium wearing their limited edition burgundy home shirt to mark their last season at Highbury before moving to the brand-new Emirates Stadium the following summer. Many Arsenal players were struggling with the cold and wore gloves, much different to the short sleeves and bare hands shown by the Bolton squad. New captain Nolan brought out his team which included youth graduate Joey O'Brien at right-back, a surprise for many. O'Brien was a central midfielder but had deputised at right-back for the injured Nicky Hunt and had done well enough to make Hunt struggle to get back into the team upon his return. N'Gotty was back along with Ben Haim in central defence in front of the ever-present Jääskeläinen in goal. Gardner at left-back as well as a midfield of Nolan, Speed and Faye supported a front three of Davies, Diouf and Stelios. Iván Campo missed out through injury and Okocha and Jaïdi were on the bench.

Allardyce, sitting with Gartside in his usual first-half seat in the hospitality area, looked down on a nervous

Wenger who chomped on chewing gum like it was going out of fashion. Sat in the row in front of Sam was Mike Forde, making notes, and Bolton legend Roy Hartle from the 1958 FA Cup-winning side. The Reebok was a cauldron by kick-off and the Arsenal players looked edgy on the ball, making some early mistakes which handed Bolton possession in dangerous areas. Bolton had an early corner from Stelios which tested the Arsenal backline but was headed away by French defender Pascal Cygan only to be quickly won back by O'Brien who crossed from the opposite wing. The ball found its way to Stelios inside the box and was still bouncing. The Greek winger, the previous season's match-winner against Arsenal, scooped it back into the penalty area towards the melee of players. Steaming in was Faye who charged at the ball and leapt high above Fàbregas to thunder it into the back of the net after 20 minutes. Initially signed as cover and not intended to be a main starter, Faye had worked incredibly hard in both central defence and midfield when asked and was now seen as a starter in defensive midfield while Campo was out injured. The Senegalese big man ran to the corner to celebrate with the Bolton players and substitutes, right in front of the travelling Arsenal fans.

Only ten minutes later, Arsenal's troubles would be compounded as Diouf and O'Brien were working well together and caused Cygan some serious issues on the right. The two combined to create space as O'Brien played a ball down the channel for Kevin Davies to run down while being closely watched by Gilberto Silva. Silva, who had won the World Cup with Brazil three years earlier, raced in front of Davies and had the bouncing ball under control. Davies didn't give up on the chase and hassled the Brazilian who was attempting to shield the ball near the corner flag. Before it could go out, Davies quickly stepped in front of Silva and outmuscled him to win the ball back on the line and cut inside which then gave him the space to drive towards the goal with acres of space and an influx of Bolton players running into the box. Jens Lehmann had come out and had left his goal wide open so Davies passed it across the six-yard line to Stelios who stepped in front of Sol Campbell and nudged the ball into the empty net to make it 2-0, haunting Arsenal once again. He ran to Davies to thank the hard work of the striker and celebrate an amazing start for Bolton. Wenger stood with his arms raised at his team as they had once again been humbled and 'bullied' at the Reebok.

Arsenal tried to hit back instantly but a looping strike from Henry on the edge of the box hit the post and went out for a goal kick. Soon after that, Faye also went close to getting a third for Bolton but was denied by a great diving save by Lehmann after a Stelios cross from deep. Nolan also came agonisingly close, but again Lehmann saved Arsenal's blushes. As the game progressed, Wenger sat in the dugout with his arms folded and a face like thunder; he knew his team had been beaten, outclassed and outmuscled and he could do nothing about it. Quality, money and skill were well and good but they were nothing compared to 'measured spirit'.

Henry hit the post again late on and Jääskeläinen denied Pires from the rebound to frustrate the Arsenal fans further. Sam came down from the stands to the dugout as the final whistle blew and Bolton had continued their Reebok hoodoo over Arsenal. He told the media that it was Bolton's most deserved win of the season as they had dominated from minute one to 90. Arsenal surrendered their three-point advantage and fell to fifth with Bolton moving up to sixth and only separated from the Gunners by goal difference after 14 games. When Sam first took over in 1999, Bolton would lose against the likes of Tranmere, Stockport and Walsall. Now, they were regularly taking points off and humbling the elite clubs of English football. Sam had picked up victories against Manchester United, Chelsea, Liverpool, Arsenal and Newcastle United at least once in Bolton's four-and-a-half-season tenure in the Premier League and they were now classed as an established top-eight team and competing in European competition.

Bolton would draw 1-1 at home to Sevilla to reach the last 32 of the UEFA Cup as Sam joked with the media that if he was called 'Allerdici' instead of Allardyce he would be being touted by Real Madrid and Barcelona. The Spanish giants may not have been looking at Sam but another giant of world football certainly was. The England national team needed a new manager and the FA were closely watching the Bolton boss. Sam had turned down Newcastle twice by this point but England was another matter and Phil Gartside and many Bolton fans worried that their fearless leader was on his way to the Three Lions.

15

The FA comes calling

FOR MANY in football, the England job is the pinnacle of any English manager's career. Many had been honoured with it and had failed on a large scale and over the years it had attracted both foreign and national names alike.

Although his playing career never reached the heights to be considered for an England cap, Sam Allardyce's managerial exploits at Bolton had caught the eye of the FA and he was being considered as one of the options to interview for the role as Sven-Göran Eriksson had declared he would leave the national team after the 2006 World Cup. Sam, Middlesbrough boss Steve McClaren – who was also assistant manager to Eriksson – Charlton Athletic manager Alan Curbishley and Brazilian Luis Felipe Scolari, the head coach of Portugal, were all being mentioned as possible replacements for the Swede. But until a formal invite to interview arrived, Sam had to concentrate on Bolton as they entered 2006 seventh in the Premier League after a mixed run of form after that confident victory over Arsenal. This run included a loss in the League Cup quarter-final to Wigan, a 4-0 win at Everton, a 4-1 loss at Manchester United and a draw at home to Liverpool over an inconsistent Christmas period.

In terms of signings in the winter window, Bolton had brought in Matt Jansen on a free from Blackburn Rovers; he was looking to restart his career after an injury sustained in a motorcycle crash had stopped his progress in which he had been close to the 2002 World Cup squad after an amazing run of form at Blackburn. Due to his accident, Jansen never ended up playing for England. He hadn't been the same since that accident but he saw what Sam had done with Kevin Davies as an example to follow, and signed on a short-term contract at the age of 29. Also incoming was Omani national goalkeeper Ali Al-Habsi from Norwegian club Lyn as cover for Jussi Jääskeläinen to add further depth in the goalkeeping department. Sam also released Fabrice Fernandes and Martin Djetou in the winter. The pair had, other than showing glimpses, offered nothing concrete in a Bolton shirt. Yet, just like in the past winter windows, Phil Gartside refused to open the purse strings to offer Sam further funds to build on his success and he still had to scrimp and save despite Bolton's lofty achievements. Sam felt with stronger funding, Bolton could build on their already amazing achievements in the season and potentially push towards the Champions League places.

Bolton were also into the fifth round of the FA Cup after beating Watford and Arsenal (again) but by mid-February, they would focus their attention back to Europe as they had drawn French superpower Marseille in the last 32 of the UEFA Cup. During the build-up to the tie, many compared the trophy cabinets of the two clubs and although Bolton had a strong FA Cup history from the 1920s and 1950s it paled into insignificance compared to Marseille's eight Ligue 1 titles, ten Coupe de France trophies and one Champions League in 1993. They truly were giants of European football and the sort of opposition the fans were dreaming of when Bolton secured qualification to the UEFA Cup back in May 2005.

By that point in the tournament, Sevilla were probably the biggest club the Wanderers had faced as the other clubs were of modest standing but Marseille would usually be in the Champions League and in the Ligue 1 title hunt in most seasons. In their side would be Franck Ribéry and Samir Nasri, both future France and Champions League stars, as well as 1998 France World Cup winner Fabien Barthez and future Bolton defender Abdoulaye Méïté. In the first leg, Bolton gave a brilliant account of themselves by keeping a clean sheet in a 0-0 draw with Jay-Jay Okocha returned to the side. They could have taken a win into the second leg if it wasn't for some dubious refereeing with their supporters feeling that Portuguese official Olegário Benquerença waved away what seemed to be two clear-cut penalties.

One week later, Bolton travelled to the hostile Stade Vélodrome to face their opponents for the second leg in one of Europe's most iconic stadiums. Supporters rushed in droves to the French city to follow their team but were disappointed with the low ticket allocation of fewer than 3,000 seats, compared to allocations on other away days in Europe which had been much higher. The fans had enjoyed some beautiful away days with Sunny Beach in Bulgaria, the coast of Turkey against Beşiktaş and a gorgeous city break in Portugal at Vitória de Guimarães, but Marseille was a different beast. Based on the southern coast of France, Marseille could be mistaken for a scenic French city from a romantic novel; however, the reality was very different. The city had a reputation for crime and violence, especially around football, and the visiting fans wouldn't receive the warm welcome that they had in previous European cities or even in their own country.

From landing in France, the Bolton supporters and officials could feel the tensions rising with the locals. Phil Gartside certainly didn't help the cagey relationship by coining Marseille as 'a bit of a dump!' upon his arrival. Many reached France with the anticipation of watching potentially the biggest and most high-profile match in Bolton's history as they boarded coaches or the Metro line to the stadium from the city and the airport. Police from Marseille and those who had come to support from Greater Manchester advised Bolton fans to get into the stadium as quick as possible and not to dawdle or be seen alone around the stadium as Marseille supporters had not hidden the fact that members of the hooligan firms were looking for trouble and wanted to add an English scalp to their list of 'victims'. The visiting faithful were placed into what could only be described as a 'holding cell' before the game for over two hours as the police wanted to avoid trouble outside and ensure the Marseille fans were in the ground before letting those backing the Wanderers in.

Marseille had given Bolton a measly 2,800 tickets but this was on purpose to avoid as much violence as possible, with the away supporters placed in the top corner of the main stand behind metal cages and away from the reach of the home fans and with the luxury of concrete slabs instead of seats to sit on. They soon realised this was no longer Blackburn away or Wigan away, this was a different animal. As the match began, the home supporters did all they could to intimidate the visitors in the stands and on the pitch with organised chanting, flares and a partisan atmosphere.

In terms of the match, Sam and his side showed no fear as they had proven themselves to be more than equal to the French side in the home leg and could go into one of Europe's fiercest cauldrons with nothing to lose. Sam decided to go full strength with a front three of Nolan, Davies and Stelios, and it was the Greek winger who silenced the Vélodrome early on in front of 38,351 fans to shock the home support. Okocha had tested Barthez in the early embers of the match before Stelios's strike. Okocha had a throw-in deep into the Marseille half, the Nigerian receiving boos and whistles from the home faithful due to his Paris Saint-Germain career. In typical Okocha fashion, the throw-in looked as if it would be a long one to go deep into the box aimed for Kevin Davies and/or Abdoulaye Faye. But Okocha quickly passed the ball short to Gardner and got it back in space on the right-hand side and chose to cross the ball into the crowded box. The ball swerved high into the area and started to float towards the left-hand. Barthez, booed by the Bolton fans due to his Old Trafford history, rushed out off his line to attempt to collect, which he did, but then dropped it near the six-yard line. Barthez lost his footing and fell over the ball, and with quick thinking, Stelios rushed in to take it away from the keeper and put it into an empty net despite attempts by Habib Beye and Abdoulaye Méïté – two players who Allardyce would one day manage – to block the shot. Stelios ran over to the Bolton supporters, who were struggling to see the match through the metal caging, with both arms aloft as Barthez looked embarrassed and was seen to be apologising to his fellow players for his error. Barthez was bothered but Bolton were not, the Trotters having scored a vital away goal at the Stade Vélodrome and taking the advantage in the match and the tie.

Captain Kevin Nolan cut the celebrations short as he called for calm and for the team to get back into playing mode. It was vital that Bolton did not get carried away as the game was still quite young and there was plenty of time for Marseille's quality to come back and hurt them. Five minutes after Stelios's goal both Mamadou Niang and Lorik Cana went close, thanks to crosses from Ribéry, and Marseille were looking to hit back instantly. Minutes after this, Joey O'Brien was marauding down the right with the ball. O'Brien had displaced Nicky Hunt from the right-back spot but would later move back into midfield to ensure Hunt's return. As the young Irishman got into the Marseille box, he switched the ball to the left where Stelios drove in a half-volley but his tame strike was easily held by Barthez.

The match was end-to-end and was totally up for grabs, but Bolton knew that a second goal would mean that Marseille would have to score three times due to the away goals rule and could take the tie away from the French side. However, Ribéry was starting to cause Bolton issues as he was finding space between O'Brien and Tal Ben Haim with ease and was exploiting the gaps due to his speed and outstanding dribbling skills. The Frenchman would eventually join German giants Bayern Munich after this stint in southern France and would haunt many Bundesliga, UEFA Cup and Champions League defences for years to come.

With half-time approaching, Bolton looked to sit in and contain their hosts so they could get into the break 1-0 up and reset. Seconds before the break, Ribéry moved the ball into the middle and drove towards the Bolton defence who were continuing to struggle with the Frenchman. Ribéry was something Wanderers had never come up against before and it was evident he was far too good for the UEFA Cup or Marseille. He passed the ball to Wilson Oruma in midfield and then on to Nasri whose shot was blocked on the edge of the box by Okocha. The blocked ball fell to Niang who played it back to Nasri in space. Nasri looked up and picked his spot with a glorious floated ball into the packed penalty area. It evaded the defence and reached the head of Ribéry on the penalty spot. Ribéry was marked by Stelios who, in all fairness, never stood a chance with his opponent who leapt high to flick the ball across Jääskeläinen and into the net. The stadium erupted with flares and fireworks set off and the floor began to tremble as the Marseille fans made the atmosphere electric. It was 1-1 on the cusp of half-time and now Marseille had the belief and momentum.

There was not much Bolton could do about it as they had been undone by two future serial winners in Nasri and Ribéry, who would become the future of French football. The Bolton players went into the dressing room deflated but still with hope. Sam knew it was vital to ensure they defended well and looked to break on the counter. The team knew that if the second half went 15 or 20 minutes without a Marseille goal then the ferocious home support would start to become restless and turn on their players which would then be a perfect time for the Trotters to pounce.

As the teams came out, the Stade Vélodrome resembled a Roman colosseum, with the supporters doing enough to try to intimidate anyone on the field and in the away section. Kevin Davies looked upon this and smiled, relishing the environment without a shred of fear in his entire body as the PA system was playing Led Zeppelin and AC/DC songs to try and inspire their team. The second half wasn't exactly total domination and lots of chances by the hosts, but they certainly had the majority of the ball and when they did go forward, they looked dangerous. Bolton looked towards Gary Speed and Okocha for their experience and resilience to help settle the team and they started to organise and dictate the pace of the game. Their efforts were strong, but Ribéry was still making the Bolton players look like Subbuteo figures as he wriggled in and out of tackles to keep the ball and go on the attack. Nasri was also showing his quality and tested Jääskeläinen from long range, the Finn turning it around the post.

Marseille pushed and pushed but the crowd were starting to turn as Allardyce had predicted and with 25 minutes remaining, Bolton started to believe. Faye had a header saved from close range after a set piece before Marseille pressed forward in the 67th minute. They moved further into the Bolton half and played through midfield, switching from left to right. Substitute Thomas Deruda played the ball across to pacy defender Habib Beye who took it past Stelios and broke into the box from the right. Beye played a slide-rule pass into the crowded six-yard box which went beyond Jääskeläinen and into the 'corridor of uncertainty'. Tal Ben Haim, who had played amazingly that season and due to his performances was the subject of an enquiry from Chelsea, was left in a difficult position as the ball bounced off his shin, past the keeper and into his own net. The young defender looked horrified as the Marseille crowd cheered, threw flares on to the pitch and sang along to 'Kashmir' by Led Zeppelin through the PA system.

Trailing 2-1 with 20 minutes to go, Bolton knew that a second away goal could keep them in the tie and also make life difficult for the French team, as the Trotters would progress to the last 16 with a draw. They went forward and Nolan came close with a half-volley which was saved and scrambled clear by Barthez. Nolan dived in to get the ball after the initial save, but also hit Barthez who had gathered it. Nolan barely clipped the French keeper who ensured he was in the running for an Oscar nomination with his theatrics before the Marseille players then tried to intimidate Nolan who laughed off their advances before receiving a cheap booking. Habib Beye in particular, a future team-mate of Nolan at Newcastle, was playing all the dark arts to try and get a reaction from the captain.

Marseille then went close to a third on 82 minutes as another long-range strike from Oruma flew past the post. It seemed inevitable that they would go through to face Zenit Saint Petersburg but in the 96th minute, Bolton had a corner and Jääskeläinen rushed into the box for one last go. Stelios swung the ball into the box and the Finnish goalkeeper flung himself at it, but Barthez was able to punch it away before the referee blew the full-time whistle much to the delight of the Marseille supporters and players. They knew they had been in a real match, but their quality had shone through. Marseille's backroom staff celebrated as if they had won the final, a real sign and show of how much they valued a win against a tough Bolton side.

The Wanderers players and staff saluted the travelling supporters as their European dream came to an end, for now at least. No one could have questioned the passion and effort of the players and 2,800 Bolton supporters sang to their heroes in white as they felt that their side's first-half performance didn't deserve the result they got. On a different day, and without Ribéry and Nasri, most agreed that Bolton would have progressed into the last 16. Marseille would go on to be knocked out 2-1 on aggregate by Zenit Saint Petersburg in the next round, before they were knocked out in the quarter-finals by eventual winners Sevilla; Bolton had gained points from both teams in the group stage.

Bolton had enjoyed a taste of the elite and so did Sam. From humble days at Notts County to managing a team at the Vélodrome, it was an experience he liked and wanted to ensure that it was not a one-off. He made it clear that he and the team needed to focus back on the Premier League to ensure they could qualify again; they were sixth by the end of February. The feeling of high-profile games was something Sam craved and as Bolton were showing to be a serious force in the top six again, he received the phone call that all supporters feared. He had been offered an interview for the England manager's role.

Early in 2006, Sven-Göran Eriksson had declared that he would leave his post after the World Cup in Germany and with this news, the FA didn't delay in their search for a new manager as they looked to get a solid hire in place as soon as possible. Early on, the FA had offered the role to 2002 World Cup-winning manager Luis Felipe Scolari who had seemed interested at first but would turn it down on the basis of the extreme media attention from the British press compared to those in Brazil. Phil Gartside, who also sat on the board of the FA, had said that he would not stand in Allardyce's way if the offer came. Sam had turned down Newcastle twice and made it very clear that it would be a great honour for Bolton to have the England manager come from their club, and it would also help the chances of Nicky Hunt, Kevin Nolan and Kevin Davies of gaining international caps.

In February, Sam received a call from FA chairman Brian Barwick for an informal chat which then progressed into an offer of interview. Sam wasn't the only man approached but knew he had a great chance compared to his contemporaries Steve McClaren and Alan Curbishley. Sam produced a presentation to show the FA board, with support from Mike Forde, which covered all bases from tactical approach to nutrition and also mental health support. It was based on his ideas and a clear plan for England moving forward, if they were to be successful in international competitions.

As Gartside and Bolton were torn over losing Sam but also their national team gaining their hero, the manager also sought the advice of then England captain David Beckham and would speak with him about getting the England fans back onside after some tournament failures and also how to create a culture of togetherness in an environment which had become famous for cliques based on club connections. By the end of their conversation, Sam felt that he convinced Beckham that he was the right man for the job, despite the midfielder's close links to McClaren with England and formerly at Manchester United. As Sam left his interview, he felt confident and had been informed later on that it was between him and McClaren. However, Sam went weeks without hearing anything. During this period of silence from the FA, McClaren's Middlesbrough would reach the final of the UEFA Cup, an amazing achievement for a smaller club. McClaren was already in the England coaching team as Eriksson's assistant and had strong links to the FA so Sam started to lose hope, and by the time Bolton played Boro in May, it was confirmed that McClaren had got the job and would take over after the World Cup. Brian Barwick rang Sam to inform him about missing out, and Gartside also called to extend his commiserations; Sam felt they were false, after pondering on the situation. However, it was time to focus on Bolton and do all he could to deliver another European tour to the Reebok.

Coinciding with the media drama over the England job, Sam's side had started to stutter as they dropped from sixth to ninth between February and May but despite this, Bolton could still qualify for Europe with maximum points in their final four games. They would end the season at a stutter and win two, draw one and lose one as they finished eighth in the Premier League, two points behind seventh-placed Newcastle who took the last league UEFA Cup spot – the place that would have gone to eighth that season instead went to FA Cup finalists West Ham United, with winners Liverpool having already qualified for the Champions League.

For many it felt like a flat end to the campaign as Bolton did not qualify for any European competition, despite a strong start which saw them push for a potential Champions League spot. However, being upset by this was a massive indication of how far the club and their expectations had grown since promotion in 2001. When Sam first took over, the fans would have been happy with sixth in the First Division, never mind in the Premier League. They may not have made Europe like the previous season, but they had managed to keep hold of Big Sam and they had secured a third successive top-eight Premier League finish. Only Chelsea, Manchester United, Liverpool, Arsenal and the Trotters had managed to do that; some company for little old Bolton.

Yes, Bolton had missed out on another season in Europe, but Sam knew they were not far off. He felt though that it was time for the board to either back him properly or not bother at all as the end of the last two seasons were beginning to feel like groundhog day after a lack of support in the January transfer window. It was vital for Sam and for Bolton not to slide and falter but to progress even more. The manager felt it was very conceivable for Wanderers to prove all doubters wrong and qualify for Europe again, maybe even pushing for the top four.

Sam had tried to sign Manchester United legend Roy Keane the previous December but lost out to Celtic. He still wanted an experienced midfielder, and had a ridiculous summer transfer drama where he signed Dietmar Hamann on a free from Liverpool for 24 hours, but the German backed out and tried to cancel the deal after signing on the dotted line. One day later, Hamann moved to Manchester City for £400,000 after not even wearing a Bolton shirt once, all based on not being impressed with the town's housing market. With this extra £400,000 in the transfer budget, Allardyce and Gartside's relationship became more frayed as they struggled to agree on what was best for Bolton with the chairman, understandably, happy with the progress the club had made with modest transfer fees and felt it was unnecessary to spend more because their current method was working by using the current financial policies whereas Sam felt that they could and should get even better and with a stronger transfer investment, would make the Champions League. However, Bolton could only do that with a stronger budget to entice younger, more in-prime elite players.

Sam spoke with Gartside and owner Eddie Davies about the need to push on in the transfer market and the chances Bolton would have of making the Champions League if they did. This would be an amazing achievement for the club but also a financial boost for all. But it would only be possible if they invested a bit more into the transfer fund to buy for the future and see the approach as a short-term sacrifice to create a long-term gain. However, Davies and Gartside both felt that it would need a huge amount of investment to reach the top four, of the size that Bolton could not handle. Sam was given it straight – if he could do it with a modest but marginally increased budget and his obvious managerial ability – yes go for it, try and reach the Champions League. Then, if they did qualify, the big bucks would be available, but Davies and Gartside made it clear that they were not willing to spend £50-100m to achieve that goal in the first place, in case they didn't and were left in financial woe. Sam's budget was increased slightly as he set his sights on improving the team ahead of the 2006/07 season.

With this in mind, he was able to identify a summer deal and a move that he felt he could pull off if given the correct backing. If so, this would be for one of the best Premier League and European strikers of all time, a World Cup and Euros winner, a Champions League winner and a scorer of over 70 goals in English football. Bolton went to meet Nicolas Anelka.

16

What's that coming over the hill?

WITH THE disappointment of the England rejection behind him, Sam and his team looked forward to try and restore Bolton's European status and improve on their eighth-placed finish from the season before. To do this, the manager knew that fresh and younger blood was needed as tired legs had potentially been one of the key reasons why the team had started to fall away towards the back end of the previous season. They had lost eight of their last 14 games and if they had been able to instead win at least three of those defeats they would have finished on the same points as fourth-placed Arsenal, and with a fourth win they would have beaten the Gunners to a Champions League place.

With that in mind, Bolton took the hard decision not to renew the contracts of Jay-Jay Okocha and Bruno N'Gotty. Both players had been crucial to the upturn in fortunes and had changed the club from a relegation yo-yo team to a Premier League force. N'Gotty gave Bolton solidity and superb experience and was Sam's very first elite continental signing, in 2001. Although many said it was Youri Djorkaeff who started it all, it could be argued that N'Gotty's signing was the first step in the evolution of Bolton Wanderers.

Okocha was undoubtedly a club legend and his form between 2002 and 2005 had gone down in Wanderers folklore. His performances to keep the club in the Premier League in 2003 as well as get them to the League Cup Final of 2004 would be fondly remembered and referred to in the years to come. N'Gotty left to join Championship side Birmingham City to extend his career in England while Okocha would move to the Middle East to join Qatar SC before returning to England a year later to join up with Phil Brown for a short-term deal at Hull City and later retiring in 2008 with 465 career appearances to his name. Both would be remembered and loved for ever by Trotters fans and those who continue to study Premier League nostalgia.

Bolton would continue their growing enrolment for the League of Nations by showing global intentions in the transfer window with the signings of Iranian midfielder Andranik Teymourian, Ivorian defender Abdoulaye Méïté, Israeli attacker Idan Tal and South African winger/full-back Quinton Fortune who joined on a free transfer from Manchester United. Leaving alongside Okocha and N'Gotty were Khalilou Fadiga and Jared Borgetti. Later in the window, Tunisian defender Radhi Jaïdi would join his former defensive partner N'Gotty at Birmingham. The powerful defender had lost his place to Tal Ben Haim and Abdoulaye Faye, and with Méïté coming in, he felt he needed to restart his English career at St Andrew's. Jaïdi would leave for £2m which was around the same fee Bolton paid Marseille for Méïté so this was seen as a piece of good business as Sam was able to upgrade his defensive unit at little extra cost.

Bolton had depended on the goals of Stelios, Kevin Davies, El Hadji Diouf, Henrik Pedersen and Kevin Nolan for a long time and although they were all averaging between seven and ten a season, Sam knew he needed a lethal striker to add to the tally and someone who could both support and also be supported by Davies. By no means did he need to replace Davies, who was still assisting on a regular basis with his flick-ons and clever box play, but he did need a more lethal striker in the side. At first, Bolton enquired about striker Andrew Johnson from Crystal Palace and along with Everton, Wigan and Newcastle had a bid of £8.6m accepted. This was a big sign from the club, and in all fairness from Phil Gartside, that Bolton were ready to challenge their rivals in the transfer window. Johnson had scored 22 goals in the Premier League the year prior and had scored 15 prior to that in the First Division which had helped him earn five England caps by the end of 2006. Sam would pull all the tricks of the trade to try and entice Johnson to Bolton as he visited all of the interested clubs. Eventually he would turn down the Trotters in favour of a move to Goodison Park so Sam decided to look elsewhere for his striker.

After the drama of the Dietmar Hamann deal, Bolton were also rejected by former Newcastle midfielder Laurent Robert who chose a move to Portsmouth instead. Sam didn't want to constantly go for a free transfer or a disgruntled loan player this time – he needed proven top-flight players who would be ready to go and he and Gartside were willing to pay upwards of £10m for the right man.

The season started with a flash of dynamite as Bolton beat Spurs 2-0 on the opening day thanks to a screamer from Iván Campo and a header from Davies, once again beginning strongly with only one defeat in their first nine. However, three games into this run, during a 2-0 loss away at Charlton Athletic, Bolton had a new face watching his new team from the bench. They had found their striker and had paid £8m for him.

Eight years earlier, a 20-year-old Nicolas Anelka had left Arsenal to join Real Madrid for £22m after scoring 23 goals for the Gunners. Between 2000 and 2006 he would also play for Paris Saint-Germain, Liverpool, Manchester City and Turkish side Fenerbahçe. Adding to this, Anelka would go on to make 69 appearances for France. By the time he met with Sam Allardyce for talks, Anelka had won the Premier League, FA Cup, Charity Shield, Intertoto Cup, Turkish Super Lig, Champions League and Euro 2000. All of this at the age of 27 too. Yet Anelka had been at Fenerbahçe since leaving Manchester City in the summer of 2005 and was struggling to settle and perform and with a reputation of being a difficult customer, due to his time at Arsenal when he was labelled 'Le Sulk'.

Anelka posed a similar challenging scenario to the one Bolton had when signing El Hadji Diouf in 2004, yet he was definitely more of an introvert than Diouf it must be said. It was heavily doubted that you would see Anelka in Bolton town centre at 4am like you might have done with Diouf. Anelka arrived at Bolton's training ground for talks in a brand-new Rolls-Royce as Sam once again sold the project to a serial winner. Anelka had turned down offers from Germany and France to speak with Bolton as he wanted to return to the Premier League to get back into the big time. Sam was realistic about this move compared to others in the past and told Anelka that they were happy to bring him back into the Premier League and if so, act as a stepping stone for Anelka before a move to a big club. This suited all parties as Sam had found his lethal striker with a proven goal record in the league, Anelka had his way back into the Premier League and Gartside could always cash in on him in the future if needs be, which he would do in 2008.

Anelka made one thing clear to Sam though – it was imperative for Bolton to get back into Europe if the move was to work. This was music to the ears of all at the club as they all felt the same. The deal had taken all summer to complete but Sam had finally got his man as Anelka signed for Bolton on the cusp of the window closing for £8m on a four-year deal. It was a club record and almost doubled the £4.5m Bolton paid for Diouf in 2005. Anelka was then showcased to fans with a signing session in the club store where he would confirm his new squad number of 39.

Bolton had signed many global stars over the last five years but this one was different; Anelka was in his prime. This wasn't an ageing star or someone past their best, this was a clinical, proven world-class player wearing a Bolton shirt. Anelka joined a team on the up and made his debut in a 1-0 victory at home to Watford thanks to a last-minute penalty from Gary Speed.

By late November, Bolton were in the top four and had picked up seven clean sheets as the signing of Abdoulaye Méïté, who was alongside Tal Ben Haim and/or Abdoulaye Faye at the back, was helping keep the goals out. Yet, despite wins once again against Liverpool and Newcastle, Bolton would be humbled and brought down to earth by a 4-0 home battering by Manchester United which then started a run of three defeats, and a draw with newly promoted Sheffield United, in the next four.

The real issue during this time was that Anelka was yet to score in the league and some fans were starting to question the signing. The Frenchman had started every game and Sam had stood by his man and knew he would come good but the former Arsenal man had gone ten league games without a goal and many, especially Gartside were getting very twitchy. Anelka had scored one goal in the League Cup against Walsall but had not repeated that in the league and needed to get his goalscoring boots on as up next to the Reebok were the old enemy, and Anelka's former club, Arsène Wenger's Arsenal. Not only were Arsenal recent league rivals of Bolton's but they were also the club that gave Anelka his start in English football in 1997, although they had also washed their hands of him after his move to Real Madrid in 1999. A lot of supporters connected to Arsenal had a lot of bad feelings towards Anelka after he left Highbury and were, seemingly, happy to see him struggling to score at the Reebok.

With each year that passed, Arsenal looked weaker and weaker as, adding to Patrick Vieira's departure the season before, they were now without talisman Thierry Henry who had joined Barcelona for £24m. Bolton may have had a happy run of form over Arsenal but they had hit some poor form of their own and were without a win in a month as the Gunners arrived in BL6. Yet they were still in the top four thanks to an amazing start and had nothing to fear as they started with a new-look 11 against Wenger's side: Jääskeläinen, Fortune, Ben Haim, Méïté, Hunt, Speed, Nolan, Faye, Diouf, Davies, Anelka.

The match had been chosen for television coverage by Sky Sports and almost 25,000 fans bought tickets and got ready to see Bolton, hopefully, end their poor form and continue their hoodoo over Arsenal. Early on, as with the previous four seasons, Bolton were in control and caused issues for Arsenal's full-backs. Since the arrival of Anelka, Davies had been moved to the right of the front three and was harassing Emmanuel Eboué. Not a natural winger, Davies used his strength and power rather than pace to his advantage against the intimidated Arsenal backline.

Seven minutes into the game Kevin Nolan found Diouf on the wing, the Senegalese controlling and crossing towards the on-running Nolan into the box. Nolan attempted to get the ball but was blocked by Philippe Senderos who cleared for a corner. The crowd cheered as the fans had seen Bolton's domination over Arsenal from set pieces over the last four years and could smell blood. They knew, no matter what, that there would be a chance about to unfold as Speed marched over to the corner flag to take the kick. Méïté and Davies were hassling the Arsenal defenders and wriggling around to find space as the ball came into the box and was met by Nolan's header which was deflected by Mathieu Flamini and out for another corner but on the other side and Diouf made his way to the left-hand corner to take the kick in front of the 'Crazy Corner'. Diouf's delivery swung in towards the near post where Faye had started a run towards the ball. Faye moved past Cesc Fàbregas and found himself unmarked as he ran towards the front post and, just like the season prior, smashed a thunderous header into the back of the net. The Senegal international was becoming the scourge of Arsenal as his only goals in a Bolton shirt had both come at home to the Gunners, and both were headers from set pieces. Within nine minutes, Bolton were 1-0 up and once again, Arsenal were falling apart at the Reebok. The young visitors were losing every 50/50 and the Bolton players were picking them off with ease.

Kevin Davies then had a moment that in 2024 could have seen him sent off but in 2006 he was lucky to get away with it. Davies, constantly causing issues to Eboué, was fouled by his marker after beating him to the ball. The striker felt that the tackle was late and dangerous so rose up and pushed Eboué to the ground with a two-handed shove. Arsène Wenger was animated on the touchline as screams of 'OFF, OFF, OFF!' came from the away end. Referee Mike Dean gave Davies a yellow, judging the shove to be below shoulder height. Wenger felt hard done by, and he may have had a point in all fairness. However, this decision by Dean would anger the Arsenal fans even more, as on the stroke of half-time, Davies had the ball on the right by the halfway line after some great work from Faye. Davies looked up and saw Anelka on the opposite side of the pitch in space. He hit a beautiful crossfield ball over to Anelka who confidently took it down with a chorus of boos from the travelling fans. Anelka, still without a league goal for Bolton, had Kolo Touré in front of him ready to tackle. The striker started to run with the ball towards the box from the left and then cut inside to lose Touré and found himself at the corner of the box with a view on goal. He unleashed a strike with all the might of his right leg as the ball moved in the air and seemed to dip up and down and left and right. The unstoppable strike flew past the Arsenal defence and up and over Jens Lehmann, then dipped into the far corner to cause a massive cheer from the home fans. He had done it, he had got his league goal and who else to score against than his former club?

Supporters looked at each other in amazement as they had witnessed one of the best goals ever scored at the Reebok Stadium. Anelka would have been forgiven for losing his cool and celebrating in an over-the-top manner but he kept his emotions in check and jogged over to his team-mates with his trademark two-handed butterfly celebration across his chest. Anelka was swamped by his colleagues who could sense his relief. He would go on to score another 11 goals that season and another 22 overall for Bolton.

The players had continued to get carried away with the celebrations of going 2-0 up and they did not reset quickly.

Little did some of them know that Arsenal had restarted the game and within seconds of Anelka's goal, they had a corner which they decided to take quickly. Fàbregas had the ball on the right-hand side of the box and acted quickly to whip it towards the penalty spot where Gilberto Silva, just like Faye before, had become unmarked and rose high to head home. Sam and the backroom team were furious, the big man coming down from the stands at half-time to tell his team exactly what he thought about their lack of concentration. They may have been winning, but they had given Arsenal hope going into the break.

The Gunners started the second half with dominance and were showing fight that they had not done at Bolton in previous years, but Méïté and Ben Haim were staying strong. When the Gunners did get through, Jääskeläinen was on hand to keep away Fàbregas and was able to tip a Freddie Ljungberg header on to the bar as Arsenal continued to push for an equaliser. The pace of Theo Walcott was starting to cause Bolton problems as he would often get away from the full-backs and put dangerous balls into the box to test the defenders. The visitors went close again with 20 minutes left as Emmanuel Adebayor took the ball past Campo but saw his strike saved by Jääskeläinen at the near post. Bolton were very much under the cosh and needed a breather. After that, they had a free kick that fell to Anelka but his strike was flicked on to the post by Lehmann and Arsenal cleared. But, on 76 minutes, Bolton hit the killer blow and it was Anelka again with the strike.

Faye won the ball in his own half and played it to Campo who was running into the Arsenal half. Campo moved forward before he played a pass that could have been made in Madrid in the late 90s. The Spaniard laid an inch-perfect through ball to his former Real Madrid team-mate Anelka. Anelka ran on, showing his amazing pace, and was through on goal. Due to the perfect timing of Campo's pass, Anelka was able to beat the defender and was one-on-one with Lehmann. Without even touching the ball first, Anelka looked up and struck his shot across Lehmann into the opposite corner to restore the two-goal lead. The pass was amazing, the finish was clinical and the result was fantastic. Anelka embraced with Diouf as the Bolton fans started their new chant for their new hero. 'What's that coming over the hill? Is it Anelka? It's Anel-KAAA!' was the chant which was a spin on the recent indie anthem 'Monster' by Welsh band the Automatic. Yet again, Bolton had Arsenal where they wanted and as the whistle blew, they had confirmed their fourth win over the Gunners in three years and cemented fourth place to continue their great form against Arsène Wenger's team and end their poor form in November.

Anelka had scored another five league goals by the time 2007 arrived as on New Year's Day, Bolton sat in third place and Bolton fans and players started to dream about a potentially imminent Champions League place. It wasn't just a dream any more but a clear reality as Sam had given Phil Gartside a very clear and obvious chance of bringing Champions League football to the Reebok but it could only be possible with the proper backing and also adding to the squad in January.

To reach third, Bolton then won five games in a row over December after that victory against Arsenal and were on the verge of greatness. However, as things were looking fantastic on the pitch, life off it was far from perfect. The BBC show *Panorama* had run a story and a programme about alleged transfer bungs from Allardyce and other high-profile managers. The BBC stated that they had run an investigation into the behaviour of managers in the transfer market and 'demanded' answers from Allardyce and others at the club before airing. The implication was that many people in the game, including Sam's son Craig, had been covertly filmed taking extra payments from agents to gain access to Bolton signings and the money was, eventually, making its way back to Sam's wallet. Sam denied this vehemently and stated that any football decision at Bolton, including transfers, was not based on corruption or payment but a democratic system which led to an approval not from the manager but from Phil Gartside and was based on what was best for the team and the club.

Sam admitted that, yes, he had used his Craig to assist in the signing of Tal Ben Haim in 2004 but it was all by the book and didn't result in any poor behaviour. Craig Allardyce would quit the elite football business due to the shame from these allegations and Sam would refuse to speak to the BBC so for the rest of the season, Sammy Lee would take BBC interview duties. Sam would also eventually sue the BBC for damages to his reputation due to the allegations, which resulted in no formal charge and no problems from the FA. However, burned by the whole situation, Sam decided to distance himself from transfer negotiations moving forward and leave it all to the board. Alongside Sam, Portsmouth manager Harry Redknapp was also accused of the same activity and even had his house searched by the police. The subsequent enquiry came to nothing for Sam other than a report which said that there was a conflict of interest between him and Craig working on deals together. Sam felt that his reputation had been ruined and he had become potentially blacklisted from big jobs in the future.

Sam, once again distracted by external factors, needed to ensure the Bolton Champions League train didn't come off the tracks as it had done in the back end of the season before. He gave his list of January targets to Gartside in a bid to confirm the Trotters as a Champions League team.

17

The beginning of the end

SAM HAD identified a clear list of areas he felt Bolton needed to strengthen in order to progress and earn a Champions League place. Third in the Premier League with 39 points, they were on target to meet Sam's dream of Champions League football but didn't have the quality in depth needed to carry that on in a large fixture build-up. Many felt, Sam included, that Wanderers had moved on from the free transfer days of old and now needed to apply more short-term investment to fulfil the long-term goal which would then give the club a luxury of both financial and football riches.

The levels that Bolton had reached were unthinkable when Sam first took over in 1999 and were laughable just a few years earlier but they were a serious force now and the levels of measured spirit, quality of the first-team and the infrastructure were at a level that meant many across England and beyond envied the club and their manager. The average age of the squad was 29 and Sam wanted to get this down even further and if possible, look to the future to ensure that Bolton would be self-sustaining but successful and continue to show consistent progression. That January, Sam identified Newcastle midfielder Antoine Sibierski and

Fulham midfielder Sylvain Legwinski among many others as the players he wanted to move the club forward and add depth to the squad. Sibierski would have cost no more than a modest £2m and would add some experience and quality to bring off the bench, with Legwinski available for even less. Sam also looked to add more depth to his full-backs and showed the board a list of key players but was knocked back.

Sam implored Phil Gartside to back him and give him the chance to make the Champions League. He had done the maths and worked out that it was near-on impossible for Bolton to finish below eighth after their strong start and had calculated the money they would receive from the Premier League for that finish would easily cover the cost of signings. If they did reach the Champions League they would receive upwards of £50m so that would be easy to recoup. Sam put it to Gartside and said that he truly believed that he could do the impossible and turn Bolton into one of the 'big four' in English football but if they got some injuries and couldn't replace them, then they would fall away and all the hard work would be for nothing.

Gartside promised to speak to Eddie Davies about this but came back to Sam later refusing to give him the money he asked for. An incensed Allardyce was furious as Gartside offered him one loan or a free transfer. He went home to vent to his wife Lynne about his decaying relationship with Gartside and how he had felt his role at Bolton had reached its ceiling. At the end of the January window Bolton signed 30-year-old former Liverpool, Portsmouth and Blackburn midfielder David Thompson on a three-month deal. Thompson was highly regarded in his younger days and had gained an England call-up in 2002 but did not feature in any games. However, he had been hit with injuries and had played only 21 games in three years due to this by the time he arrived at the Reebok Stadium. With all respect to Thompson, it was hardly the signing needed to push Bolton to Europe's elite competition – he had been seen as surplus to requirements at Wigan Athletic. Sam started to lose faith and his eyes started to look elsewhere as his resentment towards the hierarchy started to grow.

As Sam predicted, after January, the injuries started to mount and Bolton would lose steam rapidly. They were beaten 3-0 by Liverpool on New Year's Day and went on an awful run which only produced two wins in their next nine. This included a 5-1 hammering away at Middlesbrough. Despite this poor run, Bolton were still in fifth and many fans pondered where they would be without this drop-off. The team started to stagger towards the end of the season as the players became tired and Sam could not rotate due to the aforementioned lack of depth. However, one player who did come into the team due to injuries and fatigue was Slovakian defender Ľubomír Michalík. Michalík had signed with his fellow countryman Zoltán Harsányi for the reserve team in the winter and was not expected to step up to the first-team for a few years to come. However, due to the lack of numbers, Michalík was brought into first-team training and made some matchday squads towards the back end of the season. The towering 6ft 5in central defender was only 23 and had little senior experience at Senec in Slovakia before arriving in England yet his lack of fear was useful as he went toe-to-toe with some of the league's finest.

By the time Bolton got to April, they were in dire straits as Nicky Hunt, Abdoulaye Faye, Tal Ben Haim, Kevin Nolan, Stelios and El Hadji Diouf were all out injured and would not feature again before the end of the season. Sam was frustrated beyond reason and took his side to Stamford

Bridge to face Chelsea after winning only four games since the start of the new year, yet still they were sitting in fifth. Sam thought about what could have been for that season as he felt betrayed by the board of the club he loved so much. However, his side went to west London hoping to come away with some pride and set up with a mismatched team which saw Campo start at right-back, Michalík making his full debut in defence, a midfield of Thompson, Tal and Andranik and a front three of Anelka, Davies and Gary Speed on the wing. On the bench were reserve-team players James Sinclair, Júlio César Martín and Błażej Augustyn. It was embarrassing for Sam and Bolton as the refusal to strengthen the ranks had made the club look unprofessional and put vital players such as Speed and Campo in unnatural positions.

Chelsea needed a win to stay in the title race and try to retain their championship but they sat three points behind Manchester United with three games to go. The Bolton fans made the familiar journey to Stamford Bridge, a stadium they knew oh so well after relegation in 1998, a famous victory in 2003 and a happy hunting ground for Radhi Jaïdi in 2004 – it was a nostalgic place for the supporters as the second-string team looked to put in a performance to make their fans proud.

As Sam arrived in London he was holding a secret that few outside the club knew. He had seen enough and as the media outlets flocked around rumours of his joining Manchester City or Newcastle United, he decided enough was enough and came clean to the players and staff: this was to be his last match as manager of Bolton Wanderers. The legendary figure had resigned earlier on in the season. This was a decision not made in April but earlier in January after that meeting with Phil Gartside when the chairman refused him funds and after a discussion with his wife Lynne.

After meeting Gartside, Sam had gone home to Lynne and expressed his upset and inability to continue to work under the conditions which displayed a lack of matching ambitions between him and the chairman. It killed Sam to make the decision he was about to make as Bolton was home and everything he knew. However, he opted to progress beyond the club and the next day, he handed over his letter of resignation, initially with immediate effect. After this, talks ensued and Sam agreed to stay until the end of the season to support the club's efforts to reach Europe. It was agreed, however, that if the media or supporters caught wind of this, then he would have to leave his post as he couldn't deny or tell lies if he was asked if he was leaving. Manchester City and Newcastle caught wind of Sam's resignation and started to try and begin talks with him but he wanted to concentrate on leaving Bolton in a strong position. Allardyce and Gartside were able to keep it quiet for the majority of the season but a day before that visit to Stamford Bridge, their third-to-last game of the season, the newspapers had found out.

The match would be remembered as Sam's last in charge and also turned into another Chelsea-Bolton classic at the Bridge. With a weakened side, Bolton would face up against the likes of Petr Čech, John Terry, Michael Essien, Didier Drogba, Frank Lampard and Andriy Shevchenko on a beautiful day in the capital. Despite Chelsea's wealth of riches, it was Bolton who would strike first in the sun and it came from a man from much colder climates and one who didn't even expect to be in the team.

The match kicked off with the April sun beating down on the away fans, many opting to take their tops off in a true show of British style and culture, and the beating sun began to give them a lobster look as the first half progressed. Early on, Bolton were very much under pressure as the stars of SW3 were pushing for the first goal. The visitors' only chance in the first five minutes fell to Anelka on the edge of the box but he fired well over the bar. However on 18 minutes, Bolton had a free kick just outside the penalty area to the right and over it stood Bolton's makeshift midfielders, Tal and Andranik. Andranik took the free kick and put in a swerving cross. The ball reached the crowded penalty area and was flicked into the centre by Méïté where it was deflected by a mixture of Essien and Carvalho before it fell to the feet of Michalík. The Slovakian defender took a large swing with his left foot in the six-yard box as Salomon Kalou tried to block it, but his shot went underneath goalkeeper Čech and crashed into the back of the net. This was not in the script. Michalík, in true eastern European fashion, didn't even raise a smile as he wheeled away to celebrate his first goal in English football on his first start – even more to celebrate was that the Slovakian had scored past the darling of his nation's rivals, the Czech Republic, in Petr Čech. Then England captain John Terry looked around at his defence with disgust as the Chelsea team set back up into position.

Chelsea, embarrassed by being behind, hit back instantly as left-back Wayne Bridge bombed forward, passing the challenges of Campo and Andranik with ease. Bridge was in for the injured Ashley Cole and crossed into the box from deep which fell to the head of Ivorian forward Kalou who headed hard into the ground. The ball bounced in front of Jääskeläinen but then diverted and dipped past the goalkeeper and into the goal. Bolton had been in front for only two minutes before Chelsea hit back and the Stamford Bridge crowd celebrated while Kalou sprinted back into position, refusing to celebrate and eager to restart the game.

Chelsea put Bolton under great pressure and Jääskeläinen saved well from Shevchenko but just quarter of an hour after their equaliser, the home side took the lead on 34 minutes. Gardner had cleared for a corner after some great work from Kalou on the left as Bolton's makeshift side started to feel even more pressure. Lampard swung over the corner, which reached the impressive Kalou, who beat Gardner in the air to head towards the Bolton goal. The ball crashed off the post but hit Jääskeläinen and went over the line to compound Bolton's poor luck. This time Kalou did celebrate with a dance around the corner flag, and by half-time it was still 2-1 to Chelsea.

As Sam performed his final Bolton team talk, there was no anger or frustration but instead understanding as the team had shown fight, although they had come undone due to lack of cohesion and the vast gulf in quality between the two starting 11s. The Trotters came out for the second half with little expectation other than to keep fighting and ensure that they kept their integrity.

The second period started slowly but on 54 minutes, Kevin Davies went on an unconventional mazy run and went past Terry on the edge of the penalty area only to be brought down for a free kick by the home skipper. The ever-reliable Gary Speed chipped the ball into the box and just as it looked like it was going out, Davies threw himself at it and flicked his header beyond Čech and into the net. Davies ran to the Bolton support with passion and glee as he celebrated his equalising goal and what would end up being the club's last goal of the Sam Allardyce era.

At 2-2, Bolton had frustrated the champions and put a halt to their title charge and given Manchester United a huge favour. The Chelsea fans put their heads in their hands as they saw their championship defence slip through their fingers. Sam was in the dugout, still showing his passion and doing all he could to support 'his' Bolton Wanderers. By 2007 he had established an association with the club that had started in 1971 and had also grown in his heart. He never stopped and took a step back, he screamed and marshalled his side to ensure they left Stamford Bridge and his era with something to be proud of and still in the top five. There was no chance of downing tools.

As the game fizzled out and the whistle was blown for full time, the atmosphere was odd in the stadium as Chelsea knew their title chances were almost over, but also Sam knew he had taken charge of his final Bolton game. He walked over to the away fans and clapped in appreciation of them for the final time, holding back a deep feeling of sadness. From Stamford Bridge under Colin Todd in 1998 to Stamford Bridge under Sam Allardyce in 2007, what strides that club had made in just nine years.

From that moment on, it would never be the same again as the next day the club and the manager himself released statements confirming Sam's resignation. It was over.

Sam's statement read, 'It was mutually decided that I step down now rather than at the end of the season. That will give my successor the ideal opportunity to experience the preparation and build-up of matchdays in readiness for next season. After guiding the team into a position where the club is on the verge of qualifying for European football for the second time in three years, I feel it is the right moment to step down.

'I feel the club is in a great position to continue its upward trajectory, with a talented squad supported by an excellent academy programme under the guidance of a highly skilled management team. The foundations for the next phase are well and truly in place. It is with this knowledge that I feel confident that I am moving on with my life, content with a legacy that I have tried to create for this special club. I wish the owner, chairman, staff, players and all the fans every success in the future.'

From that initial wave of belief which saw minimal crowds saunter to Middlebrook and watch their team at the Reebok to see the likes of Andy Todd and Bob Taylor to the ending which saw one of Europe's greatest strikers, Nicolas Anelka, grace the stadium's turf, the journey had been like a fairytale under Allardyce. He and the club had built a dynasty and would for ever be known as a team that was a dominant force in the Premier League then and would be remembered for years to come. Nostalgic football fans would go on to often look at the team that Sam built with phrases like 'Once you arrived at the Reebok, you knew you were in for it' or 'Jay-Jay Okocha, Barclays legend'.

From the days of fights on team-bonding trips in Cheshire to walking the beaches of Bulgaria, the journey was a rollercoaster of ups and downs but the end was well worth the ride; the eight-year period would be looked upon for the manager as much as the iconic players as well as their supporters.

Twenty-four hours after Sam's resignation, his number two Sammy Lee was named as the new manager. Lee's first role in management was a big step and would eventually be seen as a step too far with his sacking in October 2007. However, Lee had inherited a team fifth in the league and close to qualification for the UEFA Cup. Yet, a shell-shocked team and fan base would see Lee lose his first game 3-1 away at West Ham and then draw at home 2-2 with Aston Villa to drop into seventh on the final day. Bolton didn't look the same; the edge, grit and motivation wasn't there as many players admitted, it just wasn't the same without Big Sam. Captain Kevin Nolan told the local press that he was 'devastated and shocked' by the resignation of the man who had 'made him the player he was today'. Later, they would be reunited on both a football and media basis, including a joint interview on TalkSport in 2024.

Oddly enough, Sam was invited to that final game of the season, as Phil Gartside's guest of honour, and would watch the team he assembled scrape a UEFA Cup place after being in the running for Champions League football only a few months earlier. Sam agreed to attend the match but instantly regretted it as Gartside refused to allow him entry to the dressing room; after Allardyce's departure, his name was near enough a banned word at the Reebok Stadium. However, Bolton were back in Europe the following season and would face giants such as Bayern Munich, Sporting Lisbon and Atlético Madrid all without Allardyce.

The team he had built, however, was about to be dismantled as a new regime looked for a different style and would decimate Sam's League of Nations and the era of 'measured spirit'. After Lee's seventh place and qualification for the UEFA Cup, many familiar faces would leave in a rejig. Bolton would lose Abdoulaye Faye, Idan Tal, Henrik Pedersen, Tal Ben Haim and eventually Gary Speed and Nicolas Anelka by the end of 2008. By the end of 2009, Kevin Nolan, Iván Campo, Abdoulaye Méïté, El Hadji Diouf and Stelios would also depart. Lee brought in ten new signings in his first summer to create a brand-new look to Bolton Wanderers, which in truth didn't come anywhere near to the team or results that Sam had built.

The good times and the golden era were well and truly over by the summer of 2007. Sam Allardyce then looked towards the north-east for his next venture.

18

Measured spirit

IN THE summer of 2007, Sammy Lee had enforced a large overhaul of playing and backroom staff as he attempted to put his own stamp on the team. With the best of intentions, Lee was out of his depth and struggled with some of the bigger egos in the team, a skill Sam Allardyce often found quite easy. Although what can't be questioned is the Liverpudlian's effort and drive to do well.

After leaving Bolton, Allardyce was a hot commodity and was under great speculation that he would join Manchester City or Newcastle. After City decided to go with former England manager Sven-Göran Eriksson, Newcastle chairman Freddy Shepherd arranged a meeting with Sam at Gordon Ramsay's Claridge's restaurant in London. Shepherd, armed and ready for a third attempt to convince Sam to join the club, was successful as there was no Phil Gartside to stand in his way this time. Two days after the end of the season, Sam was named the new manager of Newcastle United after being flown in by helicopter to be unveiled at St James' Park.

When the fixtures for the new season were released the following month, Sam couldn't believe it: his very first game as Newcastle manager was Bolton away. There was no time to settle as he couldn't afford to allow his old club to get one over on him. Sam had also taken some of his famous Bolton backroom staff as well as defender Abdoulaye Faye to St James' Park. Over that summer, Lee and Gartside were boasting about a winning formula they had cracked that would produce the same results as under Sam but with a better brand of football. This was all fuel to Allardyce as he brought his new team to the Reebok with a mixed reaction from the Bolton fans. As he got off the bus at the stadium, he was met with a mixture of boos and cheers as the supporters didn't know what to think. The sheer oddness in seeing Sam in that stadium wearing a Newcastle United tie was uncanny and a true shock to the system for all at the club. He received a lovely welcome from many of the Reebok's staff, but unfortunately his family were banned from attending the game as the security team were informed not to allow them into the hospitality box 'for their own safety'.

Bolton lined up with a very different feel as they came away from Sam's 4-3-3 into a 4-4-2. Lee's Trotters lined up with new players Gérald Cid, Jlloyd Samuel and Gavin McCann in the starting 11 with Kevin Davies and Nicolas Anelka making up the front two. There had been intense rumours that Anelka was on his way to Newcastle with Sam but Phil Gartside had put a ban on any transfer of this kind, though later he would allow the sale of Faye to the Magpies.

The game started at a frantic pace and Sam found his new team 3-0 up after 27 minutes. Previously, Bolton had been lauded for their defensive home record, but it was clear that those days could be over. Newcastle were in the faces of the home players from minute one and didn't give them a second of breathing space as Sam used the same mentality he had been famous for at Bolton. Bolton would pull one back in the second half through Anelka to make it 3-1 but the damage was done in the first half and the Wanderers would be in the bottom three of the Premier League for the first time in four years.

Lee would last just eight more games before losing his job with the team at the foot of the table. He would be replaced by Gary Megson, who would lead Bolton to the last 16 of the UEFA Cup and finish 16th, one point above the relegation zone after a battle all season. The work Sam had done was gone and Bolton were once again a team who would fight for survival season in, season out until their eventual relegation in 2012 under Owen Coyle. They had stayed in the Premier League for 11 years but as of the writing of this book in 2024, they are yet to return and have spent six of those subsequent 12 years in either League One or League Two. Sam would return to the club in 2021 to manage a charity match of Bolton legends against the then first-team. Jay-Jay Okocha, Iván Campo, Kevin Davies, Stelios, Ricardo Gardner, Jussi Jääskeläinen and many others returned with a few more wrinkles and some larger waistlines to raise money for fighting against motor neurone disease, an illness that eventually would take the life of current Bolton vice-captain Gethin Jones's mother. A sense of nostalgia filled the stadium as the current crop beat the all-star XI 7-4 with Okocha getting on the score sheet. In a moment of celebration, both he and Allardyce re-enacted their dancing celebration from that famous survival day against Middlesbrough 19 years earlier in 2003.

Sam would lose his job at Newcastle after only seven months as new ownership from Sports Direct owner Mike Ashley brought in new radical ideas. He was only given one transfer window and a short time to show what he could do before it was taken away from him. After this he would join Bolton's rivals Blackburn Rovers which allowed him to still live in his Bromley Cross home for an easy commute, but also take another stab at rebuilding another Lancashire club. He would be joined at Ewood Park by El Hadji Diouf but again lost his job due to ownership issues as Blackburn had been bought out by Indian chicken giants Venkys, who put unknown coach Steve Kean in charge, a 'yes man' who would not ask the questions Sam would.

In 2011, Sam would join relegated West Ham United where he brought Kevin Nolan, Joey O'Brien, Ricardo Vaz Tê, Jussi Jääskeläinen and Abdoulaye Faye to his 'West Ham Wanderers'. He would win promotion with the London club in his first season via the play-offs and stayed there for four years before saving Sunderland from relegation and then taking the England job. Controversially, Sam would be fired after just one game following allegations of taking financial pay-offs for insider information. After this, Sam would enjoy short stints at Crystal Palace, Everton, West Bromwich Albion and Leeds United before taking a more relaxed approach to life and starting his own successful podcast, *No Tippy Tappy Football.*

Sam is remembered as the man that changed it all for Bolton Wanderers and for many who wear a white shirt in the town, he is as much a part of the fabric of the club as anyone who has ever played for the Trotters. Many would argue that Sir Nat Lofthouse is the most important figure of Bolton Wanderers' history, and they may have a point, but for fans of a certain generation and a certain age, it is Sam Allardyce whose name will live in immortality. The towering figure of the man who would grace the Bolton dugout left an indelible mark on his beloved club. His name would be synonymous with resilience, innovation and unyielding passion for the club, which can only be labelled under the category of 'measured spirit'.

When Sam took over, Bolton were at a crossroads with no real identity and no true leadership. He arrived as a strategist with a plan and as well as this, a motivator with raw charisma, showing a deep understanding of the game and unwavering commitment to the cause. He would embark on a journey with Bolton that no one could have seen coming and would elevate the club to heights that few would or could have imagined. Bolton's ascension to and through the Premier League is in itself a testament to the man but also to the team he built. The tactical acumen and relentless drive was something to cherish as not only his impact on Bolton but his impact on English football was ahead of its time. He was seen to be a pioneer of sports science, data analytics and innovative methods to gain that extra five or ten per cent from his players and backroom team. He saw gold where others saw tired trash as shown in the cases of Kevin Davies, Youri Djorkaeff, El Hadji Diouf, Fernando Hierro and Gary Speed.

Beyond the tactical brilliance and the historic wins, what truly set Sam apart was his ability to build a team that played with heart and unity – measured spirit. He had an eye for talent, bringing in players who not only had skill but also shared his indomitable spirit. Icons like Okocha, Djorkaeff and Hierro graced the Reebok Stadium pitch, not just as stars but as integral parts of a cohesive and formidable team.

Sam's tenure was marked by unforgettable moments: the thrilling matches, the European nights that saw Bolton compete on the continental stage, and the unwavering support of fans who believed in the vision he championed.

He gave the supporters and the town not just a team to support, but a dream to believe in.

As the fans reflect on his impact, they see a legacy of resilience, innovation, and an unbreakable bond between the club and its supporters. He taught many in the game that with the right leadership, no challenge is insurmountable, and no dream too grand. His tenure was more than a chapter in the club's history; it was a transformative era that shaped the identity of Bolton Wanderers.

Sam changed the club, Sam changed the game.

Sam Allardyce was measured spirit.

Appendices

A combined Bolton Wanderers XI 1999–2007

22. Jussi Jääskeläinen

4. Guðni Bergsson 5. Bruno N'Gotty 25. Abdoulaye Faye 11. Ricardo Gardner

20. Fernando Hierro

8. Iván Campo 10. Jay-Jay Okocha ©

14. Kevin Davies 39. Nicolas Anelka 6. Youri Djorkaeff

Substitutes:
2. Nicky Hunt, 15. Radhi Jaïdi, 4. Kevin Nolan, 6. Gary Speed, 7. Stelios Giannakopoulos, 21. El Hadji Diouf, 12. Eiður Guðjohnsen.

Sam's League of Nations signings 1999–2007

Brazil: Mário Jardel, Emerson Thome, Júlio César.

Denmark: Per Frandsen, Carsten Fredgaard, Henrik Pedersen, Stig Tøfting

England: John O'Kane, Darren Holloway, David Norris, Ryan Baldaccino, Leam Richardson, Anthony Barness, Michael Ricketts, Simon Charlton, Ian Marshall, Isaiah Rankin, Tommy Wright, Nicky Summerbee, Matt Clarke, Rod Wallace, Nicky Southall, Jeff Smith, Kevin Poole, Delroy Facey, Chris Armstrong, David Holdsworth, Kevin Davies, Glen Little, Steve Howey, John Otsemobor, Michael Bridges, Les Ferdinand, Andy Oakes, Ian Walker, Matt Jansen, David Thompson

Finland: Jani Viander

France: Bruno N'Gotty, Youri Djorkaeff, Gérald Forshelet, Bernard Mendy, Pierre-Yves André, Florent Laville, Ibrahim Ba, Vincent Candela, Fabrice Fernandes, Martin Djetou, Nicolas Anelka

Germany: Fredi Bobic, Dietmar Hamann

Greece: Kostas Konstantinidis, Stelios Giannakopoulos

Guatemala: Dwight Pezzarossi

New Caledonia: John Gope-Fenepej

Iran: Andranik Teymourian

Israel: Tal Ben Haim, Idan Tal

Ivory Coast: Abdoulaye Méïté

Jamaica: Jermaine Johnson, Donovan Ricketts

Japan: Akinori Nishizawa, Hidetoshi Nakata

Nigeria: Jay-Jay Okocha, Blessing Kaku

Mexico: Jared Borgetti

Poland: Jarosław Fojut

Republic of Ireland: Gareth Farrelly, Jonathan Walters

Senegal: Djibril Diawara, El Hadji Diouf, Khalilou Fadiga, Abdoulaye Faye

Slovakia: Ľubomír Michalík

South Africa: Quinton Fortune

Scotland: Allan Johnston, Colin Hendry, Derek Niven

Spain: Iván Campo, Salva Ballesta, Javi Moreno, Fernando Hierro

Tunisia: Radhi Jaïdi

Turkey: Bülent Akın

USA: Juergen Sommer, Jeff Cassar, Johann Smith

Wales: Gary Speed

Acknowledgements

THE VAST majority of my rationale and inspiration for writing this book came from reading Chris Evans' book, *Total Belief*, about his memories of the Bruce Rioch era at Bolton Wanderers and to him, I say thank you for inspiring me to write about my own memories. His work was amazing and was something I zipped through in less than three days. His passion and love for the club made me reflect upon my own feelings but at a different era as we are from different generations of Bolton fans. Thank you Chris, and thank you for being so supportive, as well.

The main elements of this book, in truth, came from personal memories of the 2000s as well as research through various journalistic and factual channels and conversations with stakeholders of the time adding to a variety of other works. I have spent many years pondering about writing a book about the golden era of Bolton Wanderers and I have spent a lot of time dipping my toe in the waters around this idea with fan articles written to the *Bolton Evening News* in my teenage years, asking copious questions to the likes of Wanderers stalwart Andrew Dean – a long-standing member of the Bolton Wanderers in the Community team, and a director of the Bolton Wanderers Development Association – while working for the club's ticket office between 2013 and 2015, writing pieces for the Lion of Vienna and Burnden Aces fan sites, collaborating with the club regarding the anniversary and coverage of the Burnden Park disaster of 1946 (for which I wrote a first-class honours dissertation on) as well as a regular slot on the podcast *Trotter Chatter*, where I hold a weekly 'History Corner' segment as well as chatting all things Bolton Wanderers. A collective 20 or so years of researching articles, podcasts, literature, yearbooks, journals, conversations, videos, interviews and countless media outlets has come to the creation of this book. However, this would not be possible without the support of a collection of people.

First of all, thank you to Stelios Giannakopoulos for agreeing to read over my work and provide a foreword. It was quite humbling for me when Stelios agreed to do this and shows the manner and stature of the man who always keeps Bolton close to his heart. I had the pleasure of playing in a charity match with him in 2022 for the Bolton Wanderers Remembrance Group, when I also was paired in defence with Nicky Hunt, bucket list stuff. Thank you, Stelios.

Also, a huge thank you to Paul Holliday, whose support and help with the validity of some of the stories of the time helped me ensure credibility in the work as well as an inside scoop. Paul now works out of football but spent over 15 years within the media and communications team at Bolton and was a fountain of knowledge. Thank you, Paul.

To Simon Marland, the genius and guru of all things Bolton Wanderers. Simon's extensive literary works about the club helped with multiple fact-finding missions and his 'no stone unturned approach' has helped me to no end. I met Simon in 2014 as a university student writing his dissertation on the Burnden Park disaster. Simon invited me to the Euxton training ground and we spoke in the famous 'war room', where he showed me multiple pieces of evidence and historical sources to support me, including links and contact details for key people of the time. He will know far more inside scoops around the Allardyce era than I, and I imagine they will make a cracking read one day. Thank you, Simon.

A massive thank you should go to some people close to me. My wife Liz for her constant support, proofreading and for putting up with my love and sometimes obsession over Bolton Wanderers and for always believing in me. To my friends, the 'Turton lads', the group of friends for whom the away days under Big Sam were so much fun for us in our youth and helped us make lifelong nostalgic memories as we travelled up and down the country watching the Super Whites. Away days over the years with Charlie Baines, John Whipp, Dan Burrell, Dom Barker, Tom Newton, Ben Spencer, James Catherall, Gary Stones, Tommy Smith, Matt German, Tom Howard, Rik Mitchell, Lewis Leigh, Ryan Hulme, James Buckley, Erhan Ates, Adam O'Dowd and Jony Nuttall, among others, including Buckshaw's finest, David Tavener, have given me both inspiration and belief in writing about the best times we had. Cheers lads.

To my mum, Tracy, who bought me my first season ticket in 2001, and from that moment, my love for Bolton was cemented. Christ knows how much she spent over the years on tickets, shirts, scarves, etc. as well as ensuring I was at the stadium early enough to get pictures and autographs with my favourite players.

And finally, to Pitch Publishing for supporting me through the journey.

To all, thank you, it means a lot.

Bibliography

Books and literature:

Allardyce, S., & Custis, S., *Big Sam: My autobiography* (London: Headline, 2016)

Evans, C., *Total Belief: how Bruce Rioch brought the good times back to Bolton Wanderers* (Chichester: Pitch Publishing Ltd, 2024)

Flanagan, C., *Who Put the Ball in the Munich Net?: How Bolton Wanderers joined Europe's elite* (Sheffield: Vertical Editions, 2014)

Garner, T., *Bolton Wanderers: 10 years at the Reebok* (Derby: Breedon, 2007)

Halsey, M., & Ridley, I., *Added Time: Surviving cancer, death threats and the Premier League* (St Albans: Floodlit Dreams Ltd, 2013)

Hayes, D., *Bolton Wanderers* (Stroud: Sutton, 1999)

Marland, S., *Bolton Wanderers: A Complete Record, 1877–1989* (Derby: Breedon, 1989)

Marland, S., *Bolton Wanderers: One Hundred Years at Burnden Park* (Derby: Breedon, 1995)

Marland, S., *Bolton Wanderers: The Complete Record* (Derby: DB, 2011)

Orr, T., *Jay-Jay Okocha* (Hallandale, Florida: Mitchell Lane, 2020)

Richardson, J., & Speed, L., *Gary Speed: Unspoken – the family's untold story* (Liverpool: Trinity Mirror Sport Media, 2018)

Podcasts:

Undr The Cosh
I Had Trials Once
Trotter Chatter
Fore Four 2
The Wanderer (BBC)
LOV Pod
No Tippy Tappy Football

Media outlets and websites:

Bolton Wanderers official matchday programmes
TransferMarkt
Bolton Evening News
Manchester Evening News
Lion of Vienna
Burnden Aces
Getty Images
The Telegraph
TalkSport
The Guardian
Red Mist Football (YouTube)
TRIBUNA: Premier League (YouTube)
RedRoseCountyDan (YouTube)